PAPUA NEW GUINEA

GOVERNMENT, ECONOMY AND SOCIETY

PAPUA NEW GUINEA
GOVERNMENT, ECONOMY AND SOCIETY

EDITED BY STEPHEN HOWES
AND LEKSHMI N. PILLAI

ANU PRESS

PACIFIC SERIES

To all involved in the UPNG School of Business and Public Policy – ANU Crawford School of Public Policy partnership.

Published by ANU Press
The Australian National University
Canberra ACT 2600
Email: anupress@anu.edu.au

Available to download for free at press.anu.edu.au

ISBN (print): 9781760465025
ISBN (online): 9781760465032

WorldCat (print): 1297067968
WorldCat (online): 1297067837

DOI: 10.22459/PNG.2022

Cover design and layout by ANU Press. Cover photograph: University of Papua New Guinea graduands, 2019, by Dek Sum.

For more information on the partnership between the University of Papua New Guinea School of Business and Public Policy and The Australian National University Crawford School of Public Policy, see devpolicy.crawford.anu.edu.au/png-project/anu-upng-partnership.

This book is published under the aegis of the Pacific Editorial Board of ANU Press.

Contents

Acronyms ix

List of figures xi

List of tables xv

1. Introduction 1
   Stephen Howes and Lekshmi N. Pillai

Part I: Politics and Governance

2. Elections and politics 17
   Michael Kabuni, Maholopa Laveil, Geejay Milli and Terence Wood
3. Decentralisation: A political analysis 57
   Stephen Howes, Lawrence Sause and Lhawang Ugyel
4. Crime and corruption 87
   Grant W. Walton and Sinclair Dinnen

Part II: The Economy

5. PNG's economic trajectory: The long view 125
   Stephen Howes, Rohan Fox, Maholopa Laveil, Luke McKenzie, Albert Prabhakar Gudapati and Dek Sum
6. Have living standards improved in PNG over the last two decades? Evidence from Demographic and Health Surveys . . . 163
   Manoj K. Pandey and Stephen Howes

Part III: Society

7. Uneven development and its effects: Livelihoods and urban and rural spaces in Papua New Guinea 193
   John Cox, Grant W. Walton, Joshua Goa and Dunstan Lawihin
8. Communication, information and the media 223
   Amanda H. A. Watson

Contributors 261

Acronyms

ABG	Autonomous Bougainville Government
ADB	Asian Development Bank
AFP	Australian Federal Police
APEC	Asia-Pacific Economic Cooperation
ARB	Autonomous Region of Bougainville
ASFR	age-specific fertility rates
BPA	Bougainville Peace Agreement
BPNG	Bank of Papua New Guinea
CBR	crude birth rate
CEO	chief executive officer
CLRC	Constitutional and Law Reform Commission
CPC	Constitutional Planning Committee
CPI	Corruption Perceptions Index
DDA	District Development Authority
DHS	Demographic and Health Survey
DPLGA	Department of Provincial and Local Government Affairs
DPT	diphtheria, pertussis and tetanus
DSIP	District Services Improvement Program
FASU	Financial Analysis and Supervision Unit
GDP	gross domestic product
GFR	general fertility rate
GFS	Government Financial Statistics
GNI	gross national income
HRW	Human Rights Watch

ICAC	Independent Commission Against Corruption
IMF	International Monetary Fund
ITFS	Investigation Taskforce Sweep
JDPBPC	Joint District Planning and Budget Priorities Committee
LLG	local-level government
LNG	liquefied natural gas
LPV	limited preferential voting
MLAR	minimum liquid asset requirement
MP	member of parliament
MRSF	Mineral Resources Stabilisation Fund
NGO	non-governmental organisation
NSO	National Statistical Office
OECD	Organisation for Economic Co-operation and Development
OLIPPAC	*Organic Law on the Integrity of Political Parties and Candidates*
OLPG	*Organic Law on Provincial Government*
OLPGLLG	*Organic Law on Provincial Governments and Local-level Governments*
PNC	People's National Congress
PNG	Papua New Guinea
PNG–APP	Papua New Guinea–Australia Policing Partnership
PSIP	Provincial Services Improvement Program
QEB	*Quarterly Economic Bulletin*
RPNGC	Royal Papua New Guinea Constabulary
SIA	Security Industries Authority
SMDP	single member district plurality
SOE	state-owned enterprise
TFF	Tuition Fee Free
TFR	total fertility rate
TSM	Temporary Special Measure

List of figures

Figure 2.1: Electoral quality internationally. 19

Figure 2.2: Voter participation. 22

Figure 2.3: 2017 voter participation by region. 22

Figure 2.4: Average candidates per electorate by region. 24

Figure 2.5: Minimum, median and maximum winning candidate vote shares over time. 25

Figure 2.6: Incumbent turnover over time. 26

Figure 2.7: Number of women elected in general elections. 27

Figure 2.8: Share of votes that were invalid. 29

Figure 2.9: Quality of governance under SMDP (1996–2006) and under LPV (2007–18). 30

Figure 2.10: Clientelism in PNG and internationally. 40

Figure 2.11: MPs and ministers by party in 2019. 42

Figure 2.12: Length of prime ministers' tenure. 43

Figure 4.1: Growth of licensed security companies. 99

Figure 4.2: Number of licensed guards. 100

Figure 4.3: Funding for five anti-corruption organisations, 2008–22 (2021 prices). 111

Figure 5.1: Population, 1975–2020. 127

Figure 5.2: Resource dependency, 1980–2019. 129

Figure 5.3: Agriculture and manufacturing as a share of non-resource GDP, 1980–2019. 129

Figure 5.4: GDP deflators and CPI index, 1983–2019. 130

Figure 5.5: Ratio of CPI to non-resource GDP deflator, 1983–2019. 131

Figure 5.6: Annual real GDP growth, 1977–2019. 131

Figure 5.7: GDP (from 1976) and non-resource GDP (from 1983) per capita, with different deflators, to 2019. 132

Figure 5.8: Non-resource GDP per capita and the four sub-periods of PNG's economic history post-independence, 1983–2019. 133

Figure 5.9: Commodity exports as a percentage of GDP, 1976–2019. 134

Figure 5.10: The composition of commodity exports by value, 1976–2019. 134

Figure 5.11: Export volume indices of copra, copra oil, rubber, tea, cocoa and coffee, 1976–2019. 134

Figure 5.12: Export volume indices of marine products, palm oil and logs, 1976–2019. 135

Figure 5.13: Composition of non-resource commodity exports by value, 1976–78 and 2017–19. 136

Figure 5.14: Resource export volume indices, 1976–2019. 136

Figure 5.15: Composition of resource commodity exports by value, 1976–78 and 2017–19. 137

Figure 5.16: PNG's commodity export terms of trade, 1975–2019. 138

Figure 5.17: USD price indices of some important commodities, 1976–2019. 138

Figure 5.18: The value of resource, agricultural, timber and marine exports (Kina billion in 2012 prices), 1977–2019. 139

Figure 5.19: Formal sector employment, totals and population percentage, 1975–2019. 140

Figure 5.20: Formal employment by sector, 1978–2019. 140

Figure 5.21: Urban and rural minimum weekly wage (Kina per week in 2012 prices), 1977–2019. 141

Figure 5.22: Exports, imports and the current account balance (% GDP), 1976–2019. 142

Figure 5.23: The PGK–AUD and PGK–USD exchange rates, 1975–2019. 142

Figure 5.24: Real effective exchange rate index, 1980–2019. 144

Figure 5.25: Foreign exchange (FX) reserves, 1975–2019. 144

Figure 5.26: Government revenue and expenditure (% GDP), 1976–2019. 145

Figure 5.27: Non-resource revenue, resource revenue and aid (% GDP), 1976–2019. 146

Figure 5.28: (Non) resource revenue as a percentage of (non) resource GDP, 1980–2019. 146

Figure 5.29: Deficits/GDP (%), 1976–2019. 147

Figure 5.30: Debt/GDP, debt/revenue and interest/revenue (%), 1976–2019. 148

Figure 5.31: Domestic and foreign debt as percentages of total, 1975–2019. 148

Figure 5.32: Resource revenues and trust fund balances (% GDP), 1976–2019. 148

Figure 5.33: Inflation and currency depreciation, 1976–2019. 150

Figure 5.34: Deposits and lending ratios (% GDP), 1976–2019. 150

Figure 5.35: Banks' liquid asset ratios: Actual and statutory minimum, 1976–2019. 151

Figure 5.36: Weighted average lending and deposit rates and spreads, 1976–2019. 151

Figure 7.1: Percentage of urbanites: PNG, Melanesia and Oceania. 198

Figure 8.1: Mobile telephones in use in PNG over time. 239

List of tables

Table 2.1: Candidate numbers over time. 23

Table 3.1: Decentralisation legislation in PNG: A chronology from 1995 onwards. 64

Table 3.2: PNG's subnational governments. 66

Table 6.1: Share of urban and rural population according to the three DHSs (1996–2018, %). 166

Table 6.2: Engagement in non-agricultural economic activity (1996–2018, %). 167

Table 6.3: Household durable goods (1996–2018, %). 168

Table 6.4: Household floor quality and crowding (1996–2018). 169

Table 6.5: Household electrification, drinking water and sanitation (1996–2018, %). 170

Table 6.6: School attendance (1996–2018, %). 171

Table 6.7: Highest educational attainment (1996–2018, %). 172

Table 6.8: Access to mass media (1996–2018, %). 173

Table 6.9: Childhood mortality rates (1996–2018, per 1,000). 174

Table 6.10: Child health (1996–2018). 175

Table 6.11: Fertility rates and preferences (1996–2018). 176

Table 6.12: Household composition (1996–2018). 178

Table 6.13: Marriage and childbearing (1996–2018). 179

Table 6.14: Women's reproductive health and care (1996–2018). 180

Table A.1: Definitions and data notes. 185

1

Introduction

Stephen Howes and Lekshmi N. Pillai

Papua New Guinea (PNG), a nation of now almost nine million people, continues to evolve and adapt. While there is no shortage of recent data and research on PNG, the two most recent social science volumes on PNG were both written more than a decade ago. Ron May's edited volume *Policy making and implementation: Studies from Papua New Guinea* was published in 2009 by ANU Press, and Thomas Webster and Linda Duncan's edited volume *Papua New Guinea's development performance 1975–2008* was published in 2010 as a National Research Institute report. More than a decade on, much has changed, much has been learned, and there is a clear need for a volume that brings together the most recent research and reports on the most recent data.

This volume, *Papua New Guinea: Government, economy and society*, written by experts at the University of Papua New Guinea, The Australian National University (ANU) and other universities, does just that.

The book includes seven chapters, in addition to this introduction. The first part, 'Politics and Governance', includes chapters on elections and politics, decentralisation, and crime and corruption. The second part, 'The Economy', includes two chapters that track trends in the macroeconomy and household living standards. The third part, 'Society', interrogates uneven development and communications.

The chapters are a mix of literature surveys and data analyses. The surveys provide up-to-date summaries of the vast amount of research undertaken, research the authors have themselves often been involved in generating in their respective fields. Most take a historical perspective, looking at changes over time, mainly since, but sometimes also from before, independence. Among their many fine contributions, the reference lists of these chapters are invaluable. The chapter on politics and the two economics chapters (i.e. Chapters 2, 5 and 6) are more data-based. They look at a range of data, collected over time, to assess, respectively, electoral and political trends, macroeconomic performance and changes in living standards. Our introduction provides a summary of each chapter and briefly draws out some common themes and links.[1]

Part I. Politics and Governance

Elections and politics

Nothing is more important for a country than its political system. It is appropriate, therefore, that the book begins with an overview of PNG's political system and, since PNG is a democracy, an analysis of the country's electoral politics.

The authors of Chapter 2, 'Elections and politics', Michael Kabuni, Maholopa Laveil, Geejay Milli and Terence Wood, begin with an analysis of electoral quality, and show that PNG ranks poorly on international comparisons of electoral quality due to violence, problems with the roll and polling fraud, vote buying, and violence and coercion. It is certainly sobering to read that in 2017 one-third of voters reported that they were intimidated when voting. On the positive side of the ledger, electoral quality is higher in some parts of the country than others, and the actual process of vote counting is generally fair.

Moving on to a more general discussion of electoral trends and patterns, the chapter shows that voter participation is high, and that the number of candidates per seat has grown over time and is now very high. Winner vote shares are very low (less than 20 per cent in 2002, but, with the shift from first-past-the-post to limited preferential voting, up to around 30 per cent more recently) and incumbent turnover is high (about 50 per cent at most elections).

1 The summaries of Chapters 3 and 6 are taken largely from the introductions to the relevant chapter.

One feature of PNG politics is that very few women have been elected to parliament. There are 111 members of parliament (MPs). At any one time, at most three have been women. In the current parliament there are none. The authors provide three reasons: cultural factors, insufficient finance, and violence and intimidation. They argue in favour of Temporary Special Measures designed to lift the number of women in parliament.

A unifying theme for this chapter is provided by the idea of clientelism: politics based on local, personal benefits rather than on national issues. Again looking at international rankings, PNG appears to be one of the most clientelistic countries in the world. This has fundamental implications for the country's political system and in particular explains why its political party system is so weak: since a candidate's party affiliation is not normally relevant to voters, candidates do not feel much loyalty to the party they run for.

Because no one party dominates in PNG and because party allegiances are fluid, it is not surprising that the country has, since independence, been governed by coalitions rather than individual parties. As the authors show, these shifting, ruling coalitions are bound by interests in gaining positions of power rather than by policy commonalities. The inevitable outcome would seem to be political instability and, indeed, this was a characteristic of the country's political system until the turn of the century. Since then the average tenure of the position of prime minister has increased greatly. The authors explain the reasons for this, while wisely leaving open the question of whether political instability has been permanently or only temporarily banished.

Decentralisation

Chapter 3, 'Decentralisation: A political analysis', is by Stephen Howes, Lawrence Sause and Lhawang Ugyel. They provide an updated historical account of decentralisation in PNG, with a focus, as their title suggests, on political decentralisation. They argue that the country's decentralised system has several distinctive and, in some cases, unique features. First, it is constantly evolving – in fact, heading in different directions – with major reforms in 1977 and 1995, and other important changes before, since and proposed. Second, the system has evolved to be highly complex. At independence, PNG was a unitary state. Since then it has provided constitutional recognition to another three tiers of government: first provincial, then local-level and then district. Third, PNG's system of decentralisation relies heavily, perhaps uniquely heavily, on indirect representation, with no one actually being elected, as against appointed, to provincial assemblies or district boards, both of which are dominated by national politicians from that province and/or district.

Why is PNG's decentralisation experience so distinctive? The authors note that, given the clientelistic, fragmented and unstable nature of PNG's politics, political contestation is intense, and shaped almost exclusively by local factors. Therefore, it is hardly surprising that decentralisation has been the site of deep political conflicts. Four political forces, they argue, have shaped and will continue to shape PNG's decentralisation reforms: the political dominance within the country of national MPs; the dominance, within that group, of district over provincial MPs; as a countervailing force, strong, though variable, political support for provincial autonomy; and the aforementioned underlying clientelistic, fragmented and unstable nature of PNG politics. While these findings are consistent with generalisations across Western countries (Spina [2013] finds that stable governments subject to ethno-regionalist forces are more likely to decentralise), the specific combination of these four forces, often pulling in opposite directions, has set PNG on a decentralisation journey that is as unique as it is incomplete.

The authors' aim is to explain decentralisation in PNG, not to predict its future nor to make policy recommendations. However, their analysis does clarify a number of important questions that need to be asked in relation to decentralisation policy, and they conclude that PNG's decentralisation arrangements will continue to evolve for many years to come.

Crime and corruption

In Chapter 4, Grant Walton and Sinclair Dinnen tackle what are sometimes regarded as PNG's twin curses: crime and corruption. Both topics are colossal, but the authors provide a masterful survey.

As the authors show, concerns about both violent crime and corruption predate independence. Trends in both are very difficult to define with any confidence due to data weaknesses and the diffuse, multifaceted and difficult-to-quantify nature of both problems. Certainly, the two regularly rate among the top concerns of businesses whenever they are surveyed.

Urban crime levels appear to be stabilising, and may even be falling. Conversely, tribal conflict appears to be intensifying, with greater use of high-powered weapons, local mercenaries ('hire-men') and guerrilla tactics. The authors also note that violence against women and girls, including rape and other sexual offences, has been a longstanding concern in PNG, and that there is a growing problem of sorcery-related violence.

Corruption has certainly worsened since independence, the authors argue. Whether it is still worsening is unclear, but it has become widespread. The authors cite one survey of citizens in five provinces that found that 51 per cent of respondents had witnessed some sort of corruption. Another survey found that two-thirds of public servants across four provinces agreed that it is difficult to get things done without bribing government officials. While PNG's international corruption rankings have improved modestly in recent years, in a 2015 survey of citizens, 90 per cent of respondents reported worsening corruption over the past decade.

The drivers of both phenomena are complex and interrelated. Various theories explain them in terms of culture, poor governance and limited economic opportunities. The authors argue that a complete explanation must also take into account international forces, given the prevalence of transnational crime and corruption.

Both crime and corruption are serious and longstanding enough to have generated a significant response, but, interestingly, a very different response in each of the two areas. Despite much donor support, the police response to violent crime has been ineffectual. Police numbers have increased by only around 30 per cent since independence, while the overall population has more than tripled. There is little public confidence in the police, and police brutality and prison breakouts both constitute major failings. Inadequate policing has led to a dramatic growth in the private security industry. More than two-thirds of businesses in PNG employ private security staff. The number of licensed security companies grew from 174 in 2006 to 566 in 2018, and the number of security guards working for these licensed firms is now over 30,000, four times the number of serving police officers.

One limit of this reliance on security guards is that it does nothing to improve security in areas that are irrelevant to the formal private sector. The authors argue that community responses have been effective in some urban settlements and rural areas, and advocate for a rebalancing of donor support away from police reform (something of a lost cause) towards community groups.

Corruption, also perceived to be a threat even before independence, has been the subject of various government prevention and containment strategies, starting with the Leadership Code and Ombudsman Commission, both of which were written into the PNG constitution. In general, however, none of these strategies has been effective, at least over a sustained period. Unlike violent crime, official corruption is not a problem susceptible to private sector solutions. Drawing on recent research, the authors argue for focusing efforts on transnational corruption networks, improving the mandate and resources of anti-corruption institutions, enhancing educational efforts and highlighting the impact corruption has on local communities.

Part II. The Economy

The two economic chapters in the book are complementary in nature. Chapter 5 looks at macroeconomic trends (i.e. at the economy-wide level), while Chapter 6 looks at microeconomic trends (i.e. at the household level).

PNG's economic trajectory

Chapter 5, 'PNG's economic trajectory: The long view', by Stephen Howes, Rohan Fox, Maholopa Laveil, Luke McKenzie, Albert Prabhakar Gudapati and Dek Sum, is based on a new database put together by the authors to solve the problem of a lack of time series data from independence to the current time. While there are some longer time series for PNG on international databases, many are missing, and some of those available are not consistent over time. To fill this gap, the authors have created the PNG Economics Database (available at devpolicy.org/pngeconomic), which is used in the chapter to tell a data-based story of PNG's post-independence economic history.

The chapter's authors note that, given the heavily capital-intensive nature of PNG's resource projects and their high levels of foreign ownership, development in the resources sector may have little impact on the broader economy. On this basis, they argue that non-resource GDP (excluding the resources sector but including its spillover effects to the broader economy) is a better indicator of the state of the PNG national economy than GDP as a whole. (Ideally, we would use gross national income, but this is not available for PNG.)

Looking at non-resource GDP per capita, the authors divide the post-independence era in PNG into four periods: 1975–88, a period of slow but stable growth; 1989–2003, a period of instability; 2004–13, the resource boom; and 2014–19, the post-boom bust.

The authors reach a number of interesting conclusions on the basis of the new time series they have collated and, in some cases, constructed. They summarise their findings through a list of 15 claims. Here we highlight four of the less expected findings.

One is that the minimum wage paid to urban workers is half its level at independence, taking account of inflation. This shows just how relatively difficult life has become for those working in unskilled labour jobs in PNG's urban areas, such as cleaners and security guards. Given falling formal sector employment rates, the authors caution against an increase in the minimum wage at the current time, however.

A second point of particular interest is that, at independence, the value derived from the export of agricultural commodities and from the export of resources (minerals and petroleum) were roughly equivalent. Now resources make up 90 per cent of commodity exports. One can only speculate on how different PNG would be today if that 50:50 ratio had been sustained.

A third point is that the import-to-GDP ratio is at its lowest level since independence. PNG's high dependence on imported goods is often commented on, but this trend away from imports is rarely noted. The authors argue that it is a telling indicator of how little spillover there is now from the resources sector to the broader economy, since resource exports are booming.

Fourth and finally, PNG's banking system is famous for its profitability and the large spread between lending and deposit rates. But this has not always been the case. At independence, the banking sector was highly regulated. The main effect of deregulation seems to have been a decline in deposit rates to virtually zero. The spread between deposit and lending rates has risen from well under 5 per cent to well above it, meaning lending rates have not fallen by nearly as much as deposit rates. This is perhaps a lesson on the dangers of deregulation in a non-competitive environment. Getting those spreads down is one of the major economic challenges facing the country today.

Poverty and the standard of living

The lack of consistent, reliable and up-to-date data remains a major obstacle to assessing progress in living standards in PNG. The chapter by Manoj K. Pandey and Stephen Howes, 'Have living standards improved in PNG over the last two decades? Evidence from Demographic and Health Surveys', draws upon three PNG Demographic and Health Surveys (DHSs) for 1996, 2006 and 2016–18 to examine whether the standard of living in PNG has improved over the last two decades.

The last two DHSs are of particular value because they were collected either side of PNG's resource boom. High commodity prices and the construction of the large PNG liquefied natural gas project led to the strongest period of economic growth seen in PNG post-independence. Did it make a difference in terms of living standards?

The findings of this chapter can be divided into three groups. First, there are clearly some ways in which living standards have improved over the last two decades: many more households have cars and rainwater tanks; more children are at school, albeit from a low base; and childhood mortality rates have continued to fall. These improvements reflect the positive impacts of economic growth on household income, and on increased government revenue and therefore spending in the case of education.

The second group of results are areas of regress. Vaccination rates and access to traditional media have both plummeted. These would seem to be cases of worsening governance leading to poorer service delivery (e.g. radio broadcasting capacity) despite economic growth.

Finally, there are areas of stagnation. There is no growth in the share of non-agricultural jobs post-2006, a key indicator of economic transformation. There is also little sign of significantly improved status for women. Women are more likely to be heads of households, but they are hardly marrying later, or having children later, or having fewer children. While access to contraception has improved, it remains very low, and women are no more likely to receive antenatal care now than they were 20 years ago, and hardly more likely to give birth in a health facility. This third group of results is perhaps the most worrying, as it suggests that, despite some short-term benefits from growth, there is little sign of the structural transformation needed for sustained and successful development.

Interestingly, the analysis also shows that urban areas are less likely to show improvements in living standards and are more likely to show declines than rural areas. The authors interpret this as being due to the growth of urban settlements. The result is a tendency towards convergence between urban and rural living standards.

Part III: Society

Uneven development

The third part of the book moves beyond politics, governance and the economy to consider a number of what could be described as social issues. Chapter 7, 'Uneven developments and its effects: Livelihoods and urban and rural spaces in Papua New Guinea', by John Cox, Grant Walton, Joshua Goa and Dunstan Lawihin, moves beyond what the authors call 'methodological nationalism' and tackles issues of spatial inequality and social diversity in PNG. As the authors note, PNG is, according to World Bank data, the most rural country in the world. But it is also a top-20 country for resource dependency and very ethnically and geographically diverse. It is not surprising, therefore, that it is a country that both defies generalisation and shows high inequality.

Although PNG remains a predominantly rural country, for several decades people from all areas of the country have been making their homes in Port Moresby, Lae and other cities. New generations have made cities their permanent homes. Nevertheless, the authors comment, the 'legitimacy of Melanesian urbanism is yet to be established'. While, in general, urban conditions are better than rural, the life of an urban resident is often not an easy one, with high costs of living, and often a large number of extended family dependents. Financial hardship and a sense of relative deprivation fuel, on the positive side, urban engagement in microenterprises, but also, on the negative side, the widespread practice of (extortionary) payday loans and various pyramid or Ponzi schemes.

Regarding rural areas, the authors write that:

> In public discourse, rural people in PNG are often spoken about (by development agencies or by the national middle class) as if they were frozen in a pre-colonial past, living on customary land according to the ways of their ancestors and providing for themselves without money.

In fact, as the authors show, the reality is that 'a range of capitalist enterprises interact with rural life in various ways and rural people actually move from place to place in significant numbers'. Rural people engage with plantations, smallholder commodity and fresh food production, and (sometimes with far-reaching consequences, for better or worse) large-scale resource projects. Rural development has been a constant preoccupation for government, but the means by which it might be promoted remain controversial and elusive, as the various attempts to introduce free education have shown.

Development might be uneven in PNG, but the nation is increasingly connected, whether through internal migration, the nationwide betel nut trade, or the growing phenomenon of 'mixed marriages' of people from different parts of the country. Interconnectivity itself is a good thing, but it also means that many are more aware of their own deprivation.

Not only is inequality high, but increasingly PNG appears a land of contrasts. The boom years of the 2000s and early 2010s reshaped parts of the country, especially the capital. This peaked in 2018, when the country splurged on buildings and luxury cars to host the Asia-Pacific Economic Cooperation (APEC) summit. But the boom also heightened inequalities and disparities. At the same time as it was preparing for APEC, PNG became one of the few countries of the world where polio has mounted a comeback.

The authors conclude by: stressing the importance of capturing the fluid nature of uneven development and moving beyond analysis that is bound to administrative territories or particular places; highlighting the need to prioritise the needs of rural communities, by far the largest section of PNG's population, and the poorest; and suggesting that it is unlikely that the radical reshaping of urban spaces associated with the resource boom of the 2000s will be repeated any time soon.

Communication and the media

In the final chapter, 'Communication, information and the media', Amanda H. A. Watson covers a range of critical issues that are too often ignored or sidelined in social investigations. Watson shows that, while there have been some examples of a decrease of media availability, such as the end of Radio Australia shortwave broadcasts, there have also been concurrent increases in the number of television stations, in the amount of PNG-related material that is available online, and in terms of types of media offerings available.

Watson argues that access to the media in PNG is becoming increasingly unequal. The level of access to a variety of news sources is increasing for urban internet users, with the establishment of various online news outlets as well as additional weekly newspapers and television services. However, even in urban areas, some people have limited or no access to the internet, and in rural areas, communication options continue to stagnate or even decline.

Freedom of the media is a strength in PNG, but not an unmitigated one. The author is particularly concerned about the weakness of investigative journalism in PNG, which she attributes to a mix of funding, cultural and political factors.

Watson also explores the role of gender in the media. The gender composition of the media workforce has improved – a survey as long ago as 2001 found that about half of PNG's journalists were female – but female journalists are still disadvantaged in a range of ways, and the portrayal of women in the media needs to be enhanced.

The author also explores the dramatic changes relating to mobile telephony since 2007 (when Digicel started operations). The explosive growth in the number of mobile phones from 60,000 in 2006 to 2,650,000 in 2013 tells the story. But there are also many challenges ahead. Digicel (with a 92 per cent market share) has emerged as a monopoly provider, and prices its services accordingly. Competition from state-run providers is weak. One-third of PNG's people still live without mobile network coverage, and internet access is slow, costly and unreliable – though this has not stopped 600,000 people buying smart phones and 750,000 using Facebook.

Watson is largely positive about the social benefits of the mobile phone and internet revolution, and the greater connectivity it has provided. She summarises various experiments in using mobiles for development (e.g. to improve learning at school or to report corruption), and finds a mix of failures and successes. With regards to social media, misinformation can be a problem, but research has shown that in many cases social media has been used to share factual, useful information among and between communities. The distribution of pornographic and abusive material, however, is a real concern.

Conclusion

We conclude by drawing out some of the common themes of this book. First, the chapters in this book point to the many and rapid changes PNG is undergoing. Twenty years ago, the job of a political scientist writing on PNG was to explain endemic political instability. Now one has to explain why instability was replaced by stability in the 2000s and wonder about whether the change will last. Fifteen years ago, PNG was a country that had missed out on the mobile revolution; today, mobile phones are a transformative feature of PNG life.

Second, it is not easy to reach an overall assessment about progress in PNG. As the chapter on uneven development (Chapter 7) shows us, PNG is a country on which one generalises at one's peril. Further, as the chapter on living standards (Chapter 6) shows, one observes a mix of progress and regress over different dimensions. Other areas of interest are not easy to measure. How does one tell if corruption has worsened or not? It is also unclear how to weigh achievements (the maintenance of democracy) relative to shortcomings (the low quality of the electoral system). All that said, we do take from the two economics chapters (Chapters 5 and 6) support for the position advanced by John Connell (1997, p. 317) in the late 1990s that 'neither consistent growth nor sustainable development have been achieved' in post-independence PNG.

Third, there is a clear value to looking at interlinkages between disparate topics and disciplines. Clearly, if one wants to explain poor economic performance one should look at politics. If, as is argued in Chapter 2, politics in PNG is clientelistic, then citizens will not be voting on the basis of economic policies. In such a scenario, why would one expect good economic policies to emerge? Two-way linkages are also common: poor economic performance fuels crime and crime undermines the economy.

Fourth, gender is a major issue in contemporary PNG – and in this book. It features prominently in the chapters on politics, the media, crime and living standards. There are certainly signs of progress: for example, more women in the media and more concern with gender-based violence. But there are also signs of resistance to change and of inertia. There are no women in the current PNG parliament, and there are few signs of progress in key areas of women's empowerment, such as women marrying later, having children later or having fewer children.

Fifth and finally, there are often complaints that PNG lacks adequate data, but what this book suggests is that, in fact, if you go out and look for it, you can find plenty of data, and more broadly research into PNG. What has been missing in recent years – or really over the last decade – is much of an attempt to summarise and synthesise existing data and research. It is that gap which this book aims to fill.

We hope that *Papua New Guinea: Government, economy and society* will be an asset especially to students in and of PNG, but also to policymakers and researchers looking for overviews of particular topics or a starting point for further research. That this volume is open access (available to download for free) should greatly add to its utility and use.

Of course, we make no claim to be comprehensive. There are many other important topics deserving of their own chapters, and one can only hope that our efforts inspire others to follow suit. For our part, we would like to end by thanking all the individuals and institutions involved in this enterprise: the contributors for their chapters; all those who commented on chapter outlines and drafts, especially at our book workshop in October 2020 (see each chapter for individual acknowledgements); ANU Press, in particular Pacific Editorial Board Chair Dr Stewart Firth; ANU Development Policy Centre Managing Editor Lydia Papandrea and the volume's copyeditor, Rani Kerin; and the PNG–Australia Partnership for its financial support to the partnership between the University of Papua New Guinea School of Business and Public Policy and The Australian National University Crawford School of Public Policy.

References

Connell, J. (1997). *Papua New Guinea: The struggle for development*. Routledge.

May, R. I. (Ed.). (2009). *Policy making and implementation: Studies from Papua New Guinea*. ANU Press. doi.org/10.22459/PMI.09.2009.

Spina, N. (2013). Explaining political decentralisation in parliamentary democracies. *Comparative European Politics*, *11*(4), 428–57. doi.org/10.1057/cep.2012.23.

Webster, T. and Duncan, L. (Eds). (2010). *Papua New Guinea's development performance 1975–2008*. PNG National Research Institute. pngnri.org/images/Publications/MG41---201009---Webster---PNGs-development-performance.pdf.

Part I: Politics and Governance

2

Elections and politics

Michael Kabuni, Maholopa Laveil, Geejay Milli
and Terence Wood

Abstract

In this chapter we provide an overview of electoral and parliamentary politics in Papua New Guinea (PNG). We cover electoral quality and trends. We examine voter choices. And we study the dynamics of parliamentary politics. As we do this, we pay particular attention to the challenges faced by female candidates. We also look for evidence of improvements stemming from the two most significant changes to post-independence electoral and political rules in PNG: the introduction of limited preferential voting and the *Organic Law on the Integrity of Political Parties and Candidates*. Little evidence exists that these rule changes have brought improvements. At present, many challenges plague electoral politics and political governance in PNG. Yet there are some signs of potentially positive social changes. There are also good grounds to believe that other rule changes, such as the proposed introduction of Temporary Special Measures to ensure women's representation, can help.

Introduction

In the 45 years between independence in 1975 and 2020, Papua New Guinea (PNG) held nine general elections. It is one of only a small number of formerly colonised countries to have remained democratic throughout its history as an independent state. This is a proud record, yet democracy has not delivered everything hoped of it – poor governance is a problem in PNG, and most of the country's citizens have failed to see real development gains. In parts of the country elections have been marred by violence and cheating. Women have rarely been elected.

PNG is a parliamentary democracy with a unicameral parliament. At general elections voters vote twice: once to select a candidate to represent their open seat (open seats typically share borders with PNG's administrative districts) and once to select a candidate to represent their province. Members of parliament (MPs) from both open and provincial seats sit together in the same house of parliament. There are 89 open seats and 22 provincial seats in PNG's parliament.

Over the years, major changes have been made to PNG's electoral and parliamentary rules in an attempt to improve democratic governance. Most notably, after the 2002 elections, PNG exchanged its first-past-the-post electoral system for limited preferential voting (LPV) and, in 2001, parliament passed the *Organic Law on the Integrity of Political Parties and Candidates* (OLIPPAC), which was subsequently amended in 2003.

In this chapter we provide an overview of electoral and parliamentary politics in PNG. We start with the quality of elections. We then look at electoral trends and patterns. Then we cover female candidates. We subsequently examine why voters vote for the candidates that they do, and the consequences of their choices. Finally, we look at parliamentary politics, focusing on how PNG's elected representatives interact once in parliament. As we do this, we pay particular attention to rule changes, such as the shift to LPV and OLIPPAC, and ask whether they have changed politics in helpful ways. We also look at proposed future changes such as Temporary Special Measures (TSMs) (rule changes to bring more women into parliament) and discuss their potential.

Throughout the chapter we provide facts and figures about elections in PNG. Unless these figures are attributed to another source, the numbers come from the PNG election results database (Wood, 2019).[1]

1 Readers can access these data online at devpolicy.org/pngelections.

Electoral quality

Before we cover electoral politics in detail, it is worth asking two basic questions about the nature of elections in PNG. First, are elections free? Or, to put it another way, are voters safely able to choose who they want to vote for? Second, are elections fair? Are winning candidates really the most popular candidates in their electorates, or do they win by cheating in some way?

Figure 2.1 is based on data from the Electoral Integrity Project (Norris and Grömping, 2019). It shows the quality of 121 developing countries' most recent elections based on expert assessments. (Data for PNG are from 2017.) Each country is represented with a bar. Higher bars mean better run elections. As can be seen, in comparison to the quality of elections globally, electoral quality in the 2017 election in PNG was very poor.

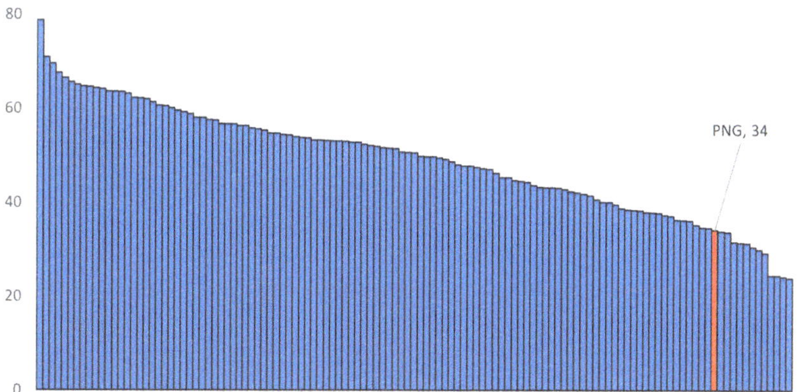

Figure 2.1: Electoral quality internationally.

Note: Each bar is a country. PNG is highlighted in red. Higher scores are better.

Source: Data from the Electoral Integrity Project (Norris and Grömping, 2019).

PNG's poor score stems from a range of issues and we look at each in turn. As we do this, we draw on analysis from the 2017 election. However, while problems were particularly bad in 2017, similar issues have been present in other recent elections, particularly 2002 (Gibbs et al., 2004; Haley, 1997; Haley and Zubrinich, 2013, 2018; May et al., 2011).

Violence and coercion

The 2017 PNG elections triggered violent conflict in places and led to over 200 deaths (Haley and Zubrinich, 2018; Lyons, 2018; Transparency International PNG, 2017). Violence occurred throughout the electoral period, including protracted conflict in some places after results were announced. A clear problem in parts of PNG during the 2017 elections was inadequate security at important times (Haley and Zubrinich, 2018).

Even when there was no actual violence, sometimes threats were enough to influence who people voted for. One survey in 2017 found that just over a third of people reported that they were intimidated when voting (Haley and Zubrinich, 2018, p. 60). In parts of the country, polling officials also reported being intimidated and threatened by candidates (Markiewicz and Wood, 2018).

Problems with the roll and polling fraud

There were major problems with the roll in 2017. There were many more names on the roll than could reasonably be expected based on estimates of PNG's population (Markiewicz and Wood, 2018). This roll inflation allowed people to vote more than once in some places and ineligible voters to vote in others. In 2017, the roll was not just inflated but also inaccurate: there were many instances of eligible voters not being able to vote because their names were missing from the roll (Markiewicz and Wood, 2018).

Polling was also problematic. Proper polling procedures were often neglected. In some instances, polling officials turned a blind eye to, or were complicit in, candidates cheating. In some electorates, supporters of particular candidates were able to take control of polling stations to ensure all votes were cast for their candidates (Haley and Zubrinich, 2018; Transparency International PNG, 2017).

Vote buying

In 2017, as in earlier elections, in many parts of PNG voters reported being offered money to vote for candidates. Although not everyone sells their vote in PNG, vote buying is common enough to influence election results in some electorates (Haley and Zubrinich, 2013, 2018; Transparency International PNG, 2017).

Better news

This is a worrying list of problems, but not the whole story. Most of the worst problems in 2017 came from parts of the Highlands or from large cities. In much of the country the election was peaceful and cheating less common. Many people were free to choose who to vote for. Also, in most of PNG the actual process of vote counting, while slow, has generally been fair (Markiewicz and Wood, 2018; Wood, 2014). Most electoral officials do their jobs well. The electoral process has not completely collapsed in PNG. This has an important ramification for this chapter: it means that we can still meaningfully talk about election results and the nature of electoral competition. Elections are not completely fraudulent.

Electoral trends and patterns

Voter participation

As discussed above, in recent years PNG has suffered significant roll inflation (i.e. more people being on the electoral roll than are eligible to vote). Given how inflated the roll has been, rather than calculate voter participation in the conventional manner, comparing votes cast to the number of names on the roll, a more appropriate calculation is the ratio of votes cast to the estimated voting-age population. Based on this calculation, voter participation is higher in PNG than in PNG's closest neighbours. Nationally, the average voter participation rate in the most recent election in PNG was 90 per cent, higher than Indonesia (73 per cent) and Solomon Islands (80 per cent). It is only marginally lower than Australia (92 per cent) where voting is compulsory (International IDEA, 2020; and authors' calculations for Solomon Islands). Trends in voter participation over time in PNG are shown in Figure 2.2. Voter participation reached its highest (we estimate it was over 100 per cent) in 2002.

Voter participation nationally masks variation across regions. Variation can be seen in Figure 2.3, using the 2017 election as an example. Voter participation in the Highlands in 2017 was about 120 per cent. Voter participation was lower in the other three regions, with 60 per cent in the Islands Region, 77 per cent in Momase Region, and 69 per cent in the Southern Region. The Highlands Region has seen votes exceed the voting-age population in the previous five elections. High voter participation in the Highlands is probably a product of intense electoral competition, roll inflation and issues with electoral fraud. It remains a puzzle, though, why voter participation is comparatively low in the Islands Region.

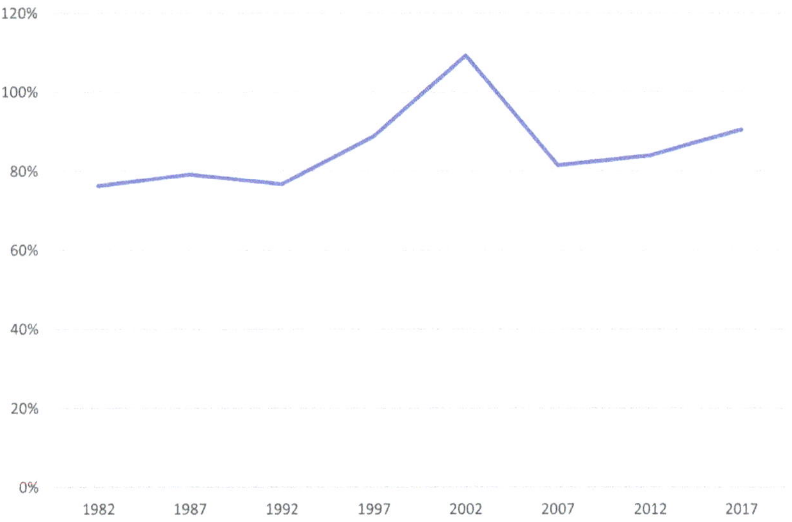

Figure 2.2: Voter participation.

Source: For full details on sources and calculations, see Laveil (2020).

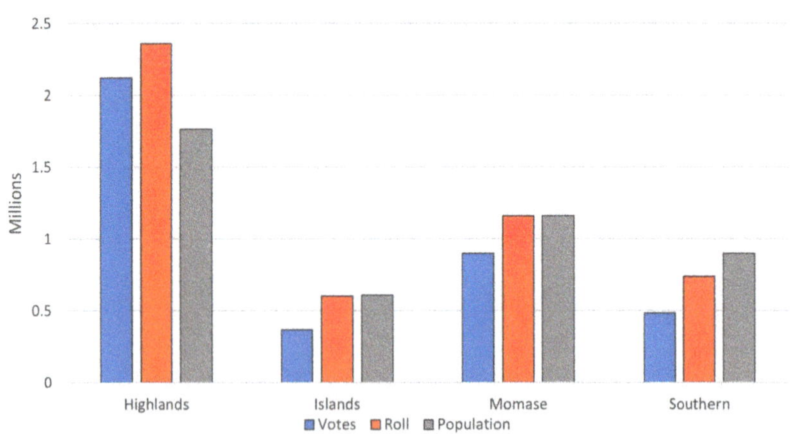

Figure 2.3: 2017 voter participation by region.

Source: For full details on sources and calculations, see Laveil (2020).

Candidates

As can be seen in Table 2.1, candidate numbers have grown with each election except 2007 and 2017. The total number of candidates that contested the 1977 election was 878, and by 2017 candidates numbered 3,335. The voting-age population only grew by 293 per cent in the same period. One possible reason for growing candidate numbers is that political parties are of limited electoral importance, and local issues dominate, thus allowing more independents to run, free of the need for party endorsement. However, this does not appear to be the main driver of increasing candidate numbers: in 2017 the share of all candidates who were independents was lower than in 1992. Another plausible explanation for increased candidate numbers is increased fracturing and less cohesion in communities, which prevents cooperation and coordinated support for candidates. This is just a possibility, however, and more research is required in this area.

Table 2.1: Candidate numbers over time.

Year	Seat numbers	Candidate numbers	Increase (%)	Candidates/ electorate	Share of independents (%)
1977	109	878		8	No data
1982	109	1,124	28	10	No data
1987	109	1,515	35	14	No data
1992	109	1,644	9	15	74
1997	109	2,373	44	22	73
2002	109	2,875	21	26	43
2007	109	2,748	–4	25	No data
2012	111	3,443	25	31	64
2017	111	3,335	–3	30	57

Source: PNG Elections Database (Wood, 2019).

Average candidate numbers vary across regions but, as can be seen in Figure 2.4, all have increased considerably since 1977. Although the Highlands Region has the most candidates in total, since 1992 the Southern Region has had the highest number of candidates contesting per seat. The Islands have the lowest number of candidates per seat. Chimbu provincial seat in 2012 had the highest number of candidates ever (73). Looking at open seats only, Kerema open in 2012 had the highest number of candidates ever (70), while Namatanai open in 1992 and Pomio open in 1977 both only had two candidates.

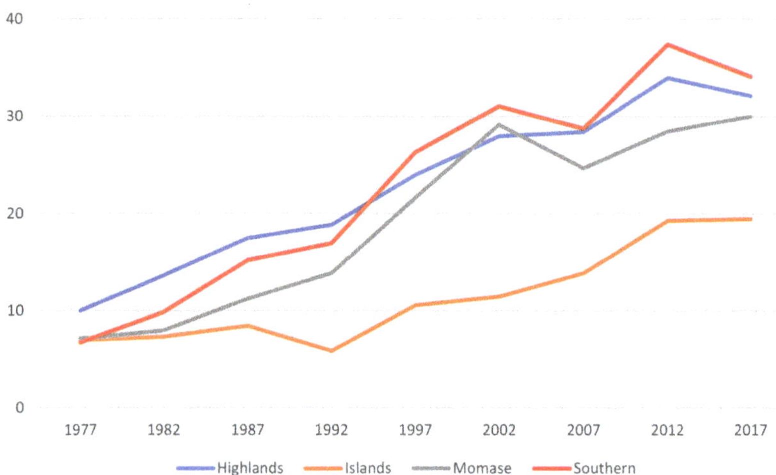

Figure 2.4: Average candidates per electorate by region.

Source: Data from the PNG Elections Database (Wood, 2019).

It is unclear why candidate numbers vary so much between electorates. One obvious explanation for variation would seem to be variation in electorate size. Using roll numbers for 2017, Laveil and Wood (2019) found that the largest electorate (Laigap-Porgera in the Highlands) is six times larger than the smallest electorate (Rabaul in the Islands). However, Wood (2017) found that larger electorates and provinces did not tend to have more candidates on average.

Winner vote shares

Figure 2.5 shows the lowest, median and highest winning candidate's vote share in each post-independence election in PNG. At times, candidates have won elections with incredibly low vote shares. The lowest vote share won by a candidate was 6 per cent, which has happened twice: Ben Kerenga Okoro in Sinasina-Yungomugl open seat in 1992, and Bani Hoivo in the Northern provincial seat in 2002. Since the introduction of the LPV electoral system, the minimum winning vote share has lifted somewhat. It was 13 per cent in 2007, 15 per cent in 2012 and 18 per cent in 2017. This is an increase, but it is a small gain considering winners' vote shares now include second and third preferences too.

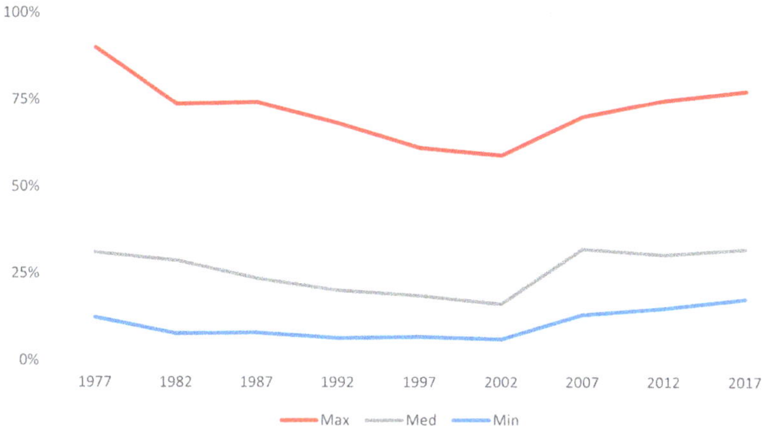

Figure 2.5: Minimum, median and maximum winning candidate vote shares over time.

Source: Data from the PNG Elections Database (Wood, 2019).

There is considerable variation in winning candidate vote shares between electorates. This variation can be seen when comparing maximum, median and minimum winner vote shares in each election (see Figure 2.5). Sir John Guise won the Milne Bay provincial seat with 90 per cent of total votes in 1977. Winner vote shares are typically highest when there are fewer candidates, as evidenced in 2017 when the winning candidate with the highest vote share of 77 per cent was the incumbent prime minister, Peter O'Neill, who contested the Ialibu-Pangia open seat, the seat with the second lowest number of candidates.

Incumbent turnover

Incumbent turnover (the rate at which sitting MPs lose their seats) has been high in all of PNG's nine elections. Figure 2.6 shows incumbent turnover in different elections. There is no clear national trend, but the highest incumbent turnover rate was experienced in 2002, when almost three-quarters of sitting MPs lost their seats. Turnover rates have averaged 54.8 per cent: on average, more than half of MPs lose their seats in every election. A few notable politicians such as Sir Michael Somare (East Sepik provincial), Sir Julius Chan (Namatanai open) and Sir Peter Lus (Maprik open) have been successful in consecutive elections. Sir Michael Somare, in particular, was triumphant in all elections before retiring from politics prior to the 2017 elections.

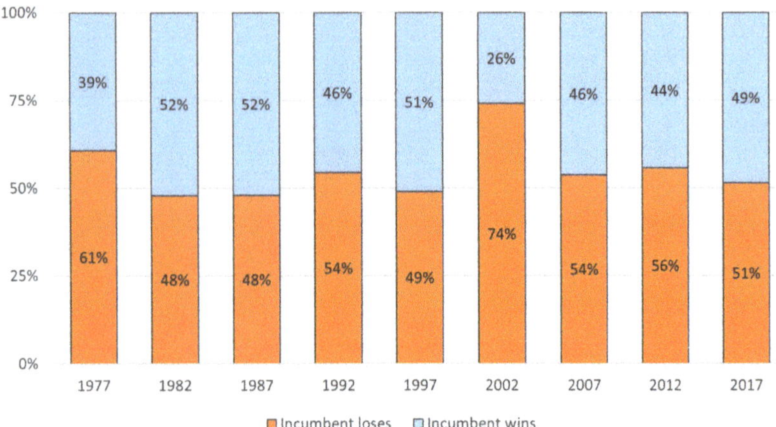

Figure 2.6: Incumbent turnover over time.

Source: Data from the PNG Elections Database (Wood, 2019).

Unlike some other aspects of elections, incumbent turnover rates do not vary much between regions: sitting members everywhere have a high chance of losing their seats.

In the early 1980s, David Hegarty (1982) noticed a correlation at each election between candidate numbers and the likelihood an MP would lose their seat. Recent statistical analysis by Wood (2017) shows that this relationship can still be found. When more candidates stand, the sitting member is more likely to lose their seat. What remains unclear though is why this relationship exists. Do more candidates stand when they think an MP is weak? Or is it the case that more candidates weaken an MP's chances of re-election by eating into their support base? Future case study research could shed light on this.

Women candidates

Since independence, PNG's parliament has seen a total of only seven women parliamentarians. At present, there are no women in PNG's parliament. PNG sits alongside Micronesia and Vanuatu as one of the few countries on earth that does not have any female representation in parliament (IPU, 2020). The number of women MPs elected in each post-independence general election in PNG is shown in Figure 2.7. The absence of women in PNG's parliament does not reflect disinterest on behalf of women candidates. Candidate numbers have risen: 10 women stood in the 1977 elections; in 2007, 105 women stood; in 2017, 179 women contested the elections (Laveil and Wood, 2019, p. 22; Sepoe, 2002, p. 39). Yet, the number of women elected at each election is not growing.

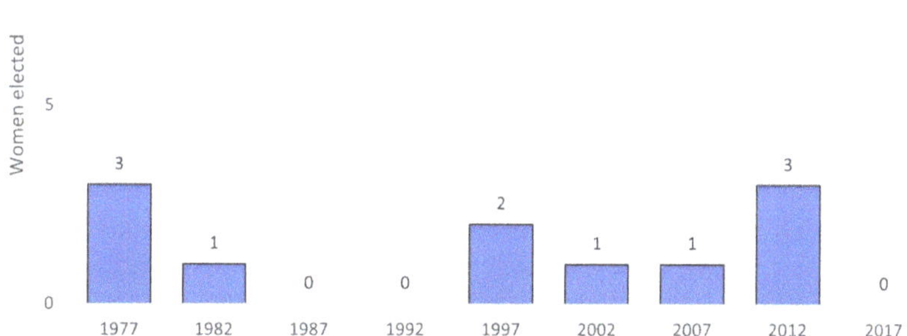

Figure 2.7: Number of women elected in general elections.

Source: Data from the PNG Elections Database (Wood, 2019).

The impact of LPV

PNG has used two electoral systems in its time as an independent nation.[2] The first electoral system, used from 1977 to 2002, was a single member district plurality (SMDP) system, commonly known as first-past-the-post. Voters were allowed a single preference under this system. The second electoral system, first used in a 2003 by-election (Reilly, 2006), is the LPV system, which allows voters three preferences. Winning candidates under the LPV are those who earn more than 50 per cent of those ballots that have not yet been exhausted.[3] In this section we examine whether changing electoral systems has changed electoral politics in PNG.

2 A third system, similar to LPV, was used in national elections prior to independence. SMDP was adopted at independence on the recommendation of the constitutional commission, which concluded it would be simpler logistically (Reilly, 2002).

3 The LPV electoral system has two counting phases: one in which first preferences are counted, and another where second and third preferences are counted. A winning candidate is one who receives either more than 50 per cent of total valid first preference votes or, failing this, receives more than 50 per cent of those ballots not yet exhausted. A ballot is said to be exhausted once a voter's first, second and third preference candidates have already been eliminated from the count. In practice a significant number of ballots are eliminated in most electorates, meaning the total ballots counted in the round in which a winner is selected is usually considerably lower than the total number of ballots cast.

Violence

Election-related violence does not appear to have changed much when elections under the SMDP and LPV systems are compared. SMDP elections had been believed to encourage clan-based candidates, with violence a reflection of ethnic differences (Reilly, 2002, 2006). Violence was an issue in SMDP elections and was particularly bad in 2002 (May et al., 2011). The 2007 elections, the first general elections run under LPV, were relatively peaceful. This seemed like an early achievement for LPV. Violence has increased since then, however, with the 2017 elections recording 204 election-related deaths (Haley and Zubrinich, 2018).

It is possible that the 2007 improvement was driven largely by an increased security presence in the Highlands in that election. Another possibility is that while LPV initially triggered a reduction in violence as approaches to campaigning changed, the changes were not sustained, and the norm of electoral violence, particularly in parts of the Highlands, ultimately proved resistant to changes in electoral rules.

Invalid ballots

Figure 2.8 shows invalid ballots for elections with available data. Unfortunately, spoiled ballot data are not available for 2007, the year LPV was first used in a general election. However, comparing numbers in the previous elections with those after 2007 is instructive.

Comparing the last election that the SMDP system was used (2002), and the first election under the LPV system for which data are available (2012), invalid ballots increased from 0.7 per cent in 2002 to 2.6 per cent in 2012. The more complex system of LPV where voters have to choose three preferences seems to have increased invalid ballots. Possibly, however, the share of ballots that are spoiled is now decreasing as more voters understand the LPV system: only 2 per cent of ballots were invalid in 2017.

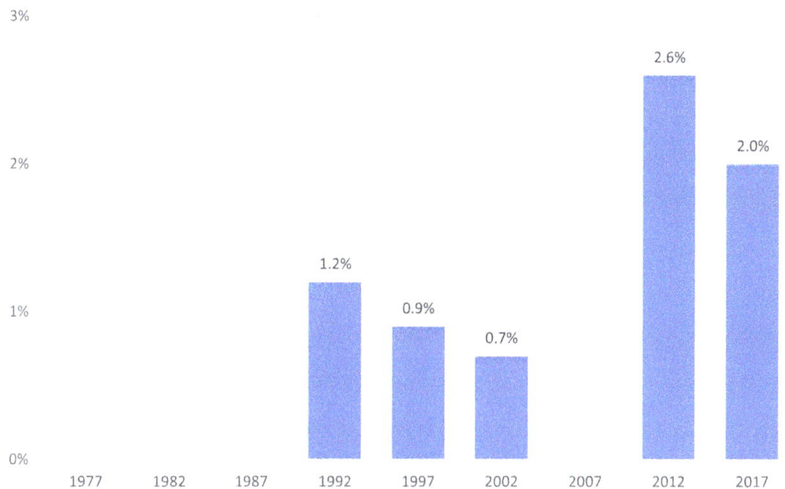

Figure 2.8: Share of votes that were invalid.

Source: Data from the PNG Elections Database (Wood, 2019). Years with no bars are missing data.

MPs' electoral mandates

One argument made in favour of LPV was that it would increase MPs' electoral mandates. It was thought that because MPs would win votes from a larger share of their electorates under LPV they would govern in a manner that better served their whole electorate, rather than just their supporters. As the median winner's vote share line in Figure 2.5 above shows, LPV has clearly increased the typical MP's mandate in the sense that they have won with the support of more voters. However, as the figure also shows, contrary to a common mistaken belief about LPV, the typical winner in elections since LPV was introduced has not won with more than 50 per cent of the total number of votes cast in their electorate (the actual figure for the median winning candidate is closer to 30 per cent).

Nevertheless, the increase in winner vote share under LPV suggests the system is more representative in the sense that MPs are now being elected to parliament with the support of more voters. Even so, persistent high incumbent turnover suggests a continued dissatisfaction with MPs' performance. LPV does not seem to have left voters much more satisfied with their MPs on average.

Governance

Another claim sometimes made for LPV was that it would improve the quality of governance in PNG. Figure 2.9 shows the average of five governance indicators provided by the World Bank: political stability and the absence of violence, government effectiveness, regulatory quality, rule of law, and control of corruption (World Bank, 2019). In the figure, these are measured in global percentile rankings for years when data are available.

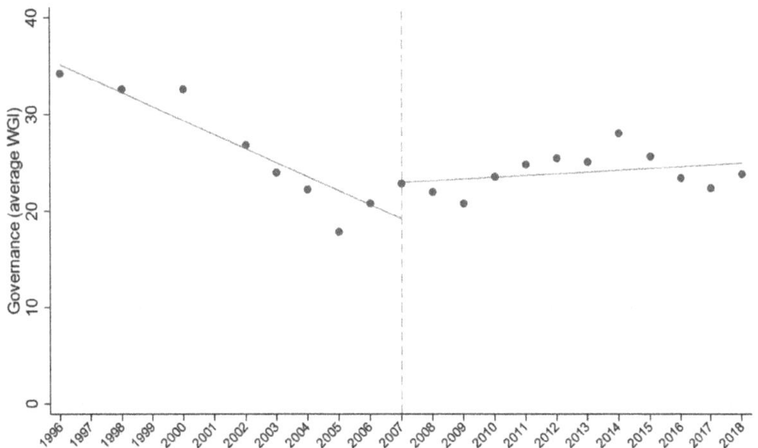

Figure 2.9: Quality of governance under SMDP (1996–2006) and under LPV (2007–18).

Note: WGI = Worldwide Governance Indicators.

Source: Data from World Bank (2019).

Although the average appears volatile, a simple comparison suggests PNG's governance score is marginally better now than it was in 2007 (the first general election with LPV). This would also seem to be a reversal of a previous trend of deterioration. However, a closer look at trends reveals more. In particular, governance started improving in 2005, before LPV was first used in a general election, and the trend of improvement also appears to have reversed again since 2014.[4] In 2018, governance was still worse than it had been under SMDP in 1996. If LPV has improved governance in PNG, there is no clear evidence in the available data.

4 There are two plausible alternative explanations for improving governance in this period. First, it coincides with the period of improved economic performance stemming from PNG's resource boom. It is plausible the resource boom is the source of better governance scores, either because more government revenue afforded improved scope for better services, or because perceptions of governance (the indicators are largely perception based) were influenced by PNG's rising affluence. Second, improvement may have stemmed from reforms introduced by Sir Mekere Morauta's 1999–2002 government.

Has LPV helped women?

Another hope was that LPV would improve the electoral fortunes of female candidates. At this point, limited data have been an impediment to research on the question of whether LPV has worked to help women candidates or not. When we examine the number of women elected to parliament, as we did in Figure 2.7, it seems clear that LPV has not yet brought any change to the number of female MPs who have been elected. However, it is also true that the average performance of women who stood in the 2017 elections tells a more positive story than the one that emerges if we look at winners alone. Average performance suggests women candidates became slightly more competitive between 2012 and 2017 (Laveil and Wood, 2019). This trend is more encouraging, although, unfortunately, insufficient data exist on women candidates in pre-LPV elections to state for sure that the trend is a result of the change in electoral systems.

The belief that LPV might help women candidates hinges on the assumption that women might win by the second and third preferences, or the '*sori* vote' (the sympathy vote, a concept many female candidates would view as patronising). Empirical analysis of election results suggests female candidates have benefited somewhat more from second and third preference votes than men have (Laveil and Wood, 2019, p. 21). This is encouraging and once again suggests LPV may have helped women candidates. However, gains have been small and there is no evidence LPV has seriously addressed the challenges female candidates face (Baker, 2018).

Ultimately, it will need more than three elections to get a clear picture of LPV's effect on female candidates. Thus far, however, if it has helped women candidates, any benefits of LPV have been modest at best.

Women's political participation and Temporary Special Measures

PNG's constitution strongly advocates for equality for all citizens. The second National Goal and Directive Principle, 'Equality and Participation', stipulates that citizens should have equal opportunity to participate in and benefit from the country's development. The principle makes explicit mention of women's political participation (Government of Papua New Guinea, 1975). However, as we have shown, election results strongly suggest women candidates have not been able to participate equally in elections.

Three key impediments serve as common challenges for nearly all women aspiring to political office in PNG: cultural factors, insufficient finance, and violence and intimidation.

Being a predominantly patriarchal society with strong cultural norms contributes significantly to low female representation in parliament. Patriarchal societies, particularly in the Highlands, still have conservative attitudes regarding a woman's 'place', which is not in positions of leadership. The challenge is not limited to the Highlands either. During observations of the 2017 national elections in Madang Province, strong patriarchal norms were observed. Many of the women voters interviewed indicated their family and tribal affiliations dictated who they voted for. Voters' comments often suggested strong opposition to women candidates with the argument that women did not belong in a 'men's house' (parliament).

As we highlighted earlier in this chapter, elections in PNG have been marred by electoral corruption and money politics. The costs of money politics, combined with legitimate expenses, make campaigning an expensive exercise. Costs associated with running a successful campaign include, but are not limited to, posters, advertisements, logistics and transportation, security, supplying 'campaign houses' with food and beverages, meeting the demands of voters, financing vote buying, hiring sing-sing and supporter groups, and allowances for scrutineers. Funding all of this can easily exhaust candidates who do not possess substantial financial resources. The gendered nature of PNG's economy makes it harder for women than men to obtain much-needed electoral finances. This puts female candidates at a great disadvantage.

Election-related violence and intimidation of female candidates are recurring problems. Policing is usually reserved for polling stations and during counting. With insufficient resources, female candidates are not guaranteed security and are prone to intimidation and violence. Sarah Garap, who contested in 2002 in Simbu Province, faced violence and intimidation from supporters of male candidates (Radio New Zealand, 2002). Mary Kaman, who has run for the Madang provincial seat four times, has spoken of how her supporters and those of other women candidates in Madang were openly intimidated.

Temporary Special Measures – a pathway to change

There is need for serious action at the national level to adequately address the issue of women's representation in parliament. Given all the constraints to women winning elections, introducing some form of TSM has been proposed as an action the government should take if it is serious about including women in national decision-making.

TSMs are not new: about 40 countries have already introduced gender quotas for parliamentary elections by constitutional amendment or electoral law. These provisions include reserved seats, which set aside a certain number of places for women (Krook, 2006).

Also, in more than 50 countries, quotas requiring that a certain minimum of parties' candidates for election to national parliament must be women are now stipulated in major political parties' own statutes (Dahlerup and Freidenvall, 2005).

In 2011, the then minister for community development and three-term parliamentarian Dame Carol Kidu spearheaded the push to introduce 22 reserved (regional) seats for women in the national parliament. Elections since the early 1980s had brought disappointing results for women, and Dame Carol was the only woman in parliament at the time.

The Equality and Participation Bill was tabled in parliament on 9 September 2011 and passed by 72 votes to 2 on 23 November 2011. This resulted in an amendment of the constitution to include the provision for 22 reserved seats for women, one for each province (Baker, 2014a). However, for the act to be implemented, a constitutional amendment on the *Organic Law on National and Local-level Government Elections* (amendment no. 2) also had to be passed. This amendment failed to get the two-thirds majority of 73 needed to pass it. Only 58 members voted for the Bill, while 21 members walked out of the chamber and one member voted against it (Elapa, 2012). With this effective shelving of the Equality and Participation Bill, the push for 22 reserved seats was not pursued, even when three women were elected to parliament in the 2012 elections.

One persistent argument against reserved seats is that it would give women an unfair advantage. According to this argument, if women truly want equality, they should contest elections without special privileges. As shown above, however, electoral contests are already unequal: female candidates face more challenges than men.

Despite the failure of the 2011 initiative, PNG does have experience of TSMs at the subnational level. With the finalisation of the Bougainville constitution in 2004, three seats in the Bougainville House of Representatives were reserved for women, along with three seats for ex-combatants (Bougainville has a 39-seat legislature) (Baker, 2014b). The existence of reserved seats in the Autonomous Region of Bougainville has helped increase women's political participation.

The 2020 Bougainville elections yielded positive and promising results for women's representation, with a total of four women elected to the Bougainville House of Representatives. In addition to the three women elected to reserved seats, 29-year-old activist, social worker and mother Theonilla Roka Matbob was elected to represent the Loro Constituency, which includes the Panguna mine, where fighting in Bougainville's civil conflict first started in the 1980s (Whiting, 2020). Matbob's win is significant, as she is only the second woman to win an open seat in Bougainville.

When the first woman to win an open seat in Bougainville, Josephine Getsi, won in 2015, her success was celebrated and credited as an indication of the growing understanding of the role women can play in politics (Radio New Zealand, 2016). The 2020 election results suggest this understanding is continuing to grow. More than 40 women contested the 2020 elections in Bougainville (SBS News, 2020). This represents a significant increase from 2015 and is evidence that more women than ever are interested in vying for leadership positions in the region.

Francesca Semoso, former deputy speaker for the third Bougainville House of Representatives, was elected twice to the north Bougainville reserved seat (in 2005 and 2015); she took second place in the 2010 elections and third in the 2020 elections for an open seat. She is an ardent advocate for TSMs. Semoso describes reserved seats as a 'launching pad' for women politicians who face challenges that men do not often face when they enter politics (Pacific Women, 2016).

PNG can learn a lot from the measures Bougainville has taken to increase equal political representation.

What is the way forward for the inclusion of women in politics?

Although female electoral success in PNG appears elusive, there are many small victories that must be acknowledged. First, the awareness around TSMs that was brought to the national consciousness in late 2011 as well as the successful use of TSMs in the Autonomous Region of Bougainville. Second, the 2012 victory of three women: Loujaya Toni (Lae open), Delilah Gore (Sohe open) and Julie Soso (Eastern Highlands provincial). Soso's win was testimony to years of planning that eventually ensured victory in a seat that demands widespread popularity in a particularly patriarchal part of the country.

The 45 years of independence and the nine elections that have occurred have brought useful lessons on equal political representation. There are two points that aspiring women politicians, advocates of equal political participation, civil society and international organisations should take into account in their attempts to get more women into parliament. The first point is for individual candidates themselves; the second point relates to the broader collective task of changing electoral rules.

Aspiring female candidates need to focus on the long-term planning associated with the challenge of winning elections. Given the disadvantages posed by culture and lack of finance, female candidates must be willing to plan ahead, putting in extra effort. In particular, female candidates need to maximise their financial resources to sustain their campaigns.

Candidates also need to get to know their community's needs by being on the ground and being involved. Winning takes groundwork. When interviewed in 2017, Dame Carol Kidu recalled how she would visit settlement communities in Port Moresby South and villages frequently as part of her groundwork to get a sense of the issues people faced. Research by the National Research Institute also confirms voters stated they valued *hanmak* as a show of concern with the community's affairs (Fario et al., 2020). In addition, candidates need to focus on networking and utilising connections with community groups. There are many examples of how women used their networks and connections to help their campaigns.

Long-term strategising is an arduous journey, and there is no guarantee that the efforts put in over the years will translate into earning a seat in parliament. Yet female candidates can improve their chances by campaigning strategically and over the long-term.

The collective task associated with improving women's representation involves lobbying and increasing parliamentary support for TSMs. To do this, reserved seats for women must be aggressively pursued. Despite its rejection by many in political office, reserved seats can be lobbied for by sitting parliamentarians, civil society and women's groups. Leaders' views can be changed. Public awareness of the nature of TSMs also needs to be raised. TSMs are not unequal as is sometimes claimed. They are designed to correct existing inequalities in electoral competition and to boost the equality of political participation until other changes occur. When these changes do occur, TSMs can be discontinued, hence the 'temporary' nature of these quotas.

Another approach would be to push for party gender quotas. The Integrity of Political Parties and Candidates Commission registrar, Dr Alphonse Gelu, has stated that proposed revisions to OLIPPAC include a provision that 20 per cent of a political party's nominated candidates must be female candidates. If the revised law is passed, it will be a big improvement (Radio New Zealand, 2020).

Whatever the mechanism, the aim must be that through collaboration, consultation and lobbying, PNG moves towards measures that will allow women more representation in parliament.

Voter choice and clientelism

As we have discussed, voters are not always free to choose who they vote for in PNG. Sometimes they are forced or intimidated into voting for a candidate. This is a real problem in parts of PNG. However, when they were surveyed after the 2012 election, the majority of surveyed voters said they were free to choose who to vote for. And in 2017 the majority of voters said they were free to choose except in the Highlands Region and National Capital District (Haley and Zubrinich, 2018, p. 61). Voter coercion is a real problem in PNG, but enough voters appear free to choose for the question 'why do voters vote for the candidates they vote for?' to be an important one for study.

What are voters looking for when they vote?

Before going any further, one point needs to be clarified: not all voters think or behave in the same way. For every rule there is an exception. In this section we are going to talk about the choices of the majority of voters. There is an obvious reason for doing this: in elections, in most circumstances, majorities decide the results.

In 1989, an academic who ran a large voter survey in PNG wrote the following about voter choice based on the survey findings: 'Recurring themes are the overwhelming importance of local factors in candidate evaluation, the corresponding insignificance of party, and the virtual absence of [national] issues in the decision calculus' (Saffu, 1989, p. 15). Nearly 40 years later, the authors of another large survey-based election study summarised their findings about voter choice by stating that: 'voter choice remains driven by local politics, personal interest and personal gain, and not by party policies' (Haley and Zubrinich, 2018, p. 41).

These survey-related findings are corroborated by the findings of case study research (e.g. Anere, 1997; Osi, 2013; Standish, 2007).[5] When voters are free to vote in PNG, most make choices based on local factors. They do not normally choose their preferred candidates based on national politics or national issues. Typically, voters vote for candidates who they think will help them, their family or their community if they are elected (Wood, 2018).

Under these circumstances, parties – as the quotations from Haley and Saffu suggest – are much less important than they are in many democracies. In PNG very few voters vote for candidates because they like their party's national policy platform or share its ideology (Okole, 2001). As we discuss in the section on parliamentary politics, parties are still important in government formation. And parties can still play a role in elections in PNG. In the past, parties sometimes provided candidates with a network of contacts who could help win votes (e.g. Filer, 1996). In more recent years, parties have sometimes served as vehicles through

5 Many of the best qualitative studies on elections in PNG, along with Yaw Saffu's quantitative work, can be found for free online in a series of downloadable books on PNG elections. To access these books, go to pacificinstitute.anu.edu.au/resources, then scroll down to 'PNG Elections'. This is a fantastic resource if you are interested in elections in PNG.

which powerful politicians provide resources to aspiring candidates. But it has been rare for voters to vote for candidates simply because they like their party.

Interestingly, in 2017 it seems as if voters were willing to vote against a party – the People's National Congress (PNC) – to punish it for what they saw as poor performance in government. Particularly, voters appeared to show their displeasure with PNC candidates by not giving them second and third preference votes, and this caused a number of PNC candidates to lose electoral contests (Laveil and Wood, 2019). This 'protest' vote is interesting and may be evidence that voters in PNG are starting to think about politics in different ways. However, the protest only involved second and third preferences, not first preferences, and it may be a one-off, stemming from unusual circumstances. For now, most of the time, most voters do not normally vote along party lines or consider national issues.

How do people choose who to vote for?

If most voters do not vote for candidates on the basis of national issues or on related grounds such as their party, how do they choose who to vote for? Researchers have identified a number of different influences. Some of these are stronger in some parts of PNG than in others and some influences are becoming more or less important with time.

Often people vote for candidates who they are in some way related to (colloquially, their *wantoks*). In parts of the country this can be a central organising principle. In some parts of the Highlands, for example, voters are expected to vote for the candidate from their *haus lain* (clan), and entire communities will vote as a bloc for an individual candidate. Often, however, when people vote for relatives or people who they share similar ties with, they are making a well-considered calculation. All candidates promise voters they will help them if elected, but not all candidates follow up on those promises. Rules of reciprocity within extended families are not always honoured, but they can be a strong cultural force. This means candidates are often more likely to help supporters who are their *wantoks* if they are elected. As a result, voters often vote for *wantoks* because they think they can trust them to help if they win (Okole, 2002, 2005; Wood, 2016). In other instances, voters simply feel obliged to vote for relatives: a voter from Central Province told one of the authors that they liked LPV because they could vote for all three of their cousins and keep each happy. Voters sometimes vote for relatives who have no chance of winning simply for the sake of maintaining good relations with the relatives in question.

Another factor influencing voters' choices can be support from community groups and recommendations from influential community figures. Strong candidates often campaign in part through support of this kind. Voters are more likely to trust a candidate if they know and trust their main, influential supporters (Filer, 1996; Osi, 2013).

Beyond relational ties, another way a voter can get a sense of whether a candidate will keep their promises and help them if elected is if a candidate has helped in the past. This is easy if the candidate they are considering voting for is the sitting MP (has the MP helped in the last five years?), but it can also be a strategy for appraising candidates who are standing for the first time. Candidates can win voter loyalty by having helped previously with community projects or with families' needs.

Closely associated to voters' considerations of whether a candidate will help in the future based on their past track record of helping is the desire among some voters for some form of *hanmak* or tangible material assistance. We have already discussed this in the context of female candidates, but the calculation is present regardless of a candidate's gender. Sometimes voters use giving of this nature as a guide as they assess candidates' longer histories and how helpful they are (Anere, 1997; Osi, 2013; Wood, 2016). At other times, giving, particularly during campaign periods, primarily serves as a form of vote buying or money politics (Haley and Zubrinich, 2018).

Clientelism and politics

The fact that voters appraise candidates based on their likelihood of helping directly, rather than on national issues, is not unique to PNG. It is a key feature of politics in many countries. Political scientists use the term 'clientelism' to refer to politics that is based on local, personal benefits rather than national issues or policies (Hicken, 2011).

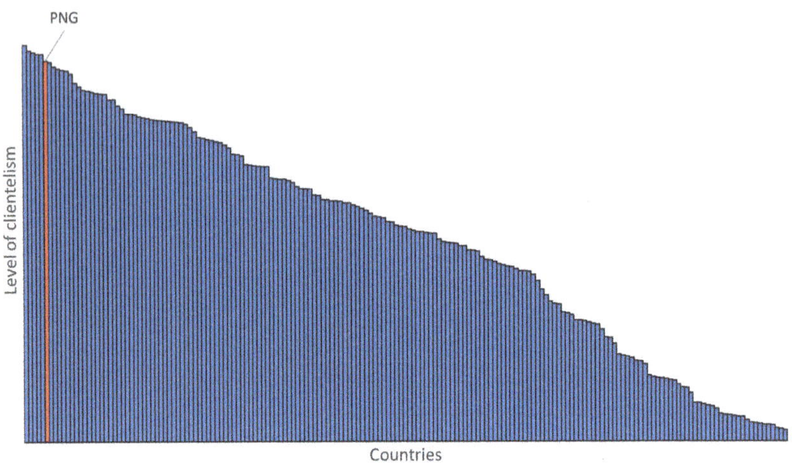

Figure 2.10: Clientelism in PNG and internationally.

Source: Varieties of Democracy (Coppedge et al., 2020).

Figure 2.10 uses data from a large international study of countries' politics (Coppedge et al., 2020). It charts countries based on how strongly clientelist their politics are. Each bar is a country. Higher bars are countries with more clientelism. All the world's countries with data are included (179 countries in total). The score is an average across the years 2015–19. PNG is shown in red. PNG has one of the highest bars on the chart, reflecting the fact that it is one of the world's most clientelist countries. However, the figure also shows that PNG is not unique – clientelism is prevalent in many other countries too.

Sometimes in discussions of voting in PNG, people blame voters for being selfish and choosing their own personal benefit over the national good. However, this view is unfair. Voting for local or personal support is a reasonable way for voters to vote in PNG. In rural areas in particular, voters have immediate material needs. They also receive very little or no support from the state. And they have never experienced politics where national policy changes have had a big impact on their lives. To further complicate matters, national change requires national political movements (to really change a country, a cohesive majority of MPs is needed in parliament). Genuinely national political movements do not exist in PNG. Under these circumstances, a rational voter wanting to see any positive change emerge from an election has good grounds to vote for someone who will help locally. This is the best they can hope for (Haque, 2012; Wood, 2016).

There is a problem, however, with voters choosing candidates based on whether they will provide direct, local support. Voting this way selects and incentivises most MPs to focus on delivering support to individuals and local communities, and to neglect national governance. This is not the only political problem PNG faces, but the dynamic does contribute to poor political governance.

Voters choosing who to vote for on the basis of whether they will help locally has other impacts too. For example, clientelism has almost certainly contributed to the rise of MP-influenced electorate funds such as the District Services Improvement Program – funds that tend to be an inefficient way of delivering services (Howes et al., 2014).

A challenge for PNG in the future will be finding a way of building genuinely national, issues-based politics. There is potential for this. New social movements and activists are starting to grow in PNG. The protest vote against the government in 2017 also suggests that voters may be increasingly willing to vote on national issues. At the same time, however, other forces, in particular the influence of money on politics and people's electoral choices, threatens to push the other way, away from issue-oriented national politics.

Parliamentary politics

Coalition governments in PNG

Since the first post-independence elections in 1977, no political party has had the majority to form the government on its own in PNG, either after a national election or a vote of no confidence. All governments have been coalition based. Reflecting the clientelist nature of PNG's politics, political parties in PNG have no clear ideological divides and, as we discussed in the section on voter choices, voters rarely vote along party lines. Parties largely operate as parliamentary factions, especially after elections, acting in the hope of forming government. Party allegiance among politicians is fluid. Parties are often based around personal ties and the financial assistance party strongmen provide to candidates (Laveil and Wood, 2019).

Governing coalitions in PNG's parliament are not normally based on similarities in parties' policies. For instance, despite having very different policies on education, Pangu Pati and the PNC formed a coalition government following a vote of no confidence in 2019 (Kabuni, 2019c). Instead, MPs and parties join coalitions with the hope of attaining positions of power, such as ministerial roles. The *Organic Law on the Number of Ministers* sets the maximum number of ministers as a quarter of the total number of MPs in the legislature, and the minimum at 18 (Government of Papua New Guinea, n.d.). This translates into a maximum of 28 ministerial portfolios as there are 111 MPs. The *Vice-Ministers Act 1994* provides 12 vice-ministers to assist the ministers (Government of Papua New Guinea, 1994). In addition, section 118 of the constitution provides for the creation of permanent parliamentary committees, without prescribing the number of committees (Government of Papua New Guinea, 1975). The chairmen of the committees are MPs from the government side who are not ministers, while deputy chairmen come from the Opposition. After the 2017 elections, 17 permanent committees were formed for the duration of the term. MPs can also be given positions on the boards of various state-owned companies and authorities.

With the exception of the roles of committee deputy chairmen, all of the above positions are reserved for MPs in the government. These positions serve as an incentive to parties and their MPs to join the government.

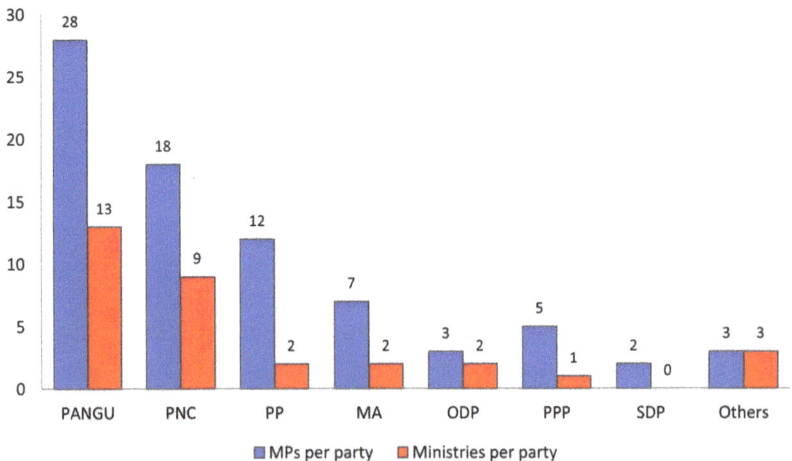

Figure 2.11: MPs and ministers by party in 2019.

Source: Data from Kabuni (2019b).

Parties with more MPs in a governing coalition usually have more portfolios. Figure 2.11 shows how ministerial portfolios were distributed when James Marape replaced Peter O'Neill as the prime minister in May 2019, and illustrates this point.

Political instability in PNG

A major consequence of coalition governments that are office oriented and not based on shared beliefs about policy is political instability. Successive votes of no confidence in PNG's parliament have led to changes in the position of the prime minister during every electoral term from 1977 until the Somare government completed the 2002 to 2007 term. As Figure 2.12 shows, between 1975 and 2020, even though PNG has had only nine national elections, there were 17 changes to the prime minister's position. Governing coalitions are rearranged with every vote of no confidence. Sometimes, changes see the cabinet replaced in its entirety. Ministerial reshuffles further add to instability, as prime ministers attempt to secure support for their position by replacing individual ministers mid-term (Ivarature, 2016).

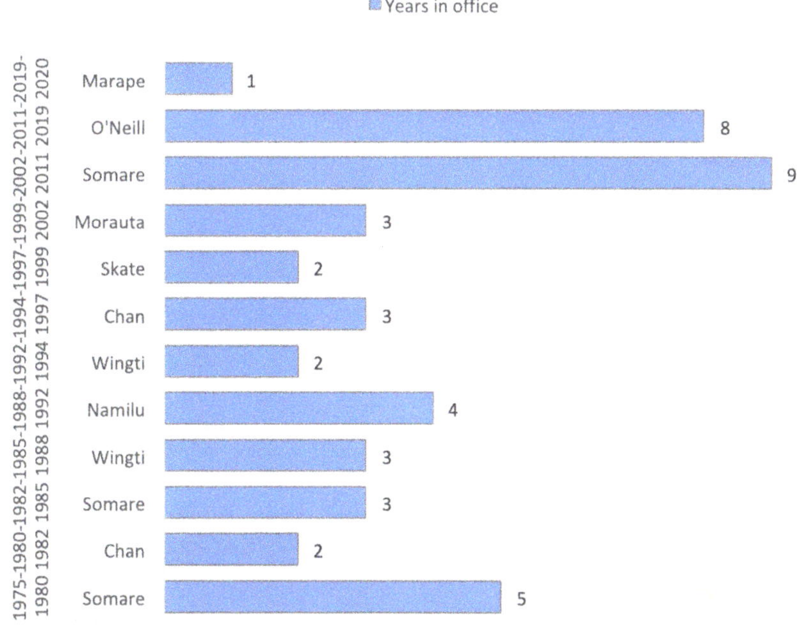

Figure 2.12: Length of prime ministers' tenure.

Source: Adapted from Kabuni (2018b). Additions were made for 2019.

In the 2000s, the prime minister's position became more stable. Michael Somare became the first prime minister to complete a parliamentary term between 2002 and 2007, and he formed government again in 2007 after re-election. His government lasted until 2011.[6] Peter O'Neill, who replaced Somare as prime minister in 2011, formed government after the 2012 elections and again in 2017. Somare and O'Neill are the only prime ministers to complete their terms and successively form government in subsequent elections. James Marape replaced Peter O'Neill as the prime minister in 2019 when O'Neill resigned in the face of a vote of no confidence (Kama, 2017; May, 2020).

Engineering political stability

OLIPPAC was passed in 2001 and amended in 2003 (Government of Papua New Guinea, 2003). It contained a number of provisions designed to promote political stability and parliamentary integrity. Section 63 stipulates that the party that has the most MPs after a national election will be invited by the governor-general to form government. The aim of section 63 is to ensure that a prime minister is appointed after a general election in an orderly manner with a direct relationship to the way voters expressed their wishes (Gelu, 2005). Only if the largest party's nominated candidate failed to win a majority of MPs' votes would the process be thrown open to other contenders, enabling any group that could pull together enough support to form government. This requirement was intended to prevent lobbying for government formation, as that had given rise to corruption and bribery in the past, as even parties with small numbers competed to form government (Okole, 2012).

However, there is no provision in the OLIPPAC requiring the party with the largest numbers to form the government if the prime minister is removed mid-term. Peter O'Neill, who replaced Somare as prime minister in 2011, had only five MPs in his PNC party. The PNG party had 25 MPs in the same coalition when O'Neill was elected prime minister (Kabuni, 2019a).

OLIPPAC was also enacted with the aim of bringing party discipline and political stability. Central to this were provisions that required:

6 The replacement of Somare by O'Neill occurred, it should be noted, under highly irregular circumstances, and in a manner that appears to have violated PNG's constitution. For a full discussion, see May (2017, 2020).

- MPs to give substantive reasons for leaving their parties, and the Ombudsman Commission to subsequently investigate these reasons. This was aimed at preventing MPs from joining other parties as this usually led to a vote of no confidence (sections 57–59).
- All MPs in a political party to remain a single cohesive body in making decisions such as to determine who will be prime minister and in supporting or opposing the prime minister during a vote of no confidence (section 65).

If MPs voted for the incumbent prime minister at the time of their nomination, they were required not to vote against the prime minister in any subsequent votes of no confidence. MPs could, however, abstain from voting against the incumbent prime minister they voted for originally in a vote of no confidence.

Votes of no confidence and the OLIPPAC

As can be seen in Figure 2.12 above, it does appear as if no confidence motions decreased after OLIPPAC was introduced. However, the effectiveness of OLIPPAC has generated considerable debate (Okole, 2012). Some scholars have claimed that OLIPPAC has had limited success (Sepoe, 2005). Others have attributed Somare's nine-year rule from 2002 to 2011 to OLIPPAC (Fairweather, 2019). In our view, recent history provides little or no evidence that OLIPPAC has played an important role in increasing the longevity of governments.

The executive government in a parliamentary democracy derives its legitimacy from the legislature and, in theory, remains accountable to the legislature. One of the ways in which the legislature exercises control over the executive is through votes of no confidence. In PNG, this process is provided for by section 145 of the constitution. In 2010, the Supreme Court ruled the OLIPPAC provisions regarding changing parties and votes of no confidence unconstitutional for, among other things, placing unreasonable restrictions on the rights and freedoms of MPs (Kabuni, 2018b). However, even before these provisions were ruled unconstitutional, MPs were moving from one party to another. Although the Ombudsman Commission was empowered to investigate these changes under OLIPPAC, it failed to do so (Gelu, 2005).

Peter O'Neill's completion of the 2012 to 2017 term is even more interesting as it was achieved after the parts of OLIPPAC intended to enhance political stability were ruled unconstitutional in 2010. The next section looks at possible explanations for this.

Peter O'Neill's term: 2012–17

The first factor that helped prevent Peter O'Neill from being removed as prime minister after the 2012 elections was the extension of the grace period. A grace period is a period in which the prime minister cannot be removed through a vote of no confidence after their election, either following a national election or after a vote of no confidence.

At independence, the grace period was six months. In 1991, this was extended to 18 months. In 2012, the O'Neill government amended the constitution to increase the grace period after the election of the prime minister to 30 months (Radio New Zealand, 2015).

There is also a rule that stipulates that if a vote of no confidence is instituted within 12 months before the fifth anniversary of the date fixed for the return of writs at the previous general election, parliament must be dissolved and national elections conducted. Because of the high incumbent turnover rate (as discussed in the section on electoral trends), MPs are usually not enthusiastic about votes of no confidence during these final 12 months.

There are 60 months in a parliamentary term of five years. Because votes of no confidence are rarely instituted within the 12 months before the next election, and another 30 months was covered by the grace period (a total of 42 months), during O'Neill's term the Opposition only had a short 18-month window to challenge the prime minister.

Also, during O'Neill's tenure, the minimum parliamentary sitting days in a year were reduced from 63 to 40 (Radio New Zealand, 2015). This left only 60 days in the 18-month window. The government then used tactics such as adjourning the parliament when there were threats of a vote of no confidence to stay in power. One such adjournment in 2016 was made as the final 12 months before the fifth anniversary of the date fixed for the return of writs at the 2012 general election drew near. The next parliamentary sitting was scheduled to fall well within the grace period, eliminating any chance of conducting a vote of no confidence without dissolving the parliament. However, the Supreme Court then ruled that both this adjournment and the increase of the grace period to 30 months were invalid (Radio New Zealand, 2015). The parliament met but the prime minister successfully overcame the vote of no confidence.

The second important factor that helped secure O'Neill in office was the increased use of the District and Provincial Services Improvement Program (DSIP/PSIP) funds. MPs have considerable discretion over the spending of these funds. They are a powerful tool that the MP can use to generate political support within their electorate. During O'Neill's time as prime minister, these funds were greatly increased. In addition, MPs in the Opposition complained that the O'Neill government deliberately withheld their DSIP and PSIP funds, while releasing the funds to MPs who supported the government. For instance, Opposition MPs Basil and Juffa, who were critical of the O'Neill government in 2016, claimed that they did not receive their full share of the funds (Kabuni, 2018a). O'Neill was not the first prime minister to use DSIP and PSIP funds in this way (Ketan, 2007); however, O'Neill appears to have been particularly astute in his use of this tool and was able to further strengthen his governing coalition. MPs had a clear financial incentive not to cross the floor.

The third factor aiding O'Neill's tenure was the politicisation of some parts of the public service (Kama, 2017; May, 2017, 2020). The executive arm of the government secured control of appointments of senior civil service positions (Kama, 2017). This can be seen in the appointment of the police commissioners. In 2014, the O'Neill government dismissed Tom Kulunga when he signed the necessary documents to effect the arrest of Prime Minister Peter O'Neill in relation to alleged illegal payments made to Paul Paraka lawyers. Geoffrey Vaki replaced Tom Kulunga. Geoffrey Vaki prevented the arrest of the prime minister, but when he became embroiled in a contempt of court case in the same year for conspiring to prevent that arrest, the O'Neill government appointed Gary Baki again as the police commissioner. Gary Baki then again prevented the arrest of the prime minister. Arguably, were it not for political appointments in key roles, O'Neill's term would have been truncated sooner on legal grounds.

Finally, it is possible that the resource boom from about 2003 to 2014 helped both O'Neill and Somare stay in office by providing funding for increasing constituency funds, and more generally by providing increased resources that could be used to help cohere governing coalitions.

The consequences of political instability

Fraenkel et al. (2008) attribute political instability in Melanesia to MPs' belief that access to elected office is a major avenue to power and wealth, and the outcome of a struggle by those MPs not in control of the resources to oust those in power. This constant struggle for power diverts parliament from its main task, which is to debate and devise legislation for the country. Instead, the MPs are occupied by the desire to form government or maintain their portfolios in the existing governing coalition. MPs in the Opposition await the expiry of the grace period and plot to replace the government. OLIPPAC was intended as a means of legislating political stability, but key provisions have been struck down by the courts and it is unclear whether OLIPPAC achieved its goals. Rather, recent political stability appears to have stemmed from recent prime ministers being particularly astute in their use of DSIP and PSIP funds, alongside lengthened grace periods and the proroguing of parliament. As O'Neill's defeat in 2019 shows, these tools do not render sitting prime ministers invulnerable. Whether the political stability seen between 2002 and 2019 will be the new normal or whether PNG will return to more frequent changes of prime minister remains to be seen. Yet one fact is clear, the tools used by prime ministers in their quest to stay on top have further detracted from the important role that parliament should be playing.

Conclusion

In this chapter we have described democratic politics as it currently exists in PNG. We have highlighted a number of problems. We have also argued that ambitious reforms to PNG's electoral system and its parliamentary rules have largely been ineffective: neither LPV nor OLIPPAC has delivered as hoped. And yet, we have also shown that a different type of reform – TSMs – could help in increasing the number of women elected to PNG's parliament. In the case of TSMs, there is a clear link between the law change and the desired outcome. There is also a precedent: such approaches have succeeded in other countries and have had a very promising start in the Autonomous Region of Bougainville.

We also have demonstrated that many of PNG's electoral and political problems do not stem from the shortcomings of voters. Rather they stem from structural issues, such as the clientelism that characterises the relationship between voters and the state in PNG, and the unstable dynamics of parliamentary coalition politics. Such structural problems may be hard to shift. They would require voters, whose needs are immediate and significant, to forego the short-term assistance currently on offer, and vote in search of something less tangible and less likely to be achieved: genuine national change. Change would also require sustained parliamentary cooperation from reformers. All of this would have to occur in the face of growing problems, such as electoral fraud and the influence of money on politics. Nevertheless, there is some cause for hope: other countries have changed the dynamics of their electoral politics through concerted efforts from both political reformers and civil society. And in PNG at present, both reformers and change-oriented civil society groups do exist. It would be naive to claim that democracy in PNG has delivered all that was hoped of it. Yet it would be unduly pessimistic to abandon hope in the democratic process. PNG's future is yet to be written. There is scope for positive change in the country's politics. Democracy is messy, but its future in PNG is still one of potential.

Acknowledgements

We are very grateful to Stephen Howes for detailed and helpful comments on earlier drafts of this chapter. We would also like to thank Dr Kerryn Baker for her insightful comments and assistance. We are similarly grateful to Ron May for his review and insights. We are also grateful to participants in two virtual University of Papua New Guinea/The Australian National University workshops for their feedback. As always, any errors or omissions are ours alone.

References

Anere, R. (1997). Milne Bay Provincial: Independents versus parties. In R. May and R. Anere (Eds), *Maintaining democracy: The 1997 elections in Papua New Guinea* (pp. 88–97). University of Papua New Guinea.

Baker, K. (2014a). Explaining the outcome of gender quota campaigns in Samoa and Papua New Guinea. *Political Science*, *66*(1), 63–83. doi.org/10.1177/0032318714531428.

Baker, K. (2014b). *Women's representation and the use of reserved seats in Bougainville*. SSGM In Brief Series, 2014/2. dpa.bellschool.anu.edu.au/sites/default/files/publications/attachments/2015-12/SSGM_IB_2014_2_0.pdf.

Baker, K. (2018). Women's representation and electoral system reform in Papua New Guinea: The limitations of limited preferential voting. *Asia & the Pacific Policy Studies*, *5*(2), 208–19. doi.org/10.1002/app5.235.

Coppedge, M., Gerring, J., Lindberg, S., Skaaning, S-E., Teorell, J., Altman, D., Bernhard, M., Fish, M. S., Glynn, A., Hicken, A., Knutsen, C. H., Krusell, J., Lührmann, A., Marquardt, K. L., McMann, K., Mechkova, V., Olin, M., Paxton, P., Pemstein, D., Pernes, J. … Wilson, S. (2020). *V-Dem Dataset v10.* Varieties of Democracy (V-Dem) Project. doi.org/10.23696/vdemds20.

Dahlerup, D. and Freidenvall, L. (2005). Quotas as a 'fast track' to equal representation for women. *International Feminist Journal of Politics*, *7*(1), 26–48. doi.org/10.1080/1461674042000324673.

Elapa, J. (2012, 23 February). Reserved seats for women bill shelved. *The National.* www.thenational.com.pg/reserved-seats-for-women-bill-shelved/.

Fairio, M., Kaut Nasengom, S. and Keimelo, C. (2020). *Challenges and critical factors affecting women in the 2017 national elections: Case of Lae and Huon Gulf.* National Research Institute Discussion Papers, 178. www.pngnri.org/images/Publications/DPNo178_Challenges_and_critical_factors_affecting_women_in_the_2017_national_elections-_Case_of_Lae_and_Huon_Gulf_.pdf.

Fairweather, K. (2019). *Farewell white man.* Jabiru Publishing.

Filer, C. (1996). 'Steak and grease': A short history of political competition in Nuku. In Y. Saffu (Ed.), *The 1992 Papua New Guinea elections: Change and continuity in electoral politics* (pp. 168–218). The Australian National University Department of Political and Social Change.

Fraenkel, J., Regan, A. and Hegarty, D. (2008). *The dangers of political party strengthening in Solomon Islands.* SSGM Working Paper Series, 2008/2. dpa.bellschool.anu.edu.au/sites/default/files/publications/attachments/2015-12/08_02wp_Fraenkel_0.pdf.

Gelu, A. (2005). Failure of the Organic Law on the Integrity of Political Parties and Candidates (OLIPPAC). *Pacific Economic Bulletin*, *20*(1), 83–97. devpolicy.org/PEB/2019/06/09/the-failure-of-the-organic-law-on-the-integrity-of-political-parties-and-candidates-olippac/.

Gibbs, P., Haley, N. and McLeod, A. (2004). *Politicking and voting in the Highlands: The 2002 Papua New Guinea national elections*. State, Society and Governance in Melanesia Discussion Paper, 1. hdl.handle.net/1885/42056.

Government of Papua New Guinea. (1975). *Constitution of the Independent State of Papua New Guinea*. www.paclii.org/pg/legis/consol_act/cotisopng534/.

Government of Papua New Guinea. (1994). *Vice-Ministers Act*. www.paclii.org/pg/legis/consol_act/va1994173/.

Government of Papua New Guinea. (2003). *Organic Law on the Integrity of Political Parties and Candidates*. www.paclii.org/pg/legis/consol_act/olotioppac2003542/.

Government of Papua New Guinea. (n.d.). *Organic Law on the Number of Ministers*. www.paclii.org/pg/legis/consol_act/olotnom353/.

Haley, N. (1997). Election fraud on a grand scale: The case of the Koroba-Kopiago Open Electorate. In R. May and R. Anere (Eds), *Maintaining democracy: The 1997 elections in Papua New Guinea* (pp. 123–39). University of Papua New Guinea.

Haley, N. and Zubrinich, K. (2013). *2012 Papua New Guinea general elections domestic observation report*. Cardno Emerging Markets.

Haley, N. and Zubrinich, K. (2018). *2017 Papua New Guinea general elections: Election observation report*. Department of Pacific Affairs.

Haque, T. A. (2012). *The influence of culture on economic development in Solomon Islands: A political-economy perspective*. SSGM Discussion Paper, 2021/1. dpa.bellschool.anu.edu.au/sites/default/files/publications/attachments/2015-12/2012_03_tobias_a_haque_0.pdf.

Hegarty, D. (1982). *Electoral vulnerability in Papua New Guinea. Political studies seminar.* University of Papua New Guinea.

Hicken, A. (2011). Clientelism. *Annual Review of Political Science, 14*(1), 289–310. doi.org/10.1146/annurev.polisci.031908.220508.

Howes, S., Mako, A., Swan, A., Walton, G., Webster, T. and Wiltshire, C. (2014). *A lost decade? Service delivery and reforms in Papua New Guinea 2002–2012*. The National Research Institute and the Development Policy Centre.

International IDEA. (2020). *Voter turnout database*. www.idea.int/data-tools/data/voter-turnout.

IPU. (2020). *Monthly ranking of women in national parliaments*. data.ipu.org/women-ranking?month=10&year=2020.

Ivarature, H. (2016). *Unravelling parliamentary instability: Ministerial durations in Papua New Guinea, 1972–2012*. International IDEA Discussion Paper, 18. www.idea.int/publications/catalogue/unravelling-parliamentary-instability-ministerial-durations-papua-new-guinea.

Kabuni, M. (2018a, 16 July). Does political stability make governments unaccountable? *Devpolicy Blog*. devpolicy.org/does-political-stability-consolidate-irresponsible-government-png-2012-2018-20180716/.

Kabuni, M. (2018b). Explaining the paradox of internal party instability and political stability in PNG: 2012–2017. *Journal of South Pacific Culture and Philosophy*, *13*, 50–63.

Kabuni, M. (2019a, 9 May). Changing prime ministers in PNG: Does party size matter? *Devpolicy Blog*. devpolicy.org/changing-prime-ministers-in-png-does-party-size-matter-20190509/.

Kabuni, M. (2019b, 19 June). PNG's fluid politics: Winners and losers from O'Neil to Marape. *Devpolicy Blog*. devpolicy.org/pngs-fluid-politics-winners-and-losers-from-oneill-to-marape-20190619/.

Kabuni, M. (2019c, 23 September). Assorted MPs, assorted parties: James Marape's coalition. *Devpolicy Blog*. devpolicy.org/assorted-mps-assorted-parties-james-marapes-coalition-20190923/.

Kama, B. (2017). *PNG in 2017: An analysis of Papua New Guinea's political condition and trends through to 2025*. Lowy Institute. interactives.lowyinstitute.org/archive/png-in-2017/png-in-2017-png-political-condition-to-2025.html.

Ketan, J. (2007). *The use and abuse of electoral development funds and their impact on electoral politics and governance in Papua New Guinea*. CDI Policy Papers on Political Governance, 2007/2. archives.cap.anu.edu.au/cdi_anu_edu_au/.png/2007-08/2007_07_PPS_4_Ketan.htm.

Krook, M. L. (2006). Reforming representation: The diffusion of candidate gender quotas worldwide. *Politics & Gender*, *2*(3), 303–27. doi.org/10.1017/S1743923X06060107.

Laveil, M. (2020, 16 September). PNG: Where voter turnout is too high. *Devpolicy Blog*. devpolicy.org/png-where-voter-turnout-is-too-high-20200916/.

Laveil, M. and Wood, T. (2019). *The 2017 election in Papua New Guinea*. Development Policy Centre Discussion Paper, 83. doi.org/10.2139/ssrn.3422550.

Lyons, K. (2018, 20 June). 'Pushing for civil war': Fears riots could turn into widespread conflict in PNG. *The Guardian*. www.theguardian.com/world/2018/jun/20/pushing-for-civil-war-fears-riots-could-turn-into-widespread-conflict-in-png.

Markiewicz, A. and Wood, T. (2018). *Evaluation of Australia's electoral assistance to Papua New Guinea 2015–2017*. DFAT.

May, R. J. (2017). *Papua New Guinea under the O'Neill government: Has there been a shift in political style?* SSGM Discussion Paper, 2017/6. dpa.bellschool.anu.edu.au/sites/default/files/publications/attachments/2017-08/dp_2017_6_may.pdf.

May, R. J. (2020). *Politics in Papua New Guinea 2017–20: From O'Neill to Marape.* DPA Discussion Paper, 2020/3. dpa.bellschool.anu.edu.au/sites/default/files/publications/attachments/2020-11/dpa_dp_may_20203.pdf.

May, R. J., Anere, R., Haley, N. and Wheen, K. (2011). *Election 2007: The shift to limited preferential voting in Papua New Guinea.* National Research Institute.

Norris, P. and Grömping, M. (2019). *Perceptions of electoral integrity (PEI-7.0).* Electoral Integrity Project. dataverse.harvard.edu/dataset.xhtml?persistentId=doi:10.7910/DVN/PDYRWL.

Okole, H. (2001). *The fluid party system of Papua New Guinea: Continuity and change in a third wave democracy* [Unpublished doctoral dissertation]. Northern Illinois University.

Okole, H. (2002). Political participation in a fragmented democracy: Ethnic and religious appeal in Papua New Guinea. *Development Bulletin, 59*, 31–34.

Okole, H. (2005). The 'fluid' party system of Papua New Guinea. *Commonwealth & Comparative Politics, 43*(3), 362–81. doi.org/10.1080/14662040500304924.

Okole, H. (2012). *A critical review of Papua New Guinea's Organic Law on the Integrity of Political Parties and Candidates: 2001–2010.* SSGM Discussion Paper, 2012/5. ssgm.bellschool.anu.edu.au/sites/default/files/publications/attachments/2015-12/2012_5_0.pdf.

Osi, H. (2013). *The 2012 elections in Oro Province: The emerging candidate and voter behaviour and distinct differences between the open constituencies, vis-à-vis the provincial constituency.* Paper Presented at the SSGM Pacific Week, Canberra.

Pacific Women. (2016). Deputy Speaker of the House: 'Women leaders vital for Bougainville'. pacificwomen.org/news/deputy-speaker-of-the-house-women-leaders-vital-for-bougainville/.

Radio New Zealand. (2002, 7 August). Women in PNG's Chimbu Province say successful candidates won through violence and intimidation. www.rnz.co.nz/international/pacific-news/140356/women-in-png%27s-chimbu-province-say-successful-candidates-won-through-violence-and-intimidation.

Radio New Zealand. (2015, 7 September). PNG Supreme Court overturns grace period extension. www.rnz.co.nz/international/pacific-news/283484/png-supreme-court-overturns-grace-period-extension.

Radio New Zealand. (2016, 31 May). Greater understanding of women in politics in Bougainville. www.rnz.co.nz/international/pacific-news/305281/greater-understanding-of-women-in-politics-in-bougainville.

Radio New Zealand. (2020, 12 March). PNG moves to get more women into parliament. www.rnz.co.nz/international/pacific-news/411521/png-moves-to-get-more-women-into-parliament.

Reilly, B. (2002). Political engineering and party politics in Papua New Guinea. *Party Politics*, *8*(6), 701–18. doi.org/10.1177/1354068802008006004.

Reilly, B. (2006). *Democracy and diversity: Political engineering in the Asia-Pacific*. Oxford University Press.

Saffu, Y. (1989). Survey evidence on electoral behaviour in Papua New Guinea. In M. Oliver (Ed.), *Eleksin: The 1987 national election in Papua New Guinea* (pp. 15–36). University of Papua New Guinea. hdl.handle.net/1885/133355.

SBS News. (2020, 13 August). Elections on the island of Bougainville this month feature a record number of women candidates. www.sbs.com.au/news/a-record-number-of-women-are-contesting-elections-in-bougainville-this-month.

Sepoe, O. (2002). To make a difference: Realities of women's participation in Papua New Guinea politics. *Development Bulletin*, *59*, 39–42.

Sepoe, O. (2005). *Organic Law on the Integrity of Political Parties and Candidates: A tool for political stability*. SSGM Working Paper Series, 2005/4. dpa.bellschool.anu.edu.au/sites/default/files/publications/attachments/2015-12/05_04wp_Sepoe_0.pdf.

Standish, B. (2007). The dynamics of Papua New Guinea's democracy: An essay. *Pacific Economic Bulletin*, *22*(1), 135–57. devpolicy.org/PEB/2019/06/29/the-dynamics-of-papua-new-guineas-democracy-an-essay/.

Transparency International PNG. (2017). *TIPNG observation report: 10th national parliamentary elections*. Transparency International Papua New Guinea Inc.

Whiting, N. (2020, 23 September). Bougainville elects new president Ishmael Toroama as negotiations on independence from PNG ramp up. ABC News. www.abc.net.au/news/2020-09-23/bougainville-elects-new-president-ishmael-toroama/12692158.

Wood, T. (2014). *The three political economies of electoral quality in Papua New Guinea and Solomon Islands*. Challenges of electoral integrity in Asia-Pacific workshop, 28 September, Sydney. doi.org/10.2139/ssrn.2497206.

Wood, T. (2016). Is culture the cause? Choices, expectations, and electoral politics in Solomon Islands and Papua New Guinea. *Pacific Affairs*, *89*(1), 31–52. doi.org/10.5509/201689131.

Wood, T. (2017). *Papua New Guinea election results: Trends and patterns 1972–2012*. Development Policy Centre Discussion Paper, 55. doi.org/10.2139/ssrn.2926707.

Wood, T. (2018). The clientelism trap in Solomon Islands and Papua New Guinea, and its impact on aid policy. *Asia & the Pacific Policy Studies*, *5*(3), 481–94. doi.org/10.1002/app5.239.

Wood, T. (2019). *The Papua New Guinea election results database*. devpolicy.org/pngelections/.

World Bank. (2019). *Worldwide governance indicators*. www.govindicators.org.

3

Decentralisation: A political analysis

Stephen Howes, Lawrence Sause and Lhawang Ugyel

Abstract

This chapter provides an overview of decentralisation in Papua New Guinea (PNG) since independence, with a focus on political decentralisation. We show that PNG's decentralised system has several distinctive and, in some cases, unique features. It is constantly evolving – in fact, heading in different directions. PNG's system of decentralisation has become highly complex, with four tiers of government. It relies heavily, perhaps uniquely so, on indirect representation, with both provincial assemblies and district boards dominated by national politicians. We argue that four political forces have shaped, and will continue to shape, PNG's decentralisation reforms: the political dominance within the country of national members of parliament (MPs); the dominance, within that group, of district over provincial MPs; as a countervailing force, strong, though variable, political support for provincial autonomy; and, finally, the underlying clientelistic, fragmented and unstable nature of PNG politics. These findings are consistent with those of Spina (2013) in a very different Organisation for Economic Co-operation and Development (OECD) context.

Introduction

Decentralisation involves the transfer of powers from the central to lower levels of government. Decentralisation reforms have been a prominent feature of many developing countries, driven by a perceived excessive concentration of authority (Turner and Hulme, 1997). It is often argued that decentralisation plays an important role in attaining good governance (Kuhlmann and Wayenberg, 2016). Decentralisation strives to bring the state closer to the citizen, to enhance efficiency and effectiveness in the provision of public services, and to promote accountability and participation. Countries seeking greater participation from their rural majority in decision-making, and intending to strengthen service delivery in the periphery, have used decentralisation as a tool to advance these goals. For many developing countries, however, securing the goals of decentralisation continues to be elusive due to problems of systemic corruption and poor governance. Despite this, faith in the virtues of decentralisation has not diminished and many governments, including Papua New Guinea's, have continued to implement reforms to try to make decentralisation work.

The powers transferred via decentralisation can be fiscal, administrative and/or political (Schneider, 2003). Fiscal decentralisation relates to the management of budgets and accounting, expenditure and revenue generation. Administrative decentralisation relates to roles and responsibilities, functions and staffing. Political decentralisation relates to decision-making and enforcement, citizen participation, accountability and transparency. These three aspects of decentralisation, according to the Organisation for Economic Co-operation and Development (OECD, 2019), although distinct, are interrelated, and getting the correct balance between them is essential for decentralisation to work.

The decentralisation literature primarily focuses on administrative and fiscal reforms, with less attention paid to political decentralisation (Spina, 2013) and institutions such as legislatures, elections, political parties and patronage systems (Hutchcroft, 2001). Political decentralisation is the focus of this chapter for two reasons. First, decentralisation in any country is complex, but it is especially so in PNG. In a single chapter, we cannot be comprehensive and cover in depth all three areas of political, fiscal and administrative decentralisation. Second, if we have to be selective, it makes sense to focus on political decentralisation, given the importance of politics to institutions more generally (Acemoglu and Robinson, 2012).

Spina (2013) studied the determinants of political decentralisation in OECD countries. He found that the ideology of parties makes little difference to the prospects for decentralisation, and that more stable governments and parliaments with strong ethno-regionalist parties are more likely to engage in political decentralisation. We ask of PNG: How should political decentralisation be explained? What has driven decentralisation and what has constrained it? As will become clear, our findings support those of Spina, though in a completely different, non-OECD context.

The contribution of the chapter is twofold. First, there has been no survey of decentralisation in PNG for several years. The extensive and excellent analysis of earlier years (including Axline, 1986; Gelu and Axline, 2008; Kwa, 2016; May, 1999, 2009; May and Regan, 1997; Reilly et al., 2015) needs updating, especially given how dynamic decentralisation is in PNG and the important changes and proposals seen in recent years. Second, too much analysis of decentralisation, both in PNG and elsewhere, is apolitical. To understand why decentralisation unfolds the way it does, and to think about how it might unfold in the future, we need to apply a political lens.

This chapter therefore provides a broad overview of decentralisation in PNG since independence, with a focus on political decentralisation and related factors. We show that PNG's decentralised system has several distinctive and, in some cases, unique features (May, 2009). First, it is constantly evolving – in fact, heading in different directions – with major reforms in 1977 and 1995, and other important changes before, since and proposed. Second, the system has evolved to be highly complex. At independence, PNG (a relatively small country with a population now approaching nine million people) was a unitary state. Since then it has provided constitutional recognition to another three tiers of representative government: provincial, local level and district. Third, PNG's system of decentralisation relies heavily, perhaps uniquely so, on indirect representation, with no one actually being elected, as against appointed, to provincial assemblies and district boards, both of which are dominated by national politicians from that province and/or district.

Why is PNG's decentralisation experience so distinctive? The answer, as to many questions, is politics. Given the clientelistic, fragmented and unstable nature of PNG's politics, political contestation is intense, and shaped almost exclusively by local factors. Therefore, it is hardly surprising that decentralisation has been the site of deep political conflicts.

We argue that four political forces have shaped and will continue to shape PNG's decentralisation reforms: first, the political dominance within the country of national members of parliament (MPs); second, the dominance, within that group, of district over provincial MPs; third, as a countervailing force, strong, though variable, political support for provincial autonomy; and, finally, the aforementioned clientelistic, fragmented and unstable nature of PNG politics. While, in general terms, these findings are consistent with Spina's (2013) conclusions for the OECD, the specific combination of these four forces, often pulling in opposite directions, has set PNG on a decentralisation journey that is as unique as it is incomplete.

The evolution of decentralisation in PNG

Decentralisation was included in the terms of reference of the Constitutional Planning Committee (CPC) established to write the constitution of a soon-to-be independent PNG. The CPC's final report was presented to the national government in August 1974. In its tenth chapter, it proposed a new level of elected government at the existing administrative district level (to become the provincial level) with the intention that districts (in the future, provinces) should enjoy a high level of autonomy.

There were two driving forces behind the CPC's proposals for decentralisation. The first was independence itself. Independence was about self-rule and giving, or returning, power to the people. For PNG's leaders, this meant not just national self-rule, but a strong emphasis on local government. As the CPC itself put it:

> Power must be returned to the people. Government services must be accessible to them. Decisions should be made by the people to whom the issues at stake are meaningful, easily understood, and relevant. The existing system of government should therefore be restructured, and power should be decentralised, so that the energies and aspirations of our people can play their full part in promoting our country's development. (CPC, 1974, para. 10.8)

The second reason for decentralisation was Bougainville, one of the then 19 districts (now 22 provinces) of PNG.[1] As PNG approached independence, Bougainville was home to both the country's single largest mine and to strong successionist tendencies. To keep Bougainville as part of PNG, it was necessary to put forward a model of government that allowed it a high level of autonomy.

At the same time, the CPC's decentralisation proposals sparked 'fierce controversy' with strong opposition from key bureaucrats and ministers who perceived that they would have less influence under a provincial government system (Regan, 1997, p. 13). Some leaders, mindful of PNG's extreme ethnic diversity, also feared that decentralisation would promote disunity. Others, however, countered that without decentralisation it would be impossible to keep the country together. Looking back some 40 years later, PNG's first prime minister, Sir Michael Somare, said that decentralisation was introduced 'to appease the Bougainvillians and to promote unity in a culturally diverse and young country' (Constitutional and Law Reform Commission – Department of Provincial and Local Government Affairs [CLRC–DPLGA], 2015a, p. 26).

It was not, however, easy to reach agreement with Bougainville's leaders and, just before PNG's independence, Bougainville attempted to break away. Negotiations broke down and PNG went into independence in September 1975 with a unitary government. One of PNG's 'five national goals', as written into the constitution, made clear the commitment to decentralisation with its call for:

> The creation of political structures that will enable effective, meaningful participation by our people … and in view of the rich cultural and ethnic diversity of our people for those structures to provide for substantial decentralisation of all forms of government activity. (*Constitution of the Independent State of Papua New Guinea*: Government of Papua New Guinea, 1975, section 2(2))

Negotiations resumed after independence. The draft *Organic Law on Provincial Government* (OLPG) was introduced into parliament in November 1976 and came into effect in April 1977 (Premdas, 1985). (In PNG, an organic law is one that amends the constitution.)

1 Two provinces have been divided in two, and the capital, Port Moresby, has been given provincial status.

The key objective of the OLPG was to create provincial governments with directly elected provincial parliaments (assemblies), premiers and ministers, and with potentially extensive powers to implement policies and plans in response to their needs rather than functioning under direction from the national government.

Provincial elections were to be held every five years, starting in some provinces as early as 1977. Axline (1986) and Regan (1985a) have provided balanced accounts of the first decade of decentralised government. Axline (1986, p. 222) commented:

> It is the generally held view that the delivery of services in the provinces has declined over the past decade, but it is by no means clear that this is wholly or partially the result of the decentralisation of political power.

What can be said is that, in most provinces, the provincial assemblies had little public support, and provincial governance was often criticised as poor, especially by national MPs. Regan (1985b, p. 170) wrote of 'the national government perception of poor performance of the provincial government system'.

In 1983, the national government passed an amendment to allow for the suspension of provincial governments for non-performance, and, over the next decade, most were suspended. According to May (2009, p. 211), 'by 1995 all but five provinces had been suspended at least once, mostly on the ground of financial mismanagement'. By the mid-1980s, national leaders started talking about abolishing the provincial government system altogether.[2] In the early 1990s, two parliamentary committees recommended the abolition of directly elected provincial governments. In 1993, this proposal was endorsed by cabinet, and the Constitutional Review Commission was tasked with coming up with a new approach (May, 2009).

The end result was the replacement in 1995 of the OLPG with a new constitutional law, the *Organic Law on Provincial Governments and Local-level Governments* (OLPGLLG). This was a pivotal moment in PNG's decentralisation history. With the justification that the focus should be service delivery not politics, the OLPGLLG did away with provincial

2 In 1985, reflecting on a decade of independence, 'Somare put decentralisation at the top of his list of mistakes he believed the country had made' (Saffu, 1998, p. 412).

elections and directly elected assemblies, replacing them with indirectly elected assemblies, which the national politicians of that province dominated. It is important for this point, and subsequent arguments, to note that PNG has two types of national MPs. There are 111 in total. Twenty-two represent one each of PNG's 22 provinces. The other 89 represent districts, which are situated within provinces; these district MPs are called 'open' MPs.[3] The OLPGLLG made the provincial MP the governor of their province. Each open MP from the province also got a seat in the provincial assembly. These members got to choose the other provincial assembly members – three representatives from local governments, up to three traditional leaders, a women's representative and up to three others.

Another important reform of the OLPGLLG (the one that gave the law its distinctively long name) was to provide a national mandate and template for local-level government, which previously had been a provincial government responsibility, and which had generally languished. Doing away with directly elected provincial assemblies was rightly seen as weakening provincial governments, and thus a centralising rather than decentralising reform. Giving constitutional recognition to local governments was an offsetting measure, intended in part to show that the new law was also about decentralising power, just in a new way and to a different, lower level – closer to the people and their communities, the new law's proponents claimed.

The OLPGLLG recognised local-level governments (LLGs) within districts, and mandated local government elections every five years at the national level. There are currently 318 LLGs or about three per district. They exist in both urban and rural areas, though in 2015 a few LLGs in major cities were replaced by city authorities (in Lae, Mt Hagen and Kokopo), based on the governance model for the nation's capital (though, in addition, Port Moresby has provincial status). To date, the three new city authorities are still finding their feet, and, like many LLGs, have yet to secure a solid financial base to carry out their operation.

3 A few electorates contain more than one district. Generally, however, electorates and districts are aligned, and the words are synonymous in the PNG context.

While important, the OLPGLLG was more of a staging post than end point for PNG's decentralisation reforms. Table 3.1 provides a summary of relevant legislation from 1995 onwards.[4]

Table 3.1: Decentralisation legislation in PNG: A chronology from 1995 onwards.

Year	Type of change	Nature of change
1995	*Organic Law on Provincial Governments and Local-level Governments* (OLPGLLG)	Repealed the *Organic Law on Provincial Government* (OLPG) and established new provincial and local-level governments (LLGs)
1996	Constitutional amendment to the OLPGLLG (section 33A)	Established the Joint District Planning and Budget Priorities Committee (JDPBPC) and equivalent provincial bodies (JPPBPCs)
1997	*Provincial Government Administration Act*	Complementary to the OLPGLLG; provided the operational framework for the administration of provincial governments
1997	*Local-Level Governments Administration Act*	Complementary to the OLPGLLG; provided the framework for LLGs' operations; established the creation of special purpose authorities as implementation units of LLGs in special circumstances deemed necessary by the minister for provincial and local government affairs
2009	*Intergovernmental Relations (Functions and Funding) Act* (IRA)	Complementary to the OLPGLLG; strengthened inter-government fiscal arrangements and the funding of subnational governments
2012	Amendment to IRA 2009	Provided clarity on the distribution of GST between the national and subnational governments, and imposed penalties on subnational governments for varying GST
2014	Constitutional amendment to the OLPGLLG	Repealed the JDPBPC amendment of 1996; enabled the creation of District Development Authorities (DDAs)
2014	*District Development Authority Act*	Established DDAs, their operating powers and functions
2015	*City Authority Acts* for Lae, Kokopo and Mt Hagen	Created city authorities with specific powers and functions to politically manage cities from previously urban LLGs that were given city status

4 Changes to Bougainville and its autonomy status starting mainly in 2001 are left out in this table and discussed separately.

A comprehensive analysis of all the changes in decentralisation since 1995 is beyond the scope of the chapter. Here we highlight four key developments.

The first is the growth in the importance of the district (open MP electorate) as a level in PNG's decentralised system. This trend started only a year after the 1995 OLPGLLG with an amendment to that law that created the Joint District Planning and Budget Priorities Committee (JDPBPC), to be headed by the district or open member of the national parliament and including as members the LLG heads from that district and up to three other nominated members.

PNG's prime minister from 2011 to 2019, Peter O'Neill, is a strong proponent of the importance of the district and advocated as early as 2006 for the replacement of the JDPBPC by a statutory corporate body, the District Development Authority or DDA (O'Neill, 2006). The combination of bills he put forward (to amend the OLPGLLG and establish the DDAs) was passed by parliament in 2006, but, for some reason, never gazetted. The process was repeated a few years later, and DDAs finally came into existence in 2014 (though, even then, with little consultation). The district or open MP is now the chair of the DDA board. DDAs cannot pass laws, but they can buy and own assets, sue and be sued, and set up their own procurement systems. The executive head of the DDA is the district CEO.

Importantly, first the JDPBPCs and then the DDAs have also been given extensive funding. The history of electorate funds in PNG (i.e. government money put under the control of MPs, often referred to as slush funds) goes back to the 1980s (Ketan, 2007). The amounts of funding have increased over time. In the most recent budgets, K10 million has been given to each MP to be spent either as determined by the DDA (chaired by open MPs) or as determined by the provincial assembly (chaired by provincial MPs). These amounts total K1.07 billion or about 10 per cent of government revenue.[5] Since there are four times as many DDAs as provincial assemblies, this funding goes predominately to DDAs.

5 No electorate funding is provided for Bougainville: hence the total of K1.07 billion not K1.11 billion. The 2021 budget estimates 2020 revenue at K11.4 billion.

Although PNG's system is still often referred to as three-tier, excluding districts (e.g. DPLGA, 2018), in reality the DDA provides a fourth tier to PNG's decentralised architecture (i.e. fourth in chronological terms),[6] between provinces and LLGs. Though DDAs are not law-making bodies, nor subject to direct elections, they are not only constitutional but also powerful representative bodies, and a challenge to the authority of both the provincial governments above and the LLGs below them.

With DDAs now part of the mix, Table 3.2 provides a quantitative summary of the current state of play of decentralisation in PNG.

Table 3.2: PNG's subnational governments.

Region	Provinces (and provincial governments)	Districts and DDAs	Urban LLGs	Rural LLGs	Total LLGs	Population (2011 Census)
Southern	6	18	14	5	19	1,302,887
Highlands	7	34	6	97	103	3,001,598
Momase	4	25	5	90	95	1,795,474
Islands	5	12	6	73	79	959,694
TOTAL	22	89	31	265	296	7,059,653

Source: Modified from Commonwealth Local Government Forum (2020).

A second critical part of PNG's decentralisation voyage (and one not covered by Table 3.1) is Bougainville's own journey towards greater autonomy and perhaps independence. Dissatisfaction with the environmental impact of and the distribution of profits from the province's Panguna copper mine led to the closing of the mine in 1989 and a decade of conflict, resolved finally by the Bougainville Peace Agreement (BPA), signed on 30 August 2001 at Arawa.[7] The BPA led to an agreement that, for the first time, enshrined a separate treatment for the province (now the Autonomous Region of Bougainville [ARB]) in PNG's constitution. There were three main pillars of the BPA: a deferred referendum on the future political status of Bougainville (including an independence option) ten years after the creation of the Autonomous

6 Though note that the *Electoral Development Authority Act 1982* (May, 2009, p. 213) established bodies very similar to the DDAs. The fate of the Electoral Development Authorities requires further research.

7 The Bougainville civil conflict, which paved the way for the creation of the ARB and Bougainville's autonomy arrangements, has been discussed elsewhere (Chand, 2018b; Chand and Sause, 2015; Dziedzic and Saunders, 2019; Regan, 2013).

Bougainville Government (ABG); a uniquely high level of autonomy, including its own constitution, and, once again, an elected provincial assembly; and the demilitarisation of Bougainville through the withdrawal of the PNG security forces and an agreed weapons disposal plan. We further discuss the Bougainville case and its lessons and implications later in the chapter.

A third and related trend concerns the rising calls for, and incipient moves towards, greater provincial autonomy from, and for, provinces other than Bougainville. In July 2018, Prime Minister Peter O'Neill signed the Inter-Government Agreement on Greater Autonomy with the governors of East New Britain, New Ireland and Enga Provinces (Loop PNG, 2018). Two of these provinces (Enga and New Ireland) have their own mine and, therefore, robust provincial finances. East New Britain, like Bougainville, has long had a strong self-identity. All three provinces have had governors who have been strong advocates of provincial autonomy. What the greater autonomy arrangements will actually imply has not been clarified, though the focus seems to be on greater administrative and financial autonomy and on gradual reform (O'Keeffe, 2018). There is also a clear sense that some provinces will be given more autonomy than others.

The final, and again related, trend is growing dissatisfaction with PNG's decentralisation Mark II, as shaped by the OLPGLLG and DDAs. Recent research has revealed the structural and operational shortcomings of the DDA (Duncan and Banga, 2018; Ugyel et al., 2021), and has shown that, while the *District Development Authority Act 2014* has enabled the creation of autonomous corporate entities, it has also created multiple and confusing lines of reporting and accountability, failed to consider resource capacity, and may be creating a rival administrative structure undermining the role of provincial and local governments (Duncan et al., 2017). Generally, the current system of decentralisation is seen as overly complex, poorly coordinated and at least in part responsible for the decline of service delivery in PNG (CLRC–DPLGA, 2015a).

Dissatisfaction with the current state of affairs led the O'Neill government to commission a Constitutional and Law Reform Commission report on the OLPGLLG in May 2013. The result of this inquiry, which included extensive provincial consultations, was a report written jointly with the Department of Provincial and Local Government Affairs (CLRC–DPLGA, 2015a, 2015b) recommending a third overhaul of decentralisation in PNG, and a third organic law, the *Organic Law on*

Decentralisation. This would abolish local governments, relying instead on the DDAs. It would restore provincial elections, but the provincial MPs would remain as governors. And it would allow for more autonomy for those provinces who wanted it and were capable of exercising it.

The recommendations of the CLRC and DPLGA had a mixed reception. They were opposed by a number of governors at the annual Governors' Conference in October 2014. The PNG National Executive Council (or cabinet) in February 2015 established a bipartisan parliamentary committee to review the CLRC–DPLGA report and recommendations, under the chair of Sir Peter Ipatas, the governor of Enga. The resulting report (Ipatas Parliamentary Bipartisan Committee, 2015), while supporting calls for selective provincial autonomy, rejected the key recommendations of the CLRC and DPLGA for provincial elections, and the abolition of LLGs. It also called for tighter controls on DDAs.

In October 2020, the government indicated that the National Executive Council had accepted the CLRC–DPLGA proposals, and that it would move to introduce the new organic law the latter had recommended (*Post-Courier*, 2020). However, according to press reports, the provincial MPs once again signalled their opposition to this approach as recently as August 2020 (Tarawa, 2020). It is too early to predict with confidence whether and when there will be further major legislative changes to PNG's decentralisation regime.

An overall assessment of decentralisation trends in PNG since independence would require a detailed assessment of both fiscal and administrative aspects to supplement the analysis of political decentralisation provided in this section. In fiscal terms, more funding has certainly been provided to subnational governments. We have already talked about the growth of District Services Improvement Program (DSIP) and Provincial Services Improvement Program (PSIP) funding under the control of MPs (see p. 65 and Chapter 2, this volume). In addition, the *Intergovernmental Relations (Functions and Funding) Act 2009* provided for additional funding to provincial governments in the form of function grants. Funding 'for provinces and local-level government has increased significantly from K134 million in 2009 to K547.3 million in 2018' (National Economic and Fiscal Commission [NEFC], 2018, p. iii). Administratively, nearly all public servants are still on the national government payroll, even when they are regarded as provincial and district staff. However, the provincial administrators and district CEOs have certainly become powerful civil servants.

Even after a comprehensive analysis covering all three areas of political, fiscal and administrative decentralisation, an overall assessment of PNG's decentralisation trajectory would be difficult given its complexity and non-linear nature.

There is no doubt though that, at the provincial level, decentralisation has weakened. Bray (1982, p. 282) described PNG's post-independence (OLPG) arrangements as among the 'most decentralised in the world'. One certainly could not say that now. Looking at formal lists of responsibilities for different tiers of government is uninformative, since these are vague and may bear little or no relationship to the reality on the ground. Shifting to indirect elections has reduced both the legitimacy and the strength of provincial governments. Two concrete examples of the reversal of decentralisation at the provincial level involve health and education. Bray (1982) related that, in 1981, the PNG parliament passed a motion to make school education free. This proved to be a controversial decision as:

> It was pointed out that control of both community (primary) and secondary schools had been decentralised to provincial governments, and the national government actually had no legal authority in the field. (Bray, 1982, p. 281)

Even when the national government offered financial compensation to provincial governments for the abolition of fees, five provinces refused to accept the compensation, and even more refused to abolish school fees. Ultimately, the effort to make education free was abandoned, but there have been several more attempts, the most recent in 2012. Then, when the central government again moved to abolish school fees, there was no question of provinces having any say in this policy at all.

Regarding health, the major reform of the last decade has been the creation of Provincial Health Authorities under the *Provincial Health Authorities Act 2007*. These authorities have now been created in most provinces, and are responsible, where they have been created, for all health services in the province they serve. Provincial governments have to agree to their creation, but, once they do, health services are no longer under their control. Provincial Health Authorities report to their boards, not to provincial governments. While the provincial administration has some say in the composition of the board, the nomination of the chair is a matter for the health minister. Most provinces thus no longer have responsibility for health. Whether this is an improvement or not can be debated; at the very least it shows that provinces have much less power than they used to.

Thus one can certainly conclude that PNG's provinces are less autonomous than in the early years of independence. Considering the various other reforms at the district and local government level, whether PNG as a whole is more or less decentralised under the OLPGLLG is too difficult a question to answer. In any case, our interest is in why PNG has taken the unique and non-linear route to decentralisation that it has. That is the subject of the next section.

The drivers of decentralisation in PNG

In this section we argue that there are four key explanatory factors that have shaped, and will continue to shape, decentralisation in PNG over time: the dominance of PNG's national politicians; the dominance within that group of open or district MPs; the countervailing force of provincial autonomy; and the nature of PNG politics as clientelistic, fragmented and unstable.

1. Dominance of national members of parliament

The course of decentralisation in PNG has been fundamentally shaped by the intolerance of national politicians for, and their dominance over, any actual or potential provincial rivals. The most obvious case of national politicians acting as a group or class to impose their will on PNG's decentralisation arrangements is the 1995 abolition of provincial elections that removed the category of provincial politicians entirely and put national politicians in charge of provincial assemblies through an indirect election system that, as far as we can tell, is unique worldwide. As has been recently noted, the introduction of the OLPGLLG was driven by:

> [a] political agenda to eradicate political competition created by Provincial Assembly members contesting national elections, competing against incumbent national MPs, and provincial government Premiers in different parties opposing national governments led by rival parties. (CLRC–DPLGA, 2015a, p. 34)

Likewise, as May (1999, p. 202) observed four years after the passage of the OLPGLLG, 'the new system is likely to increase substantially the role of national MPs'. Indeed, 'this was the real objective of the reform' (May, 1999, p. 202; see also Edmiston, 2002; Reilly et al., 2015).[8]

National politicians have been able to exercise a decisive influence over decentralisation arrangements at this and other points of time because of the fact that the PNG constitution can be changed by a two-thirds vote in its unicameral parliament. Neither a referendum nor assent from any lower level of government is required. Moreover, it has not been hard, at least on issues that do not threaten the power of national politicians, to obtain a two-thirds majority. The party system is weak in PNG and politicians will rally behind causes that suit them. With the constitution exclusively in their hands, national politicians set the rules of the decentralised game, and determine how much should be decentralised and to whom.

The extensive legislating at the constitutional level on decentralisation is testimony to this, including the two organic (i.e. constitution-amending) laws relating to decentralisation, the 1977 OLPG and the 1995 OLPGLLG, and a number of amendments to them, as well as a number of pieces of regular legislation (see Table 3.1).

Compare this situation to one prevailing in countries where there is a constitution that enables provincial governments and is hard to change because changes require either a popular referendum or assent from the provinces themselves. In such a regime, subnational governments are in effect protected by the constitution. Subnational governments have no such protection in PNG. They are at the mercy of national politicians. As Reilly et al. (2015, p. 38) put it, PNG is a 'quasi-federal system'. Subnational governments are given autonomy but within a constitutional framework that can be altered by the central government – the unrivalled powerbroker on decentralisation matters, which decides on the type, manner and timing of the decentralisation reforms.

The dominance of national MPs is something that has developed over time. Writing in 1986, Axline concluded that:

8 May (1997, pp. 391–92) notes that a national government briefing paper explaining the legislation said that the new law sends a clear message that provincial governments 'are not a second source of political or governmental power'.

> While the national government has the formal authority to determine the future of provincial government, it is likely that changes will be the result of political co-operation and compromise rather than unilateral action on its part. (Axline, 1986, p. 223).

The abolition of provincial assemblies a decade on showed how things had changed: national MPs did indeed take unilateral action, and successfully too.

One constraint on change outside of the national parliament is the Supreme Court, which has taken on the role of defender of the constitution and is liable to strike down constitutional amendments if they are judged to be contrary to the intent of the original. However, perhaps because PNG's original constitution contained no detailed decentralisation arrangements, and perhaps because it is such an arcane subject matter, the courts have not been active in relation to decentralisation, with only one exception as far as we are aware, which we recount in the next section.

2. Dominance of district members of parliament

If the first force shaping decentralisation in PNG is the dominance of national politicians as a class, the second is the dominance within that class of the 'open' or district MPs. There are four times as many open MPs as provincial MPs (89 to 22), so it is not surprising that, over time, the former have exerted their influence.

The fruit of the efforts of PNG's district MPs can be seen by the fact that districts have gained in power as provinces have been diminished. Okole et al. (2016, p. 151) made this clear, writing that 'the intention … for District Authorities was to remove Provincial Authorities'. The creation of DDAs is indeed an impressive show of political strength. Although DDAs cannot pass laws, provincial assemblies have, in general, made little use of their law-making powers. Meanwhile, DDAs have become an important, well-funded and constitutionally recognised representative tier of government.

The motivation of open MPs can be understood from the simple fact that provincial assemblies are chaired by the provincial MP and district authorities by the district MP. Put differently, district or open MPs felt that their role was marginalised by the OLPGLLG (and before it the OLPG) and acted to remedy that, starting as early as a year after the passage of the OLPGLLG with an amendment to create JDPBPCs. They followed that up over the next two decades with the establishment of DDAs, which, in the words of Wiltshire (2014), 'help open MPs to consolidate influence and power across their electorate'.

Looking at changes in funding patterns over time shows how district MPs are asserting themselves relative to other politicians. From 2013 to 2015, provincial MPs received K5 million per district in their province. But from 2016, they receive only K10 million each, as district MPs do. As a result, the share of electorate funding going to provincial MPs fell from 30 per cent of that going to all MPs in 2014 to 20 per cent in 2018. It is true that, as noted earlier, recurrent funding to provinces has greatly expanded. Nevertheless, the amount of K492 million going to the provincial governments in 2018 in the form of function grants (NEFC, 2018, p. 5) is less than three-fifths of the amount that goes to DDAs through the DSIP (for the last few years, K860 million).

The rise of the districts is also at the expense of LLGs, that, by contrast, have been starved of funding. Reilly et al. (2015, p. 24) commented that: 'LLGs have had insignificant funding and usually lacked committed staff'. Ketan (2016) wrote that 'the LLG Presidents are the poor cousin of the Open MPs' (p. 264) and that 'the authority of LLG councillors, many of whom are established community leaders, has been weakened by the JDPBPC [and DDA]' (p. 266).

For a short time in the early 2010s, towards the end of PNG's resource boom years, LLGs also received electorate funding of K500,000 each, but that was a small amount compared to the K10 million per district (recall there are 3–4 LLGs per district) and, in any case, a short-lived experiment.[9] When the boom ended, this LLG funding was done away with. LLGs also get a small share of the function grants that, in general, go to provincial governments, but this amount was only K55 million in 2018 (NEFC, 2018, p. 5). This amount pales into insignificance compared to the K860 million going to national MPs via electorate funding. It is a sign of the political weakness of LLGs that the 2015 CLRC–DPLGA report, which argued that PNG is overgoverned, recommended the abolition not of DDAs but of LLGs.

9 In the past there was even electorate funding for wards (the electorates of LLGs), but this too was short-lived.

The rise of the district MPs as a political class shaping PNG's decentralisation can also be seen in two specific decentralisation reforms, one that succeeded and one that did not. First, provincial MPs had been part of the JDPBPCs (as discussed above, created in 1996), but were removed from the DDAs (in the 2006 and 2014 legislation). Clearly, district MPs did not want to be cramped by their provincial counterparts.

Second, MPs voted to remove the three local-level government members from the provincial assembly. This was arguably a move by district MPs, as provincial MPs chair provincial assemblies and would therefore be able to control the selection of, and not be threatened by, LLG representatives on those assemblies. It is also noteworthy that this reform was made as part of the 2006 legislation to introduce DDAs.

This is the one case, mentioned earlier, that the Supreme Court acted to check the power of MPs to change PNG's decentralisation arrangements. The Ombudsman Commission appealed this amendment, and that appeal was upheld by the Supreme Court, which argued that the removal of LLG heads was inconsistent with the status of provincial assemblies as indirectly elected (Supreme Court of Papua New Guinea, 2010).

3. Provincial autonomy

So far the story is of national MPs extending their influence from the national to the provincial and district levels. Given the dominance of national MPs, and open MPs in particular, one might imagine that the end point would be the abolition of provinces and LLGs altogether, and a two-tier system of national government and DDAs.

Certainly, we have seen the rise of DDAs. And with the government now endorsing the 2015 CLRC report, the days of LLGs might be numbered. However, the push by the O'Neill government, described earlier in this chapter, for greater provincial autonomy does not fit this narrative. Nor does the fact that the CLRC–DPLGA drafted organic law recently endorsed by the PNG cabinet proposes not to abolish but to strengthen provincial government with the reintroduction of directly elected provincial assemblies (albeit with the provincial MPs remaining as governors).

To explain these developments, we need to appeal to a countervailing force to the influence exercised by national (and especially district) MPs. This is the strong, albeit geographically variable, support for provincial autonomy.

We can see the influence of this countervailing force most clearly in the 1977 reforms, in which, as noted earlier, Bougainville's influence was decisive: essentially, the central government and Bougainville negotiated on what was an acceptable level of decentralisation to both sides; subsequently, that model was applied to all other provinces. As Bray (1982, p. 282) noted, Bougainville 'won for the other provinces a decentralisation which some of them neither wanted nor could cope with'.

We can also see the weakening of this countervailing force as partly responsible for the reversal of provincial decentralisation in 1995. By that time, Bougainville had been mired in conflict for several years. It had become clear that greater autonomy would need to be given to the province. But Bougainville, because it was the only region of PNG that had risen in rebellion, had also become a 'special case' that required a unique solution. This meant that greater autonomy for Bougainville would not necessitate greater autonomy for other provinces, and that, in fact, provincial autonomy could be reduced without antagonising Bougainville, since it would be subject to different rules.

Spina's (2013) distinction between two modes of political decentralisation is useful here. One is uniform: for example, the creation of a secondary level of subnational government throughout a country (as in any federation). Another is through special treatment, such as when a geographically, ethnically or linguistically distinct population receives additional autonomy (e.g. France's decision to grant Corsica a directly elected assembly in 1992 or the establishment of the Scottish Parliament in the late 1990s). PNG's treatment of Bougainville shifted from the first mode at the time of independence to the second in the 1990s after conflict broke out. The result was more autonomy for Bougainville, but less for other provinces.

It would be overly restrictive, however, only to focus on Bougainville when thinking about provincial autonomy (Okole et al., 2016). The 1995 reforms were opposed by the Island provinces of not only Bougainville, but also East and West New Britain, Manus and New Ireland, all of which at one point threatened to secede to form the Federated Melanesian

Republic. These provinces were unable to prevent the passage of the OLPGLLG, but did ensure that the proposal to abolish provincial governments altogether was not successful (Mukherjee, 2010).

Likewise, today, we see that it is not only Bougainville that is pushing for autonomy. Certainly, not all provinces are equally interested. In much of the Highlands, provincial identity seems to count for little, and smaller tribal and linguistic groups seem much more important. Enga, a province dominated by one ethnic group, is an exception. In the Islands, provincial identity seems stronger.[10]

An additional force supporting provincial decentralisation is the group of provincial MPs who are threatened by the rise of DDAs, who control provincial governments, and whose view is given voice to in the 2015 Ipatas report (Ipatas Parliamentary Bipartisan Committee, 2015).[11] While provincial MPs are greatly outnumbered by district MPs, their voice cannot be ignored entirely, bearing in mind that constitutional amendments require a two-thirds majority and that the government of the day may well need their support, especially during the unpredictable and frequent votes of no confidence that characterise PNG politics.

The push by some provinces for autonomy, the 2018 O'Neill agreement with Enga, New Ireland and East New Britain, and the recent reform proposals all point in the direction of provinces not withering away, but rather becoming stronger. The provincial autonomy now being discussed is intended to be selective (or 'gradative' in the words of CLRC–DPLGA, 2015a): to grant greater autonomy only to those provinces that want it and are able to exercise it. It is worth noting that this selective approach was also meant to be embodied in the 1977 OLPG (see the discussion of 'gradation' in Regan, 1985b, pp. 164–65). Early on in the implementation of the OLPG, however, the selective approach was abandoned (Axline, 1986, p. 18; May, 2009, pp. 205–06). All provinces got autonomy whether they wanted it or not, and it is plausible that this would ultimately happen again if a new push for selective provincial autonomy is successful.

10 See Gelu and Axline (2008, ch. 2) for an account of East New Britain's push for autonomy since the early 2000s.

11 The Ipatas Committee called for more provincial autonomy (on a selective basis) but rejected the proposal that there be provincial elections, thus supporting more power for provinces, while keeping those provinces firmly under their (provincial MPs') control.

To summarise, a centralised PNG is not an option. The original CPC and constitutional endorsement of decentralisation, as well as what Reilly et al. (2015, p. 7) referred to as the fact that 'many Papua New Guineans see virtue in decentralising governance in their country', rule it out. In any case, the clientelistic nature of PNG politics (see the discussion immediately below) is always going to push in the direction of decentralised decision-making, since local decisions are much more important for election outcomes than national ones. But, as the PNG experience itself shows, decentralisation can take many forms, and one can imagine a decentralised PNG without provinces at all, and indeed this option was explicitly mooted in the 1990s. The discussion of this section, however, shows why provincial governments survive, are likely to continue and may indeed be strengthened in the future.

4. PNG politics

We have so far identified three political forces as driving PNG's decentralisation (often in different directions): the dominant position of MPs, the dominance within that grouping of district MPs and the countervailing push for provincial autonomy. The account would be incomplete without reference to the underlying nature of politics in PNG as clientelistic, fragmented and unstable.

Kabuni et al. (Chapter 2, this volume) note that PNG is rated by experts as one of the most clientelistic countries in the world (see Figure 2.10, this volume). This means that, more than in nearly any other country, people in PNG vote on the basis of local considerations, not national policies or parties. The authors further show that politics in PNG is also highly fragmented, with a large and growing number of candidates running for elections (from an average of 8 candidates per seat in 1977 to 30 in 2017), and a median winning share of just above 25 per cent. Third, politics in PNG is unstable. There is often overall political instability, but here the reference is to individual MPs and their uncertain grip on power. About 50 per cent of incumbents lose every election. In this sense, most seats in PNG are marginal.

This nature of PNG politics is important for two reasons. First, it supercharges the rivalry between national and provincial politicians (actual or potential). To see this, consider the opposite system to the one PNG has: a system where parties are strong, few candidates compete to represent each electorate, and most incumbents are returned. In such a scenario, a provincial MP would find it difficult to break into national politics and virtually impossible to displace a sitting MP. In turn, sitting MPs would have little to fear from provincial politicians and no need to undermine decentralisation to defend themselves. That might be the case in a country like Australia. But, in PNG, where many candidates compete, and politicians have a tenuous grip on their seat, the last thing an incumbent wants is to give a potential rival a leg-up by giving them access to the profile and resources that election to a provincial assembly or local government would provide.

This is particularly the case given that in a clientelistic system all politics is local. As noted by Ketan (2007) and by Allan and Hasnain (2010), MPs, once elected to office, need substantial resources to repay debt, reward supporters and build support. Voters are unlikely to reward national MPs for being a minister and even less for sitting on a parliamentary committee. If what matters is the local delivery of goods and services, then national MPs need to ensure that they control that. Hence their establishment of local funds, which they control, and their aversion to funds being controlled by rival groupings of politicians – provincial or local.

Second, clientelistic, fragmented and unstable politics is not conducive to good governance. In fact, PNG is rated as a fragile state by the World Bank and the quality of service delivery is widely agreed to be low. A vicious cycle is at work: because of poor governance, MPs distrust the public service and want to be in charge of service delivery themselves, but this promotes clientelism, which further undermines good governance.

What this leads to is not necessarily either decentralisation or recentralisation, but a dissatisfaction with the status quo, which can be, and has been, used to argue for reform. Thus, it can be, and has been, argued that the solution to weak service delivery is more autonomy for provinces – or districts, for that matter. But, equally, it can be, and has been, argued that subnational governments are the problem.

Just as dissatisfaction with the current system is behind the latest calls for reform, so too the criticism of provincial governments in the early years of independence was a driver for the 1995 reforms. Saffu (1998, p. 424) argued then that provincial assemblies tended to replicate the problems seen at the national level: 'instability of coalitions and political alliances; the over subscription of elections and the super-rapid circulation of elites; the weakness of financial controls'. May (1999, p. 187), also writing mainly of the 1980s and early 1990s, referred to 'copious documented and anecdotal evidence of lax and inefficient administration, nepotism and outright corruption' in provincial governments.

The case of Bougainville provides illumination from PNG's more recent history. A comprehensive review of the autonomy arrangement was carried out by a combined national and international team of experts in 2013 (Government of Papua New Guinea and Autonomous Region of Bougainville Government, 2013).[12] This found that many of the powers granted to Bougainville had not been taken up. Currently, the ARB does not have its own independent court system, independent judges, police force, teaching service commission, audit and accountability institutions (except for its electoral commission), prison system or local system of government to the extent allowed for under section 49 of its constitution. While the ABG is constitutionally empowered to establish those institutions, it has not done so due to its significant capacity problems.

In particular, while section 137 of the BPA requires Bougainville to be fiscally self-reliant and generate revenue at least equal to its national government grant, a recent analysis by Chand (2018a, p. 550) revealed that, in 2017, the ARB could only generate an internal revenue of K2,379,000 or 5.7 per cent of its national government recurrent grant. Thus, 20 years since the signing of the BPA, the ARB is in no way close to being financially self-reliant.

This is not to argue against decentralisation in general or greater provincial autonomy in particular. But it does suggest that decentralisation is itself no guarantee of better service delivery. Indeed, one might conclude that better governance (though itself a formidable task) is needed to make decentralisation work rather than that decentralisation (or recentralisation for that matter) will improve governance (Reilly et el., 2015).

Conclusion

This chapter has followed, and tried to explain, the complex trajectory of decentralisation in PNG. To conclude, we relate our findings back to the academic literature. As noted in the introduction, Spina (2013)

12 The review was a constitutional requirement under both the PNG and ARB constitutions and was carried out under the auspices of both governments.

found that among OECD countries the ideology of parties makes little difference to the prospects for decentralisation, but that governments that are more stable and parliaments with strong ethno-regionalist parties are more likely to engage in political decentralisation.

Our findings, though in a very different non-OECD context, are similar. Parties are not of great importance in PNG and ethno-regionalist political forces have definitely pushed decentralisation forward: this is our third, countervailing force in favour of provincial autonomy. Also consistent with Spina (2013), we find that the inherent instability of PNG politics has worked against decentralisation. The resulting insecurity of national MPs has led them, in a context of clientelistic politics, to push back against decentralisation both to provinces and to LLGs, and to favour decentralisation to districts, as this is a level of government the majority of MPs (who represent districts) control.

Our aim in this chapter is neither to prescribe a preferred mode and level of decentralisation nor to predict the future of decentralisation in PNG. However, our analysis does lead us to make a few observations.

First, the analysis raises a number of decentralisation policy questions. If there is to be greater autonomy, should it be to provinces, districts or lower levels of government, or, indeed, to higher levels, such as a region (a grouping of provinces)? Will the implementation of greater autonomy be symmetrical (selective) or asymmetrical (universal)? How should the issues (barely touched on in this chapter) of fiscal and administrative decentralisation be addressed? Finally, and most importantly, since experience shows that autonomy is unlikely to thrive and, in fact, can be greatly undermined if poor governance and corruption continues, how should governance be improved?

Second, turning to what might happen next, perhaps the CLRC and DPLGA hit a sweet spot in its 2015 report and found a solution that promotes decentralisation (by bringing back directly elected provincial assemblies) while safeguarding the interests of national MPs (by keeping them at the head of provincial and district governments, and by abolishing LLGs altogether). Conversely, although the CLRC and DPLGA reported in 2015, its recommendations, which were finally endorsed by the PNG cabinet in 2020, continue to be opposed by provincial MPs (Tarawa,

2020) who reject the reintroduction of provincial elections. At the time of writing, the fate of the CLRC–DPLGA recommendations can only be described as uncertain.

Whatever the next reform is, however sweeping it is, and whenever it comes, it does seem likely that PNG's decentralisation arrangements will continue to evolve, as the various and contradictory political forces driving decentralisation play themselves out. In 1982 Bray wrote that PNG's directly elected provincial governments 'are probably here to stay' (p. 282). Thirteen years later they were abolished. More changes have followed since, and still more are likely to follow. PNG remains a young nation; it has a long way to go before it finds an effective and stable system of decentralised government.

Of course, PNG is not alone in this. Despite much euphoria, the actual outcomes of decentralisation policies adopted around the world have been mixed (Andersson and Ostrom, 2008). As countries continue to experiment with multiple decentralisation reforms, the evolving experience of PNG will continue to be a rich source for both scholars and practitioners alike. In particular, it is fascinating that PNG seems to have evolved, for better or worse, a unique system of decentralisation. We are aware of no other country in which, with two votes cast in the one election, electors choose all three of their national, provincial and district government representatives. This is a type of 'national decentralisation' without parallel elsewhere. We are also not aware of a country of the same, modest size as PNG that has four tiers of government.

We have argued that, consistent with Spina's (2013) OECD analysis, PNG's decentralisation journey is the result of a conflict between insecure, clientelistic national politicians on the one hand and ethno-regional forces on the other. More research on the political drivers of decentralisation in other developing countries would surely be illuminating.

Acknowledgements

The authors would like to acknowledge very useful comments from participants at the book workshop in October 2020 and, in particular, the review and assistance generously provided by Colin Wiltshire and Ron May.

References

Acemoglu, D. and Robinson, J. (2012). *Why nations fail: The origins of power, prosperity, and poverty*. Random House.

Allan, A. and Hasnain, Z. (2010). Power, pork and patronage: Decentralization and the politicization of the development budget in Papua New Guinea. *Commonwealth Journal of Local Governance*, *6*, 7–31. doi.org/10.5130/cjlg.v0i6.1617.

Andersson, K. P. and Ostrom, E. (2008). Analyzing decentralized resource regimes from a polycentric perspective. *Policy Sciences, 41*(1), 71–93. doi.org/10.1007/s11077-007-9055-6.

Axline, W. A. (1986). *Decentralisation and development policy: Provincial government and the planning process in Papua New Guinea*. PNG Institute of Applied Social and Economic Research.

Bray, M. (1982). The politics of free education in Papua New Guinea. *International Journal of Educational Development, 2*(3), 281–87. doi.org/10.1016/0738-0593(82)90007-4.

Chand, S. (2018a). Fiscal decentralisation in a divided state: Bougainville in Papua New Guinea. *Federal Law Review, 46*, 541–55. doi.org/10.1177/0067205X1804600404.

Chand, S. (2018b). *Financing for autonomy: Fiscal self-reliance in Bougainville*. The National Research Institute.

Chand, S. and Sause, L. (2015, 18–19 June). *Peace in Bougainville: The past, the present, and the prospects*. Paper presented at the 2015 PNG Update Conference, University of Papua New Guinea.

Commonwealth Local Government Forum. (2020). *The local government system in Papua New Guinea*. www.clgf.org.uk/default/assets/File/Country_profiles/Papua_New_Guinea.pdf.

Constitutional and Law Reform Commission and Department of Provincial and Local Government Affairs. (2015a). *Final report on the inquiry into the Organic Law on Provincial Governments and Local-level Governments, Volume 1: Gradative decentralisation and integration for a stronger and more prosperous Papua New Guinea*. Government of Papua New Guinea.

Constitutional and Law Reform Commission and Department of Provincial and Local Government Affairs. (2015b). *Final report on the inquiry into the Organic Law on Provincial Governments and Local-Level Governments, Volume 2: Provincial consultation report on the inquiry into the Organic Law on Provincial Governments and Local-level Governments*. Government of Papua New Guinea.

Constitutional Planning Committee. (1974). *Constitutional Planning Committee report*. Government of Papua New Guinea.

Department of Provincial and Local Government Affairs. (2018). *Corporate plan 2018–2022*. Government of Papua New Guinea.

Duncan, R. and Banga, C. (2018). Solutions to poor service delivery in Papua New Guinea. *Asia & the Pacific Policy Studies, 5*, 495–507. doi.org/10.1002/app5.260.

Duncan, R., Cairns, A. and Banga, C. (2017). *Papua New Guinea's public service delivery framework at the subnational levels*. The National Research Institute.

Dziedzic, A. and Saunders, C. (2019). *Greater autonomy and independence for Bougainville: Institutional options and issues for transition*. The National Research Institute.

Edmiston, K. D. (2002). Fostering subnational autonomy and accountability in decentralized developing countries: Lessons from the Papua New Guinea experience. *Public Administration and Development, 22*(3), 221–34. doi.org/10.1002/pad.223.

Gelu, A. and Axline, A. (2008). *Options for the restructure of decentralised government in Papua New Guinea* [NRI special publication no. 50]. The National Research Institute. www.pngnri.org/images/Publications_Archive/SP_50.pdf.

Government of Papua New Guinea. (1975). *Constitution of the Independent State of Papua New Guinea*. www.paclii.org/pg/legis/consol_act/cotisopng534/.

Government of Papua New Guinea and the Autonomous Region of Bougainville Government. (2013). *Report of the joint review of Bougainville autonomy arrangement*. Government Printer.

Hutchcroft, P. D. (2001). Centralization and decentralization in administration and politics: Assessing territorial dimensions of authority and power. *Governance: An International Journal of Policy and Administration, 14*(1), 23–53. doi.org/10.1111/0952-1895.00150.

Ipatas Parliamentary Bipartisan Committee. (2015). *Developing a policy framework to suit a decentralised political structure and for service delivery purposes for the 21st century Papua New Guinea*. Government of Papua New Guinea.

Ketan, J. (2007). *The use and abuse of electoral development funds and the impact on electoral politics and governance in Papua New Guinea*. Centre for Democratic Institutions Policy Papers on Political Governance, 2007/2. archives.cap.anu.edu.au/cdi_anu_edu_au/.png/2007-08/D_P/2007_08_PPS4_PNG_Ketan/2007_08_PPS4_KETAN.pdf.

Ketan, J. (2016). The impact of constituency development funds on the implementation of the OLPGLLG. In E. Kwa (Ed.), *Decentralisation for an integrated, strong and prosperous Papua New Guinea* (pp. 244–74). Constitutional and Law Reform Commission.

Kuhlmann, S. and Wayenberg, E. (2016). Institutional impact assessment in multi-level systems: Conceptualizing decentralization effects from a comparative perspective. *International Review of Administrative Sciences, 82*(2), 233–54. doi.org/10.1177/0020852315583194.

Kwa, E. (Ed.). (2016). *Decentralisation for an integrated, strong and prosperous Papua New Guinea*. Constitutional and Law Reform Commission.

Loop PNG. (2018, 13 July). Autonomy signing for 3 provinces. www.looppng.com/png-news/autonomy-signing-3-provinces-78212.

May, R. J. (1997). Postscript: The Organic Law on Provincial Governments and Local-Level Governments. In R. J. May and A. J. Regan (Eds), *Political decentralisation in a new state: The experience of provincial governments in Papua New Guinea* (pp. 386–95). Crawford House Publishing.

May, R. J. (1999). Decentralisation: Two steps forward, one step back. In R. May (Ed.), *State and society in Papua New Guinea: The first twenty-five years* (pp. 173–202). ANU Press. doi.org/10.22459/SSPNG.05.2004.

May, R. J. (2009). Policy making on decentralisation. In R. J. May (Ed.), *Policy making and implementation: Studies from Papua New Guinea* (pp. 203–32). ANU Press. doi.org/10.22459/PMI.09.2009.

May, R. J. and Regan, A. J. (Eds). (1997). *Political decentralisation in a new state: The experience of provincial governments in Papua New Guinea*. Crawford House Publishing.

Mukherjee, R. (2010). *Provincial secessionists and decentralisation: Papua New Guinea, 1985–1995*. Innovations for Successful Societies.

National Economic and Fiscal Commission. (2018). *2018 Budget Fiscal Report*. NEFC.

OECD. (2019). *Making decentralisation work: A handbook for policy-makers*. www.oecd.org/cfe/Policy%20highlights_decentralisation-Final.pdf. doi.org/10.1787/g2g9faa7-en.

O'Keeffe, A. (2018, 19 October). Deciding the future for PNG's provinces. *The Interpreter*. www.lowyinstitute.org/the-interpreter/deciding-future-png-provinces.

Okole, H., Songo, P., Raka, S., Payani, H., Badu, N., Winnia, X., Guba, L. and Ikosi, R. (2016). Implementing decentralisation in Papua New Guinea: The challenges. In E. Kwa (Ed.), *Decentralisation for an integrated, strong and prosperous Papua New Guinea* (pp. 80–165). Constitutional and Law Reform Commission.

O'Neill, P. (2006). *The proposal to establish district authorities in the provinces of Papua New Guinea* [Paper One in *Two papers on the proposed decentralisation in Papua New Guinea*]. SSGM Public Policy in PNG Discussion Paper 2. dpa.bellschool.anu.edu.au/sites/default/files/publications/attachments/2015-12/ONeill_Tuck_NRI_02_2006_web_0.pdf.

Post-Courier. (2020, 15 July). Organic Law on Provincial and Local-level Governments to be repealed. postcourier.com.pg/organic-law-on-provincial-and-local-level-governments-to-be-repealed/.

Premdas, R. (1985). Papua New Guinea: Decentralisation and decolonisation. In P. Lamour and R. Qalo (Eds), *Decentralisation in the South Pacific: Local, provincial and state government in twenty countries* (pp. 105–18). University of the South Pacific.

Regan, A. J. (1997). The origins of the provincial government system in Papua New Guinea. In R. J. May, A. J. Regan and A. Ley (Eds), *Political decentralisation in a new state: The experience of provincial government in Papua New Guinea* (pp. 8–20). Crawford House Publishing.

Regan, A. J. (2013). Autonomy and conflict resolution in Bougainville, Papua New Guinea. In Y. Ghai and S. Woodman (Eds), *Practising self-government: A comparative study of autonomous regions* (pp. 412–48). Cambridge University Press. doi.org/10.1017/CBO9781139088206.014.

Regan, T. (1985a). Papua New Guinea: Implementing provincial government. In P. Lamour and R. Qalo (Eds), *Decentralisation in the South Pacific: Local, provincial and state government in twenty countries* (pp. 119–54). University of the South Pacific.

Regan, T. (1985b). Papua New Guinea: National-provincial relations. In P. Lamour and R. Qalo (Eds), *Decentralisation in the South Pacific: Local, provincial and state government in twenty countries* (pp. 155–71). University of the South Pacific.

Reilly, B., Brown, M. and Flower, S. (2015). *Political governance and service delivery in Papua New Guinea: A strategic review of current and alternative governance systems to improve service delivery*. The National Research Institute.

Saffu, Y. (1998). January–December 1987. In C. Moore and M. Kooyman (Eds), *A Papua New Guinea political chronicle 1967–1991* (pp. 429–46). Crawford House Publishing.

Schneider, A. (2003). Decentralization: Conceptualization and measurement. *Studies in Comparative International Development, 38*(3), 32–56. doi.org/10.1007/BF02686198.

Spina, N. (2013). Explaining political decentralisation in parliamentary democracies. *Comparative European Politics, 11*(4), 428–57. doi.org/10.1057/cep.2012.23.

Supreme Court of Papua New Guinea. (2010). *Reference by the Ombudsman Commission of Papua New Guinea* [2010] PGSC 10; SC1058 (4 June 2010). www.paclii.org/pg/cases/PGSC/2010/10.html.

Tarawa, H. (2020, 24 August). Governors reject changes. *The National*. www.thenational.com.pg/governors-reject-changes/.

Turner, M. and Hulme, D. (1997). *Governance administration and development: Making the state work*. Macmillan. doi.org/10.1007/978-1-349-25675-4.

Ugyel, L. Sause, L. and Gorea, E. (2021). Dynamics and tensions of implementing agencification reforms: Experience of district development authorities in Papua New Guinea. *Australian Journal of Public Administration*, *80*, 138–51. doi.org/10.1111/1467-8500.12448.

Wiltshire, C. (2014, 13 January). Without fear or favour? O'Neill's district authorities to build capacity and consolidate MP powers in PNG. *Devpolicy Blog*. www.devpolicy.org/without-fear-or-favour-oneills-district-authorities-to-build-capacity-and-consolidate-mp-powers-in-png-20140113/.

4

Crime and corruption

Grant W. Walton and Sinclair Dinnen

Abstract

Concerns about crime and corruption in Papua New Guinea (PNG) predate independence and are considered by many to be a significant threat to its prosperity and stability. In this chapter, we examine understandings of, and drivers and responses to, crime and corruption in PNG's recent history. We show how manifestations of and responses to crime and corruption have changed over time and across space. While these two concepts clearly overlap (with corruption often regarded a crime and crime often facilitated by corruption), for analytical purposes they are treated here as two distinct concepts. We argue that it is important to recognise the networks and relationships that animate crime and corruption and the responses to these challenges. It is also important to understand the ways these challenges and responses change over time.

Introduction

For outsiders as well as many citizens, crime and corruption are viewed as significantly curtailing the fulfilment of Papua New Guinea's (PNG's) development goals. Reflecting on the occasion of PNG's 10th independence anniversary, the country's first prime minister, Michael Somare, remarked:

> I will now turn to what I consider to be the greatest threat to our country, crime, and here I'm referring to both street crime and official corruption. Unless we can control it, it can destroy all the advances we have made in the last ten years. It must be controlled before it destroys us. (quoted in Connell, 1997, p. 274)

The nation consistently scores poorly compared to most other countries on international indices that track perceptions about the level of crime and corruption. However, such indices say little about how the various forms of crime and corruption manifest themselves and the diverse ways government, citizens and the private sector seek to address these challenges. In this chapter, we examine understandings of, and drivers and responses to, crime and corruption in PNG in the context of its recent history. In doing so we consider crime and corruption as two overlapping though heuristically distinct concepts (Dinnen, 1993). Certain types of corruption are indeed criminal offences (as the above quotation from Somare suggests), and criminals often use corruption to achieve their nefarious objectives. In this chapter, we broadly categorise 'crime' as concerning law, order and justice. Drawing on recent empirical work, our discussion of corruption focuses on abuses of public office, power, morals and institutions, as well as the broader networks that can help facilitate corruption.

The first section focuses on key law and order trends and responses set in the context of PNG's recent history. The second section centres on corruption and anti-corruption. We conclude by highlighting the overarching themes that emerge from this analysis.

'Law and order' in the post-independence period

Concerns with violent crime and personal security feature prominently in external representations of PNG. Foreign governments regularly issue travel warnings, highlighting the risks posed to visitors by PNG's high levels of violent crime. Port Moresby, the national capital, has been depicted as one of the world's least liveable cities, largely owing to security problems. While such portrayals are contestable given their generality and the lack of reliable data on which they are based, security remains an everyday preoccupation for people throughout the country. Such concerns have a major impact on business confidence. Surveys of companies have repeatedly identified law and order as among the top constraints to doing business in PNG (Fox et al., 2018). Indeed, World Bank research indicates that security concerns among the PNG business community are more than four times the regional average for East Asia and the Pacific, and comparable with countries like El Salvador, Venezuela and the Democratic Republic of Congo (Lakhani and Willman, 2014a, p. ix).

Concerns with 'law and order' first came to prominence in the late 1960s as the pace of decolonisation accelerated in preparation for PNG's independence in 1975. Decolonisation involved a long, drawn-out process of social, political and institutional change, with a strong accent on state building. In terms of conflict stresses, this historical transition meant that the:

> Fundamental opposition between indigenous people and colonial powers was displaced by a far messier array of local divisions, relating variously to precolonial antagonisms between different indigenous populations, the simultaneous exacerbation of conflict and suppression of warfare during the colonial period, uneven development, and corruption. (Otto and Thomas, 1997, p. 4)

Some of these divisions manifested in the outbreak of localised conflicts, most dramatically on the island of Bougainville, initially around the construction of the Panguna mine and much later with the decade-long Bougainville conflict (1988–97). The lead up to independence also witnessed the revival of tribal fighting in parts of the Highlands, while a moral panic grew around rising crime rates in Port Moresby as independence loomed.

Two aspects of the decolonisation process in particular had an important bearing on the emergence of law and order concerns. The first related to the repeal of discriminatory colonial regulations that previously applied to the indigenous population. Removal of restrictions on movement opened up the towns, formerly expatriate enclaves, to migration from rural areas. Young male migrants flocked to Port Moresby in search of adventure and a better life, with the capital experiencing a 12.2 per cent annual growth rate between 1966 and 1977 and doubling again in size during the first decade after independence (King, 1992). While available data were thin, increasing crime rates were accompanied by a growing chorus of voices warning of a serious emergent crime problem in Port Moresby (Clifford, 1976). The lifting of colonial restrictions on alcohol was viewed as another contributing factor. According to Harris (1988, p. 8), who investigated Port Moresby gangs in the 1980s, the legalisation of alcohol provided 'the spark which ignited the flame' of urban gang growth from the mid-1960s.

The second aspect related to changes in government and administration, including the modernisation of the police and national justice system. The suppression of tribal fighting had been viewed as one of the Australian administration's most significant accomplishments. Its reappearance in the late 1960s was seen by some as evidence of a withdrawal of government from rural areas resulting from the replacement of the old devolved system of district administration with a bureaucratic system of centralised government (Gordon and Meggitt, 1985). The relative success of the old system in suppressing tribal conflict was attributed to its mobility and physical presence in rural areas, primarily in the form of *kiaps* and their field police, and its ability to engage pragmatically with local forms of authority and dispute resolution.

By contrast, the modern justice system was found wanting on many fronts. In the first place, its concentration in urban locations posed difficulties of access for those living in rural areas. For others, the new system was also seen as overly formalistic and cumbersome compared to the more flexible approach it replaced (Dinnen and Braithwaite, 2009). It also inadvertently weakened the standing of the formerly powerful (colonial) police, now subject to regular and humiliating 'defeats' in court, often on obscure technical grounds. From this perspective, renewed fighting in the Highlands represented a return to forms of violent self-help in the absence of effective government alternatives for managing disputes.

Concerns with violent crime and personal safety became progressively more pronounced during the 25 years after independence, particularly in the main urban centres. Signs of pervasive insecurity continue to manifest in the heavy fortifications and razor wire adorning homes and other buildings, and the ubiquitous presence of private security across PNG's urban landscapes. Streets empty as dusk approaches, and visitors are still routinely warned not to visit certain areas or walk after dark. During the 1970s, 1980s and for much of the 1990s, *raskol* gangs provided the folk devils in a prolonged moral panic around urban street crime. Port Moresby experienced cyclical patterns of outbreaks of criminal violence followed by special policing operations, entailing heavy-handed raids directed at the settlements viewed as incubators of *raskolism* (Dinnen, 2001). However, concerns with urban *raskols* appear to have diminished during the first two decades of the new millennium. Support for this proposition is provided in a review of available crime data by the World Bank in 2014 (Lakhani and Willman, 2014b). While levels of crime and violence in PNG are high compared with other parts of the world, the review concluded that these levels may be stabilising and noted that in 2010 there was an overall reduction in recorded crime compared to 2000. More attention has been placed in recent years on serious problems of violent tribal conflict in some Highlands areas. High-powered weapons, local mercenaries ('hire-men') and guerrilla tactics have fundamentally altered the ground rules of tribal conflict and fuelled prolonged cycles of violence in several provinces. These forms of conflict have been aggravated by heightened contestation around elections and large-scale natural resource projects (Dinnen et al., 2010).

Violence against women and girls, including rape and other sexual offences, has been a longstanding concern. According to the Human Rights Watch (HRW) *World Report 2017*, PNG is one the most dangerous countries in the world for women, with the majority experiencing rape or assault in their lifetime and women facing systemic discrimination (HRW, 2017). Deeply engrained social attitudes towards gender are slow to change, while the effects of economic globalisation, including growing inequalities, impact disproportionately on women and girls. The effectiveness of legal protections has long been hindered by weak enforcement. High-profile cases and persistent campaigning by local non-governmental organisations (NGOs) and activists have contributed to growing awareness of the level of violence and abuse experienced by women and girls and have prompted government, donors and civil society organisations to initiate a range of legislative, policy and emergency responses in this area. One of the most significant law reforms was the enactment of the *Family Protection Act 2013*, which made domestic violence a discrete offence for the first time. Parliament also endorsed the first National Gender-Based Violence Strategy in late 2016. An ongoing spate of sorcery-related violence, often directed against women, has also precipitated awareness, engagement and law reform campaigns, including repeal of the colonial-era *Sorcery Act 1971* (Forsyth and Eves, 2015).

The combination of weak enforcement agencies, porous borders (including a 750-kilometre land border with Indonesia), location as a regional shipping hub and rapid rate of economic globalisation renders PNG highly vulnerable to transnational crime. There have also been concerns that criminal syndicates have been using PNG as a transit point for conveying illicit goods, such as drugs and weapons, to its southern neighbour, Australia. Evidence of such activity surfaces periodically in the media, as with the recent arrests of alleged members of a major drug syndicate in PNG and Australia following the crash of a light aircraft outside Port Moresby in July 2020 (Kenneth, 2020a).

Despite the prevalence of law and order concerns, available data remain patchy and unreliable, making it hard to quantify levels of crime and violence with any precision. A review of PNG's criminal justice data in 1994 lamented the lack of systematic evidence that 'could provide a rational basis for understanding the current context of crime and promoting feasible strategies for crime prevention, development and management of the criminal justice system' (Zvekic and Wedderburn, 1994, p. 2). Not a lot has changed in the almost 30 years since. Levels of unreported crime remain extremely high, especially, but by no means exclusively, in rural areas where access to police and justice services are limited. The prevalence of informal approaches to managing disputes and infractions is another factor behind the low number of cases reported to authorities. Victimisation surveys also indicate considerable variations between urban and rural contexts, as well as within particular regional, rural and urban settings (Lakhani and Willman, 2014b).

State responses

State responses to PNG's law and order problems have relied primarily on the criminal justice system, notably the police, courts and corrections. While expectations have often been unrealistically high, the limited effectiveness of these responses on levels of crime and violence has been a concern throughout the post-independence period. The complexity of this particular sector adds to its challenges, with different departments and agencies operating with relatively little coordination. In addition, the sector shares systemic issues with other parts of government, including severe resource constraints, modest institutional capabilities, and the operational challenges presented by the country's topography and limited transport infrastructure. Over the years there have been numerous reports and policy reviews directed at improving responses to these problems.

Although undertaken almost 40 years ago, the 1984 Clifford Report remains one of the more insightful reviews (Clifford et al., 1984). It documented the shortcomings of individual agencies, noted the poor quality of data, and was critical of planning, budgeting and coordination across the sector. The report also highlighted distinctive features of PNG's broader regulatory environment, including high levels of legal pluralism and continuing reliance on informal approaches for everyday security and dispute resolution. It recognised how significant this informal layer of non-state regulation was in dealing with many kinds of problems at local levels. The report recommended further engagement with some of these informal approaches as a way of supplementing over-reliance on a fragile and expensive criminal justice system.

Despite the prescience of the Clifford Report's efforts to broaden the lens on available resources for managing disputes and security, successive governments continued to be preoccupied with crisis management, relying on special policing operations and temporary crime control measures such as curfews to suppress surges in crime and violence. In the context of rapid population growth, urbanisation and globalisation in recent years, the scale and range of PNG's law and order problems have progressively overwhelmed the criminal justice system. Although affecting all parts of the system, these pressures are most apparent in the police force, the Royal Papua New Guinea Constabulary (RPNGC).

While placing heavy reliance on the police as the frontline agency in responses to crime, no government has been prepared or able to make the necessary investment to build and sustain an effective national police organisation. Since PNG's independence in 1975, the size of the RPNGC has increased by only around 30 per cent, while the overall population has more than tripled. Recent estimates are of an organisation of around 7,383 staff (Deloitte, 2020, p. 19) and a national population close to nine million. At 1:1145, the current police-to-population ratio is significantly lower than the UN recommended level of 1:450. Government pledges to increase the size of the force are unlikely to be realised anytime soon given severe fiscal constraints as accentuated by the economic fallout from the COVID-19 pandemic. Inadequate funding has been a persistent problem for the RPNGC. A recent study undertaken on behalf of the Papua New Guinea–Australia Policing Partnership (PNG–APP) demonstrated that the RPNGC was seriously underfunded. The study found that the RPNGC experiences an average recurrent funding gap of K126 million per annum and would require a one-off capital injection of around K3.9 billion to enable the organisation to deliver its service mandate (Deloitte, 2020, p. 5). An example of how funding issues can affect police operations was the recent stalling of investigations into the massive drugs seizure following the light aircraft crash in July 2020 (see above). The media reported that this was a result of financial and other resource constraints (Kenneth, 2020b).

Household victimisation surveys confirm limited public confidence in the police (Guthrie, 2013). There is widespread scepticism about the ability of the RPNGC to carry out basic policing tasks, including responding to requests for help and investigating reported crimes. Lack of funds to buy fuel for police vehicles is a common reason provided for non-attendance. Flatlined budgets cover salaries but leave little to fund operational expenses, encouraging police to pursue rent-seeking opportunities. These can include payment for 'turning a blind eye' to infringements and illegal imposition of on-the-spot fines. It also renders the police highly susceptible to reliance on wealthy patrons, including political and business leaders, with the obvious risks this poses to police integrity.

Police performance and morale have also been affected by patronage networks and factionalism within the force, which have impacted on senior appointments and the conduct of some investigations. A 2013 baseline study of the RPNGC provides a depressing account of how these issues impact on everyday police practice, documenting low arrest rates; poor investigations, evidence collection and custody; and inadequate brief preparation, which results in low rates of successful prosecutions in the district courts and adversely affects committals to the higher courts (Coffey International Development, 2013).

Police brutality is another area of concern (Yakam, 2019). Although not all police engage in such behaviour, some have been involved in serious acts of violence, including unlawful killings, assaults and rape (HRW, 2005). As well as alienating many in the community, police abuses have also proven costly to government. A major review in 2004 found that outstanding legal claims against the state arising from unlawful police actions amounted to more than double the total police budget for that year (Government of Papua New Guinea, 2004). Recent years have seen growing debate around police brutality, in part responding to increasing coverage of such incidents in PNG's vibrant social media, as well as reflecting the reformist agenda of Bryan Kramer, who served as police minister from June 2019 to December 2020, and David Manning, appointed as police commissioner in December 2019, amid growing public demand for police reform. Kramer has been outspoken about problems of endemic corruption, illegality and brutality within the RPNGC. He recently stated that the police force he inherited on becoming police minister was:

> In complete disarray and riddled with corruption. The very organisation that was tasked with fighting corruption had become the leading agency in acts of corruption. Add to that a culture of police ill-discipline and brutality. (quoted in Doherty, 2020)

PNG's National Judicial System comprises two layers. The higher courts consist of the supreme and national courts established under the constitution and presided over by judges. The lower courts are the district courts established by legislation and presided over by magistrates. There are also a number of specialist courts, such as the coroner's court, juvenile court and land court. In relation to criminal matters, most serious cases are tried in the national court, with less serious ones dealt with by district courts. The National Judicial System has been the beneficiary of donor support over many years and, although facing many of the same systemic issues, is generally viewed as the most professional part of the law and justice sector. A persistent challenge has been long delays in court hearings, often reflecting problems in the broader criminal justice system, including, for example, the collection of evidence and preparation of case files by police. These delays, in turn, contribute to overcrowding in correctional facilities (see below).

Although not part of the National Judicial System, the most accessible and widely used court in PNG is the village court. First introduced in 1974, village courts represent a significant institutional innovation in PNG's law and justice system and, in many respects, embody the approach advocated in the Clifford Report. They were initially established to provide a form of accessible justice for predominantly rural areas, and are now also found in urban centres. In conception and design, these courts were intentionally hybrid, aimed at linking state and community approaches to dispute resolution and order maintenance at local levels. Staffed by lay magistrates, village courts are tasked with ensuring 'peace and harmony' in their respective communities, and with endeavouring to obtain 'amicable settlement of disputes' through the application of local custom. Created by statute with designated jurisdictional powers, the decisions of these courts are also subject to review by district court magistrates. They thus draw simultaneously on the authority of state law and local community norms. In recent years there has been growing appreciation of the actual and potential role of village courts, scattered across the length of the country, to bring 'substantial justice' to ordinary Papua New Guineans (Goddard, 2009). While the sheer volume of village courts massively complicates the task of providing adequate administrative support and supervision, which can in turn lead to problems associated with lack of accountability, these courts have demonstrated an openness to reform and professionalisation. This is seen in the growing number of women who now sit as village court magistrates and officials in different parts of the country.

PNG's prisons, administered by Correctional Services, have arguably been the most neglected part of the criminal justice system and have long struggled with inadequate funding. Overcrowding is a major issue and has been exacerbated by the large number of remandees (usually around a third of the prison population) awaiting trial in the courts. These have added to the pressures on staff and frustration among inmates, many of whom have to wait years before trial. The official mission of Correctional Services is to enhance public safety by providing secure and humane containment, and by rehabilitating detainees. Resource constraints and lack of specialist staff impede the latter. Activities that do take place often depend on the voluntary sector, particularly the churches. As elsewhere, PNG's prisons provide a fertile environment for building criminal identities and networks. Overcrowding, court delays and poor security practices contribute to regular mass breakouts from the largest facilities. Lae's Buimo prison is especially prone to escapes. Built to accommodate 436 inmates, it currently houses over 1,000. Since 2015, there have been six major breakouts from this prison with 11 escapees recaptured, 32 shot dead and 138 still at large (*The National*, 2020).

Capacity building and donor programs

Given constraints on government finances, donor assistance to PNG's criminal justice system has been an important source of support over many years. Most of this has been from Australia, PNG's largest bilateral donor. Initially it took the form of institutional strengthening projects with individual agencies including the police, courts, prisons, legal services and the Ombudsman Commission. Support to the RPNGC used to be delivered by civilian advisers but has now been replaced by direct police-to-police assistance provided by the Australian Federal Police (AFP). Under the short-lived Enhanced Cooperation Program, uniformed Australian officers exercising police powers worked alongside their counterparts in

Port Moresby, but that initiative was abruptly terminated after a successful constitutional challenge in the Supreme Court. Since 2008, the AFP have been providing capacity building as advisers to the RPNGC under the PNG–APP. Australian assistance to other parts of the justice system is delivered on a sector-wide basis and is currently provided through the Justice Services and Stability for Development (JSS4D) Program, which focuses on priority areas identified by the PNG Government and heads of sector agencies.

The results from decades of donor assistance have been modest in terms of substantial improvements in the performance of PNG's criminal justice system. This is particularly so in the case of the RPNGC, which has been the beneficiary of Australian support dating back to the late 1980s. While undergoing various iterations, involving changes in focus and mode of delivery, police capacity building has consisted mainly of training. Measuring the overall effect of donor efforts in this regard is difficult. Numerical indicators such as numbers of officers trained and equipment handed out do not tell us whether activities have changed policing practice. The fact that assistance continues to revolve around training and advising on broadly the same set of issues after more than three decades suggest limited impacts rather than major transformation. Capacity building has done little to address systemic challenges facing the police such as the vexed issue of resources. Recent observations, including, as we have seen, by a police minister, have drawn attention to important respects in which the organisation appears to be going backwards. Arguably the most realistic assessment of Australian support is that it has helped the RPNGC maintain a semblance of organisational functionality, rather than making a major difference to police effectiveness or improved security in the wider PNG community (Peake and Dinnen, 2014).

The limitations of organisational capacity building approaches are evident across the broader law and justice sector. A review of Australian law and justice assistance by AusAID's Office of Development Effectiveness that covered various countries concluded that it had produced patchy results without necessarily improving the overall quality of justice received by citizens (AusAID, 2012). The reasons given for these results are germane to the PNG context. In the first place, lack of capacity is not always the binding constraint on institutional performance. Other more immediate factors include the dense network of informal institutions and practices overlaying the formal justice system. Second, capacity building programs are often overambitious in scope and there may be extremely limited ability to implement them in low-capacity settings. Third, capacity building approaches often work towards best international practice and imported models, which are a poor fit in the local environment.

The issues of institutional transfer and fit are especially salient when considering donor support to the RPNGC and criminal justice system over the years. Much of capacity building has been predicated on the assumption that what 'works' in Australia and other metropolitan contexts can be transplanted directly to PNG. This raises fundamental issues around the appropriateness of the policing and justice models being transferred through donor engagements, issues that cannot be simply overcome with technical or administrative solutions and tweaked delivery modalities. Critical observers, going back to the Clifford Report over 35 years ago, have long argued that a more productive basis for reform would be to start by acknowledging the plural and networked character of security and justice provision in PNG.

The narrow focus on the RPNGC is at best only ever going to address part of the problem. For a start, this focus is almost exclusively on urban areas, even though most citizens live in rural localities, geographically and socially removed from the uniformed police. In these places, including in most urban settlements, everyday disputes and security are managed through community-based approaches that often rely more on restorative justice than investigation, prosecution and incarceration. Focusing exclusively on state policing can obscure the many examples of positive and often quite creative local responses to insecurity that draw on a mix of state and non-state resources with an emphasis on prevention and reduction (see section below on community responses to insecurity). It also neglects the increasingly prominent role of private security, which is examined in the next section.

Private security

One significant response to insecurity in PNG has been the dramatic growth in the private security industry (Dinnen, 2020). While broadly consistent with global patterns, there has been increasing demand for private security services, particularly from the business sector. According to the World Bank, more than two-thirds of businesses in PNG employ private security staff, spending on average 5 per cent of their annual costs on this, compared to an average of 3.2 per cent for firms in East Asia overall (Lakhani and Willman, 2014a). The increase in private security companies has occurred against a background of significant development in the extractive industries and rapid economic globalisation. Additional boosts to industry growth in recent years include the hosting of Australia's controversial offshore detention facilities on Manus Island and several major international events such as the Asia-Pacific Economic Cooperation (APEC) summit in 2018.

According to the industry regulator, the Security Industries Authority (SIA), the number of licensed security companies grew from 174 in 2006 to 566 in 2018 (Figure 4.1), with a workforce of over 30,000 licensed security guards (Isari, 2019; see Figure 4.2). According to the SIA the significant jump in the number of licensed companies between 2013 and 2014 resulted in part from their efforts to track down unlicensed security companies. The SIA figures do not, however, include what are believed to be a very substantial number of unlicensed companies and personnel providing private security services in different parts of the country. The number of licensed guards is, nevertheless, four times that of serving police officers, and exceeds the combined strength of PNG's three disciplined forces (the RPNGC, PNG Defence Force and Correctional Service). By any account, the private security industry is a significant employer in PNG and a major player in the provision of security services.

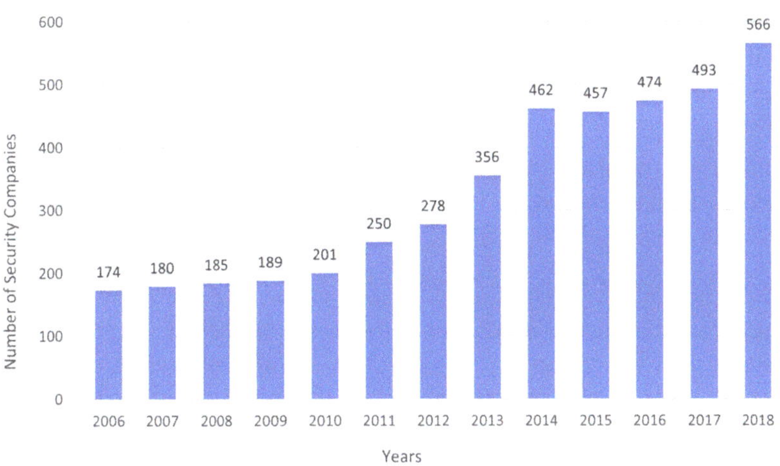

Figure 4.1: Growth of licensed security companies.

Source: Security Industries Authority; figure adapted from Isari (2019).

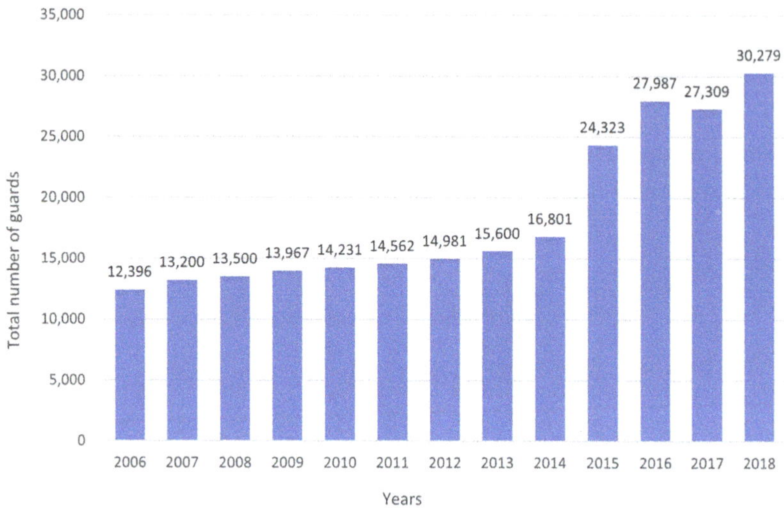

Figure 4.2: Number of licensed guards.

Source: Security Industries Authority; figure adapted from Isari (2019).

Private security companies vary in size, services offered, areas of operation, as well as national origins. They range from transnational security corporations with global reach, to large locally owned firms, through to numerous smaller and often short-lived operators. Most are based in the main urban centres, but some also operate in rural areas where major resource projects are located. As well as static asset protection, other services include close personal protection, mobile escorts, security training, security assessments, emergency evacuations, rapid response capabilities, security fences, and sophisticated electronic surveillance and satellite tracking systems. The SIA estimated the value of the industry in 2018 as between K800 million and K1 billion.

As the industry has grown, so too have stories of violence, theft and other misdeeds by some private security personnel (Walton and Dinnen, 2020). The *Security (Protection) Industry Act 2004* established the SIA to regulate the private security sector. Its key functions include:

- granting operating licences and guard permits to security companies
- specifying minimum standards of training and approving training facilities
- approving security equipment other than firearms

- ensuring that companies and guards operate in accordance with their licences and permits
- drafting a Code of Conduct covering discipline and work ethics in the industry.

The resources available to the SIA to fulfil its role are, however, woefully inadequate and, as currently constituted, it has no real powers of enforcement to ensure compliance with the Act. Many industry insiders regard it as a toothless and largely ineffectual body. While amendments have been drafted to strengthen it, these have yet to be endorsed by the SIA Council and, as legislative amendments, also need approval from the National Parliament.

A close and mutually supportive relationship exists between the police and private security industry. Both sets of security providers undertake many of the same activities, with the SIA website stating that security companies 'play an important role as a quasi-law enforcing agency beside the Police force' (SIA, 2020). Strong informal networks exist, with many senior industry employees having previous police (or military) experience in PNG or overseas. Larger operators regularly assist police by, for example, providing fuel and tyres for vehicles, while the informal networks facilitate intelligence sharing. The private sector relies on the police to respond to serious incidents, receive and process crime reports, and detain suspects. Some private security employees also serve as reserve constables and, in that capacity, exercise the same powers as regular police.

Despite extensive interaction in practice, concerns have been raised in some quarters about the potentially negative impacts of the private sector on the performance and standing of the police. These include sensitivities about private providers encroaching on areas that some believe should remain the exclusive preserve of the public police. There are also concerns that the growing prominence of private companies diverts attention away from the need for adequate government support of the RPNGC, as well as perceptions that public–private security collaborations are more likely to privilege powerful business over the security interests of ordinary citizens. There is also resentment about international security companies among some locally owned operators who view the former as diminishing their share of this growing market.

Community-based responses to insecurity

Reflecting issues of limited access, affordability and, in some cases, preference, informal community-based approaches to dispute resolution and everyday security are widespread throughout PNG in both urban and rural settings. Operating alongside, and often together with, parts of the criminal justice system, are multiple local actors and mechanisms involved in problem solving and security provision in communities across the country. These are not simply remnants of traditional forms of dispute resolution and order maintenance but are often innovative local responses to contemporary problems. Given the absence or weak presence of the state in many places, and in the face of new stresses and forms of contestation, local actors have devised their own ways of dealing with them, albeit often drawing on older traditions. Some of these initiatives have achieved promising results, while others have not and, indeed, can exacerbate existing problems. Without proper accountability, informal responses to crime and violence can end up as violent forms of vigilantism, increasing the risks faced by already vulnerable groups, such as women, children and the elderly. However, this outcome is not inevitable.

Recent research has highlighted the important and constructive role of informal governance arrangements, including mediation services, in the regulation of PNG's sprawling urban settlements (Craig and Porter, 2018a). While long depicted as dangerous places, crime surveys suggest that life in many settlements is no more violent than in non-settlement areas (Guthrie, 2013). Settlements are home to multiethnic and varied populations, including public servants and private sector employees, as well as those working in the informal economy. Residents rely on extended family, kinship and ethnic networks for managing disputes and personal safety. *Komitis* and leadership networks play a crucial role in social regulation within these localities, notably as a way of bringing together locally specific forms of authority with those of external agencies, for example through relationships with individual police officers, magistrates, private security companies or NGOs. These approaches are intentionally hybrid, drawing on available state and non-state resources. According to a recent study, it is this ability to 'combine the authority of leaders and ethnic groups inside the blok and also draw in individuals with connections to the state, police, or others whose power and respect is derived from a range of sources physically external to the settlement' that is the key to the effectiveness of these local *komitis* (Craig and Porter, 2018b, p. 5).

There are examples of responses to conflict and violence in rural areas that also draw on a mix of state and non-state resources. An example is the Gor 'community police' in Simbu Province, established in the aftermath of prolonged tribal fighting and sorcery-related violence. Tribal and church leaders, with the tacit approval and support of provincial authorities, set up their own community police. They have received support, including some training, from the RPNGC, and initial assessments indicated a noticeable reduction in violence in that area (Bal, 2015). Another example is the District Peace Management Teams in Eastern Highlands Province, formed in response to tribal conflict. District Peace Management Teams comprise provincial and district officials, police, village court officers, community and church leaders. Trained in non-violent conflict resolution, they mediate between conflicting parties, broker ceasefires and help negotiate written peace agreements. Breaches of the agreements are reported to the police and offending parties can be penalised. This initiative also reportedly led to a marked reduction in tribal conflicts in the province (Allen and Monson, 2014). Another illustration from the Highlands is the peacemaking work of Operation *Mekim Save* in Enga Province, a culturally inflected local initiative directed at preventing and resolving tribal conflicts in that province (Pupu and Wiessner, 2018).

Gender-based violence has also prompted a range of highly localised initiatives in different parts of the country (Hukula, 2020). These include the impressive and courageous work of committed community-based organisations such as Kup Women for Peace, Voices for Change, Highlands Human Rights Defenders, Kafe Women's Association, PNG Human Rights Defenders Association and Tribal Foundation. Enacting community by-laws and revitalising community governance arrangements has become a promising local response to problems of violence and social breakdown in some areas. For example, Voice for Change has worked with local leaders in Jiwaka Province to take ownership of gender-based violence and other law and order issues by creating community laws aimed at preventing and sanctioning this kind of behaviour. Local activists involved in such schemes have been supported by international NGOs and donors.

In reaffirming the value of local solutions to local problems, these initiatives also demonstrate the potential of hybrid and networked approaches that link together different actors and forms of authority (state and non-state) and enable them to work strategically to prevent, reduce and resolve violence.

Corruption

Many consider corruption in PNG a key threat to social and economic development. International indices suggest that corruption in PNG is acute, with Transparency International's Corruption Perceptions Index (CPI) ranking the country as one of the more corrupt in the world. In 2021, PNG scored 31 out of 100 (with zero being highly corrupt and 100 very clean) and was ranked as the 124th most corrupt country out of 180 countries (Transparency International, 2022). However, it is important to note that the CPI has a number of limitations. In particular, CPI scores are based on assessments from international experts who may not live in the country, focus on the public sector (ignoring the private sector) and only apply to the national scale (thus overlooking transnational corruption). In this section, we go beyond the broad brushstrokes from international assessments to examine perceptions about, manifestations of and causes of corruption in PNG.

Perceptions of corruption

While there is much discussion about corruption in PNG, it is important to note that the concept itself is contested. Scholars have long argued about how to define corruption and who should define it. On the one hand, there are those who tend to see corruption as a universal concept, which has been a feature of life and governance in all countries throughout history (see Noonan, 1984). Many believe corruption can be effectively measured and define corruption as 'the abuse of public office for private gain', which means corruption is confined to state officials. This perspective is popular among international scholars (particularly economists and political scientists), international donors and some NGOs (such as Transparency International). Given its popularity, we can refer to this position as the 'mainstream view' of corruption.

On the other hand, other scholars believe that corruption is a social construct and that interpretations of this concept vary depending on social, political, cultural and economic factors (Harrison, 2006). Some of these scholars note that what is considered corrupt in one country or community is often not in another and argue that interpreting 'corruption' requires understanding the contextual factors that shape people's lives and decisions. While increasingly popular (particularly among anthropologists and human geographers), these views are still on the margins of debates about corruption, so we can refer to this position as the 'alternative view' of corruption.

Over the past decade in PNG, researchers have sought to comprehend how Papua New Guineans interpret corruption and how these understandings differ or overlap with international definitions. Findings reveal that many Papua New Guineans do indeed reflect the mainstream view of corruption. A survey of over 1,800 people across nine provinces of the country found that 53 per cent of respondents defined corruption as 'the abuse of public office for private gain' (Walton, 2015). However, reflecting the alternative view, marginalised respondents were less likely to define corruption in this way. Rather, women, the poor and rural respondents defined corruption more broadly, focusing on local concerns and activities that did not involve public officials (Walton, 2015). Some in PNG justify corruption because of poverty and cultural obligations (see Walton and Jackson, 2020).

What do these findings tell us about corruption in PNG? Well, for a start, we need to be careful when assessing the nature of corruption in PNG. While international indices might suggest corruption is a major problem in the country, they fail to account for the lived experiences and perceptions of Papua New Guinean citizens. Taking these into account shows that, for some, particularly the marginalised, what some call 'corruption' is simply a way of responding to economic and cultural constraints. This is not to say that we should tolerate all forms of corruption. Indeed, it is difficult to justify grand corruption involving millions of kina. However, when examining corruption in PNG we need to take into account social, economic, cultural and geographical factors that might explain why some might support activities that others label 'corrupt'.

Manifestations and causes of corruption

Keeping the above discussion in mind, it is worthwhile examining the drivers and manifestations of corruption – as the mainstream view interprets it – in PNG. In the lead up to independence, the Constitutional Planning Committee's (1974) report identified corruption as a key risk to this new nation and recommended the establishment of a Leadership Code and Ombudsman Commission. Despite the concerns expressed by some of PNG's elites about these institutions – for example, Julius Chan (2016, p. 65) argued against the establishment of the Ombudsman Commission and leadership code – both were adopted, in modified form, into the nation's constitution.

When assessing the nature of corruption in the post-independence era, scholars and officials have identified two distinct time periods. The first epoch centres on the early years of independence until the early 1980s. While the newly independent country faced numerous challenges, until the early 1980s its public administration was robust and corruption was mostly kept under control (May, 2004; Pieper, 2004). This period saw smooth changes of government in 1980, 1982 and 1985 (May, 2004), and senior public administrators described public servants of this era as motivated, independent and professional (Pieper, 2004). However, by the mid-1980s service delivery had noticeably declined and by the 1990s, as May (2004) noted, corruption and nepotism had become particularly apparent. In their influential report, Clifford et al. (1984) observed numerous examples of potential corruption and warned that the extent of the problem was likely greater than available data suggested.

Since this time, there have been numerous corruption scandals involving public servants, politicians, private companies, landowner groups, citizens and non-citizens (for a list of some of these, see Barnett, 1989; Dorney, 2001; Jones, 2014; Larmour, 2012; Transparency International Papua New Guinea [TI PNG], 2017; Walton, 2018). Examples of 1980s corruption scandals include those in the logging industry forensically investigated in the Barnett Commission of Inquiry (Barnett, 1989). In 1997, concern about corruption increased after the government's failed attempt to hire foreign mercenaries to fight in its long-running war in Bougainville. This event was beset by accusations of backroom deals and became known as the 'Sandline Affair' (after Sandline International, the name of the company that provided the mercenaries), which ultimately caused the downfall of the then prime minister, Sir Julius Chan (Dinnen et al., 1997).

Corruption scandals, often involving senior public servants and politicians, continue to feature in national media and in online forums. For example, in 2020, former prime minister Peter O'Neill was arrested in relation to the purchase of generators (Davidson, 2020); he was later acquitted in the National Court (*Post-Courier*, 2021). This followed a failed attempt in 2014 to arrest the then prime minister over a government payment to a local law firm. While corruption scandals involving senior officials and, often, millions of kina, can be hard to keep track of, TI PNG endeavoured to describe the nature of these allegations in their report *Lest we forget.* It reviews 20 unresolved large-scale corruption allegations between 2007 and 2017, and shows how state investments and lease arrangements have contributed to potential corruption (TI PNG, 2017). In turn, over the past two decades PNG businesses have consistently cited corruption as a key constraint to business in the country (Fox et al., 2018).

Research with citizens and public servants also suggests that corruption is a part of many people's lives. A survey with citizens in five provinces of the country found that 51 per cent of respondents had witnessed some sort of corruption, with males more likely to witness corruption than females (TI PNG, 2016, p. 19). Most respondents (73 per cent) were concerned about bribery, particularly during elections. Respondents believed nepotism was most prevalent in tendering boards, while misappropriation (or theft of government property) was most associated with the health sector (TI PNG, 2016, p. 22). Many public servants also believe corruption is common, with research conducted in 2018 showing that two-thirds of public servants across four provinces agreed that it is difficult to get things done without bribing government officials (Walton, 2019).

It is difficult to know whether corruption in PNG is getting worse. As discussed, corruption is a contested concept making measurement difficult; in addition, it is often conducted in secret and hidden from indicators that attempt to quantify it. One indicator suggests that, over the past decade, PNG's efforts to address corruption have improved. According to the World Bank's Worldwide Governance Indicators, PNG's control of public sector corruption improved: from a percentile rank of 6.7 to 16.8 out of 100 between 2009 and 2019 (World Bank, 2020). However, the country's score on Transparency International's CPI has only marginally improved: from a score of 25 (out of 100) in 2012 to 31 in 2021 (Transparency International, 2022). A 2015 survey of citizens found that 90 per cent of respondents said that corruption had gotten worse over the past decade (TI PNG, 2016, p. 7).

The drivers of corruption in PNG are numerous, multi-scalar and complex. Reflecting on the decline in PNG's public administration from the mid-1980s, senior public servants have noted that poor governance was accompanied by a number of factors, including a move away from bureaucratic procedures, politicisation of the administration and the shift from expatriate personnel contracted within inline positions to providing advisory support (Pieper, 2004). Decentralisation policy may have also helped exacerbate corruption, with some concerned that the decentralisation reform of the 1995 *Organic Law on Provincial Governments and Local-level Governments* has politicised subnational bureaucracy and led to weaker accountability and greater opportunities for corruption and cronyism (Reilly et al., 2014). The increased District Services Improvement Program (DSIP) funding channelled to District Development Authorities (established by law in 2014) is also believed to be fuelling corruption in some districts. An auditor-general's review found an array of problems associated with DSIP funds including 'a pervasive breakdown in the DSIP governance framework; and ineffective spending of DSIP grants including potential misuse of DSIP funds', and warned there was a 'high risk of fraud' (Auditor-General's Office of Papua New Guinea, 2014, pp. 12–13).

For some, corruption is an outcome of the merging of traditional systems of governance with PNG's weak state. Ketan (2004), for example, shows how the big man politics that leads to client–patron relations reflect the reciprocal exchanges of wealth embodied in the practice of *moka* by the Melpa people of Mount Hagen. From this perspective, corruption is part of a longer tradition of reciprocity. Clifford et al. (1984, p. 80) argued that corruption is particularly possible in PNG due to *wantok* obligations of reciprocal gift exchange and 'a cultural lack of familiarity with written records'. Walton (2018) found that, because of the deficiencies of the state, it is the poor and marginalised who are most likely subject to the cultural, social and economic pressures that can drive what some label corruption. While subject to the same pressures, it is the enfranchised who are more able and likely to identify and report various forms of corruption – particularly corruption that occurs at the national scale (Walton, 2018).

Still, it is important to note that much of what is called 'grand (large-scale) corruption' involves a network of transnational elites and organisations. This is particularly the case in the logging sector, with transnational companies (especially those from Southeast Asia) long associated with corruption and human rights abuses (Barnett, 1989). Urban areas are also centres for transnational crime and corruption. Lasslett (2018) argued that urbanisation in PNG often features anti-competitive practices, corruption and violence facilitated by the state and transnational corporate interests (also see Chapter 7, this volume).

Transnational networks across the region can help facilitate the laundering of illicitly gained funds into offshore bank accounts and real estate. In 2015, an investigation by the NGO Global Witness and Australian media outlets showed how PNG politicians were investing corrupt monies into Australian banks and real estate (McKenzie et al., 2015). For its role in harbouring corrupt funds, Sam Koim, head of the now defunct anti-corruption organisation Investigation Taskforce Sweep (ITFS), described Australia as the 'Cayman Islands of the Pacific'. Focusing on its transnational elements shows that corruption is not simply associated with state officials – it also involves a network of organisations and individuals from the private sector that move illicitly gained goods and monies throughout the world. In turn, corruption in PNG involves a myriad of actors that span the globe (see Walton and Dinnen, 2020).

The poor state of the nation's integrity agencies is another key driver of corruption, which is much more likely if people think they can get away with it. We have already highlighted the challenges facing the country's police force. In the section below, we briefly examine some of the other state-based responses to fighting corruption and note that, while there are some bright spots, most agencies do not have the resources or mandate to effectively address corruption in the country.

State-based responses: Anti-corruption and integrity agencies

The PNG state funds a number of organisations to address government corruption and mismanagement. The RPNGC plays a critical role in addressing corruption – it is often the first port of call for citizens who want to report it. The Department of Justice and Attorney General also plays a role in addressing corruption, as it is the 'central agency responsible for the administration of legal services to the State and its instrumentalities, and the provision of law and justice services' (Department of Justice and Attorney General, 2020). However, unlike the aforementioned agencies, only four organisations specifically focus on investigating corruption and wrongdoing.

The first is the Ombudsman Commission, which was mandated to investigate wrongdoing by those in government leadership positions through the nation's constitution at independence in 1975. While an important anti-corruption organisation that has helped prevent 'the decline of the executive and parliament into total irresponsibility and unaccountability' (Ghai, 1997, p. 324), the Ombudsman Commission has long suffered from a lack of resources and an inadequate mandate to hold state officials to account (Walton, 2018). The second is the National Fraud and Anti-Corruption Directorate (referred to as the 'Fraud Squad'), which sits within the RPNGC. The Fraud Squad has been involved in investigating many high-profile cases of alleged corruption; for example, it was at the forefront of an attempt to arrest Prime Minister Peter O'Neill in 2014 (AAP, 2014). Third, the Financial Analysis and Supervision Unit (FASU) was created through the *Anti-Money Laundering and Counter Terrorist Financing Act 2015*. The organisation operates within the Bank of PNG, and has a mandate to detect, deter and disrupt money laundering and terrorist financing activities (FASU, 2018). Fourth, the Auditor-General's Office commenced operations in 1973 and was established as the country's supreme audit institution under section 213 of the constitution in 1975. The organisation inspects, audits and reports on accounts, finances and properties of government departments, agencies and public corporations.

In 2011 Prime Minister Peter O'Neill promised to add to these key anti-corruption organisations by establishing an Independent Commission Against Corruption (ICAC). (An ICAC was first proposed in 1997 but ultimately failed to gain political support.) To pave the way for an ICAC, the O'Neill government first established the independent ITFS to investigate corruption in the interim. ITFS was initially successful; its investigations resulted in numerous arrests and the recovery of millions of kina from the proceeds of crime. However, in 2014 the agency turned its attention to O'Neill himself, helping to organise an arrest warrant for the then prime minister over allegations of corruption. ITFS was subsequently defunded after a lengthy legal battle ended in 2016, when the court ruled the government's decision to abolish ITFS was within the law. The Marape government has recently established an ICAC. While the ICAC legislation has been finalised, the organisation has yet to start operations.

Figure 4.3 compares the relative amounts of spending on and, after 2020, budget allocations (dashed lines) for each of these key anti-corruption organisations (figures have been adjusted for inflation so are comparable over time). It shows that the Ombudsman Commission and Auditor-General's Office are by far the best funded. Funding for both organisations is set to decline under the Marape government. Continuing a trend set in 2017, the Marape government has spent more on the Ombudsman Commission than the Auditor-General's Office. In comparison, other organisations receive small sums. Building on previous analysis (Walton and Hushang, 2020), recent analysis by Walton and Hushang has found that between 2008 and 2020 key anti-corruption organisations in PNG only received between 0.37 per cent and 0.27 per cent of the overall national budget, a paltry percentage that declined over O'Neill's time as prime minister.

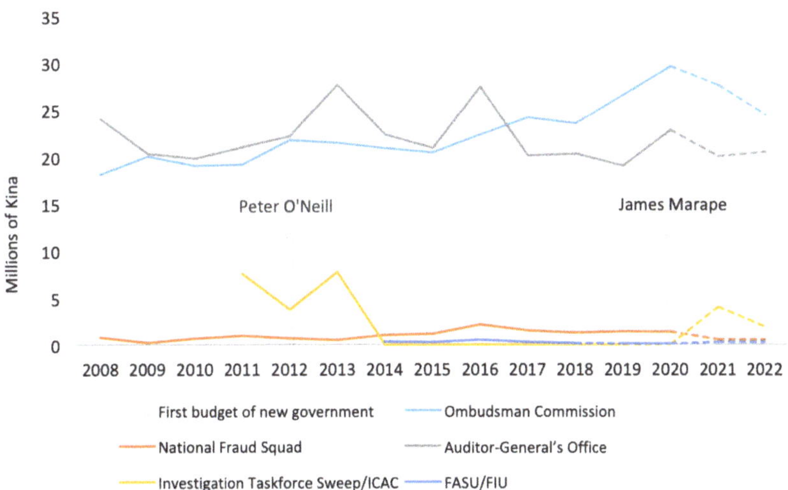

Figure 4.3: Funding for five anti-corruption organisations, 2008–22 (2021 prices).

Source: Calculations by Grant Walton and Husnia Hushang.

International donors have often augmented these anti-corruption efforts through technical support and other types of assistance. Indeed, for more than 15 years, Australia, PNG's largest donor, has spent more funding on good governance programs than in any other sector (see Department of Foreign Affairs and Trade, 2020). Some of these programs have encouraged innovative responses. For example, the United Nations Development Program and the Australian Government in partnership with PNG's Department of Finance funded an anti-corruption phone service that allowed public officials to anonymously report cases of corruption through a mobile phone text messaging service (Watson and Wiltshire, 2016).

While these organisations go some way towards addressing corruption in the country (the problem would be greater if they were not around), their effectiveness is limited due to the lack of resources and limited mandate that makes it easy for political and bureaucratic elites to avoid prosecution. Their effectiveness in addressing corruption further is undermined by two other factors. First, most anti-corruption organisations are mandated to focus on public officials rather than the private sector or civil society – two sectors that play a significant role in delivering services across the country. Second, with some exceptions (see Walton and Dinnen, 2020), most anti-corruption organisations fail to focus on transnational corruption. Like state-based anti-corruption organisations in other jurisdictions, these organisations struggle to investigate and hold to account the transnational web of actors involved in corruption.

Non-state responses: Citizens and civil society

It is important to note that, in their everyday lives, many Papua New Guineans resist corruption. In focus groups conducted with citizens across four provinces in PNG, respondents spoke of directly confronting and even physically assaulting those involved in what they thought was corrupt behaviour (Walton, 2018). Likely because they dominate the police and other public institutions, men are more likely to report corruption than women (Walton, 2019; Walton and Peiffer, 2017). While it is true that some citizens might support and participate in corrupt practices (Crocombe, 2001), particularly bribery during elections, it is important to note that many also resist these practices. Citizens are also increasingly reporting corruption through social media and other internet portals. While Facebook continues to be an important source of information, reports featured on that site are often unverified. The media also highlights corruption cases, though many journalists are threatened. In response, some have set up anonymous websites, such as pngicentral.org, that investigate and report on corruption.

Recent research on what might motivate citizens to report corruption has highlighted three key drivers. First, researchers have found that formal education is key in determining how likely it is that citizens will report corruption to authorities (Walton and Peiffer, 2017). In short, those who are educated above primary school level are more likely to report a variety of different types of corruption. Second, citizens are even more likely to report corruption if they trust that anti-corruption agencies will do something about it. Finally, citizens are far more likely to respond to corruption when they understand how it impacts on their local community (Walton and Peiffer, 2017). Overall, these findings suggest that supporting the formal education sector, strengthening anti-corruption organisations and raising awareness about how corruption impacts on local communities are likely to lead to more citizens reporting corruption.

PNG has a long tradition of civil society groups protesting against and building awareness about corruption. Mostly urban based, anti-corruption groups have involved leaders from PNG churches, political organisations and universities. For example, Melanesian Solidarity (MelSol), one of PNG's most vocal civil society activist groups, was formally launched in 1984 (King, 2004). The organisation took up a wide range of issues in the 1980s and 1990s, including supporting the West Papuan nationalist movement, environmental preservation, landowner rights and militarisation (Standish, 1999). In 1997, MelSol played a critical part in organising community protests over the government's failed attempt to hire foreign mercenaries to fight in its long-running war in Bougainville. Given that the government was negotiating with Sandline International (a company that was to provide mercenaries to the government), events around this negotiation became known as the 'Sandline Affair'. With negotiations beset by accusations of backroom deals, the Sandline Affair brought corruption to the public's consciousness like few other events before it. Groups like MelSol and the pan-denominational movement 'Brukim Skru' ('Bend the Knee') protested against the shady deals that had caused the crisis (Griffin, 1997).

While MelSol's activism petered out in the early 2000s, grassroots movements have continued to protest against corruption across the country. For example, in the late 2000s grassroots groups held regular protests across Port Moresby calling for Prime Minister Michael Somare to resign over alleged corruption (Walton, 2018). In 2016 students across the country shut down major universities as they protested the O'Neill government's alleged corruption and its undermining of anti-corruption organisations, particularly the Fraud Squad. This involved a showdown with police in Port Moresby, resulting in police shooting protestors.

These grassroots movements are joined by transnational NGOs, TI PNG being the most prominent. TI PNG commenced operations in 1997. Since its inception, the agency has campaigned against corruption and has worked with civil society organisations and the media to highlight the problems that cause corruption and offer solutions to it (Larmour, 2003). While a chapter of the broader global Transparency International network, TI PNG is managed by a local voluntary board of directors. Individuals, corporations and donors help to finance TI PNG's activities, which mean it is better funded than its grassroots counterparts (Walton, 2018).

Civil society has played an important role in highlighting corruption in PNG. However, the sector faces numerous challenges. Many local civil society organisations lack resources and, as a result, have been unable to sustain their operations. Moreover, local organisations are sometimes tied to politicians, and civic leaders themselves have a history of running for parliament and, in turn, by their absence, weakening the anti-corruption movement while they pursue – and sometimes gain – political office (Walton, 2016). Civil society is also fragmented, with schisms opening up between local and transnational organisations (which have greater access to resources) (Walton, 2016).

Conclusions

This chapter has examined key understandings of, and drivers and responses to, crime and corruption. It has provided a nuanced account of crime and corruption, an approach often obscured by the popular indices that can frame discussions about these challenges. The chapter shows how manifestations and responses to crime and corruption have changed over time and across space.

Three key themes flow from this analysis. First, while crime and corruption are contested concepts, they both represent key challenges for PNG. Crime and corruption can undermine economic activity, social harmony and state stability. Both issues are regularly cited as key challenges for business in particular – indeed, a 2012 survey of businesses in PNG found that law and order and corruption were the top two reform priorities (Asian Development Bank and Institute of National Affairs, 2014, p. 4). Still, responding to these challenges requires a nuanced understanding of the social, cultural and economic forces that allow these problems to flourish. This requires looking beyond the assessments of crime and corruption rendered by international indices.

Second, thinking about crime and corruption requires recognising the networks and relationships between a variety of individuals and organisations. Networks of politicians, bureaucrats and businesspeople often perpetuate crime and corruption. Responses to these challenges involve networks of state and non-state actors and organisations. While many focus on the way state agencies and organisations address crime and corruption, our analysis suggests effective responses involve a melange of state and non-state actors and organisations. This often involves a hybrid configuration of different sources of authority, drawing on, for example, a combination of state, custom and religious values. Thinking about the networked and hybrid nature of these challenges rather than focusing on strict divisions between state, private sector and civil society has the potential to provide a more realistic assessment of the multifaceted quality of crime and corruption in PNG and the need for similarly multilayered responses.

Finally, crime and corruption, and responses to these challenges, are far from static. While some have been prescient in their assessment of the types of law and order challenges facing PNG (e.g. Clifford et al., 1984), the character of crime and corruption are continuously evolving. At the time of writing, PNG, like nations around the world, is dealing with the COVID-19 pandemic. As Kabuni (2020) has demonstrated, the PNG Government's response to this pandemic through its state of emergency exacerbates the risk of corruption. Responses to crime and corruption have also changed considerably: citizens now report corruption and police brutality through social media and websites, and hotlines allow people to report corruption through their mobile phones. Global, regional, national and local events, as well as innovations and technological change will continue to reshape the threat of crime and corruption in the years to come. Law enforcement and anti-corruption agencies need to adapt to these changes if they are to effectively address crime and corruption, especially as efforts to date have been wholly inadequate.

Acknowledgements

We would like to thank Fiona Hukula, Miranda Forsyth, Stephen Howes, Lekshmi Pillai and workshop participants for their feedback.

References

AAP. (2014, June 16). PNG Prime Minister Peter O'Neill served with warrant by corruption watchdog. *The Australian.*

Allen, M. and Monson, R. (2014). Land and conflict in Papua New Guinea: The role of land mediation. *Security Challenges*, *10*(2), 1–14.

Asian Development Bank and Institute of National Affairs. (2014). *The challenges of doing business in Papua New Guinea.* Asian Development Bank.

Auditor-General's Office of Papua New Guinea. (2014). *District services improvement program.* Auditor-General's Office of Papua New Guinea.

AusAID. (2012). *Building on local strengths. Evaluation of Australian law and justice assistance.* AusAID.

Bal, C. (2015). Kumo Koimbo: Accounts and responses to witchcraft in Gor, Simbu Province. In M. Forsyth and R. Eves (Eds), *Talking it through: Responses to sorcery and witchcraft beliefs and practices in Melanesia* (pp. 299–307). ANU Press. doi.org/10.22459/TIT.05.2015.16.

Barnett, T. E. (1989). *Report of the commission of inquiry into aspects of the forest industry.* Government of Papua New Guinea.

Chan, J. (2016). *Playing the game: Life and politics in Papua New Guinea.* University of Queensland Press.

Clifford, W. (1976). Urban crime in Papua New Guinea. In D. Biles (Ed.), *Crime in Papua New Guinea* (pp. 1–37). Australian Institute of Criminology.

Clifford, W., Morauta, L. and Stuart B. (1984). *Law and order in Papua New Guinea, Vols 1 & 2.* Institute of National Affairs and Institute of Applied Social and Economic Research.

Coffey International Development. (2013). *Australian Federal Police baseline report.*

Connell, J. (1997). *Papua New Guinea: The struggle for development.* Routledge.

Constitutional Planning Committee. (1974). *Final report of the Constitutional Planning Committee: Part 1.* Constitutional Planning Committee.

Craig, D. and Porter, D. (2018a). *Safety and security at the edges of the state. Local regulation in Papua New Guinea's urban settlements.* World Bank. doi.org/10.1596/30260.

Craig, D. and Porter, D. (2018b). *Learning about leadership, regulation and security from Papua New Guinea's urban settlements.* World Bank.

Crocombe, R. (2001). *The South Pacific.* University of the South Pacific.

Davidson, H. (2020, 24 May). Papua New Guinea police arrest former PM Peter O'Neill over alleged corruption. *The Guardian.* www.theguardian.com/world/2020/may/24/papua-new-guinea-police-arrest-former-pm-peter-oneill-over-alleged-corruption.

Deloitte. (2020). *True cost of policing services in PNG.* Final report.

Department of Foreign Affairs and Trade. (2020). *Papua New Guinea: Development cooperation fact sheet.* www.dfat.gov.au/sites/default/files/development-cooperation-fact-sheet-papua-new-guinea.pdf.

Department of Justice and Attorney General. (2020). *About Department of Justice and Attorney General: Overview.* www.justice.gov.pg/index.php/about-us#overview.

Dinnen, S. (1993). Big men, small men and invisible women: Urban crime and inequality in Papua New Guinea. *Australian and New Zealand Journal of Criminology, 26*(1), 19–34. doi.org/10.1177/000486589302600104.

Dinnen, S. (2001). *Law and order in a weak state. Crime and politics in Papua New Guinea.* University of Hawai'i Press. doi.org/10.1515/9780824863296.

Dinnen, S. (2020). Insecurity, policing and marketization: Papua New Guinea's changing security landscape. In S. N. Amin, D. Watson and C. Girard (Eds), *Mapping security in the Pacific: A focus on context, gender and organisational culture* (pp. 186–98). Routledge. doi.org/10.4324/9780429031816-18.

Dinnen S. and Braithwaite J. (2009). Reinventing policing through the prism of the colonial kiap. *Policing & Society, 19*(2), 161–73. doi.org/10.1080/10439460802187571.

Dinnen, S., May, R. and Regan, A. J. (1997). *Challenging the State: The Sandline Affair in Papua New Guinea*. National Centre for Development Studies and Research School of Pacific and Asian Studies, The Australian National University. hdl.handle.net/1885/132682.

Dinnen, S., Porter, D. and Sage, C. (2010). *Conflict in Melanesia: Themes and lessons*. World Bank. doi.org/10.1596/27503.

Doherty, B. (2020, 18 September). Papua New Guinea police accused of gun running and drug smuggling by own minister. *The Guardian*. www.theguardian.com/world/2020/sep/18/papua-new-guinea-police-accused-of-gun-running-and-drug-smuggling-by-own-minister.

Dorney, S. (2001). *Papua New Guinea: People, politics and history since 1975*. ABC Books.

Financial Analysis and Supervision Unit. (2018). *2018 Annual report, Financial Analysis and Supervision Unit*. Bank of Papua New Guinea. www.bankpng.gov.pg/wp-content/uploads/2019/04/Annual-Report-2018.pdf.

Forsyth, M. and Eves, R. (2015). *Talking it through: Responses to sorcery and witchcraft beliefs and practices in Melanesia*. ANU Press. doi.org/10.22459/TIT.05.2015.

Fox, R., Howes, S., Nema, N. A., Nguyen, H. B. and Sum, D. K. (2018). *2018 PNG economic survey*. Development Policy Centre. devpolicy.org/2018_economic_survey_final_draft_29June.pdf.

Ghai, Y. (1997). Establishing a liberal political order through a constitution: The Papua New Guinea experience, *Development and Change*, *28*, 303–30. doi.org/10.1111/1467-7660.00044.

Goddard, M. (2009). *Substantial justice: An anthropology of village courts in Papua New Guinea*. Berghahn Books.

Gordon, R. J. and Meggitt, M. (1985). *Law and order in the New Guinea Highlands*. University Press of New England.

Government of Papua New Guinea. (2004). *Report of the administrative review of the Royal Papua New Guinea Constabulary*.

Griffin, J. (1997). The Papua New Guinea national elections 1997. *Journal of Pacific History*, *32*(3), 71–78. doi.org/10.1080/00223349708572853.

Guthrie, G. (2013). Social factors affecting violent crime victimisation in urban households. *Contemporary PNG Studies: DWU Research Journal*, *18*, 35–54.

Harris, B. M. (1988). *The rise of rascalism: Action and reaction in the evolution of rascal gangs*. Institute of Applied Social and Economic Research. Discussion Paper, 54.

Harrison, E. (2006). Unpacking the anti-corruption agenda: Dilemmas for anthropologists. *Oxford Development Studies, 34*(1), 15–29. doi.org/10.1080/13600810500495915.

Hukula, F. (2020, 10 September). Addressing gender-based violence in Papua New Guinea. *East Asia Forum*. www.eastasiaforum.org/2020/09/10/addressing-gender-based-violence-in-papua-new-guinea/.

Human Rights Watch. (2005). *Making their own rules: Police beatings, rape and torture of children in Papua New Guinea*. www.hrw.org/report/2005/08/30/making-their-own-rules/police-beatings-rape-and-torture-children-papua-new-guinea.

Human Rights Watch. (2017). *World report 2017. Papua New Guinea: Events of 2016*. www.hrw.org/world-report/2017/country-chapters/papua-new-guinea.

Isari, P. K. (2019, 15 July). *How the Security Industries Authority (SIA) is supporting the security companies address law and order issues in PNG*. Presentation to CIMC conference. Popondetta, PNG.

Jones, A. (2014). *Corruption amongst government ministers in Papua New Guinea: Leadership tribunals and their impact on re-election* [Unpublished report]. International IDEA.

Kabuni, M. (2020). *COVID-19 (coronavirus) in Papua New Guinea: The state of emergency cannot fix years of negligence*. In Brief, 2020/15. dpa.bellschool.anu.edu.au/sites/default/files/publications/attachments/2020-05/dpa_in_brief_202015_kabuni.pdf.

Kenneth, G. (2020a, 2 August). Police investigate major syndicate trading and ferrying of illicit drugs in PNG. *Post-Courier*. postcourier.com.pg/police-investigate-major-syndicate-trading-and-ferrying-of-illicit-drugs-in-png/.

Kenneth, G. (2020b, 22 September). Cocaine probe stalls. *Post-Courier*. postcourier.com.pg/342171-2/.

Ketan, J. (2004). *The name must not go down: Political competition and state-society relations in Mount Hagen, Papua New Guinea*. Institute of Pacific Studies, University of the South Pacific.

King, D. (1992). The demise of the small towns and outstations of Papua New Guinea: Trends in urban census populations and growth from 1966 to 1990. *Yagl-Ambu, 16*(3), 17–33.

King, P. (2004). *West Papua and Indonesia since Soharto: Independence, autonomy or chaos?* UNSW Press.

Lakhani, S. and Willman, A. M. (2014a). *Gates, hired guns and mistrust: Business as unusual.* World Bank.

Lakhani, S. and Willman, A. M. (2014b). *Trends in crime and violence in Papua New Guinea.* World Bank.

Larmour, P. (2003). Transparency International and policy transfer in Papua New Guinea. *Pacific Economic Bulletin, 18*(1), 115–20. devpolicy.org/PEB/2019/06/08/transparency-international-and-policy-transfer-in-papua-new-guinea/.

Larmour, P. (2012). *Interpreting corruption: Culture and politics in the Pacific Islands.* University of Hawai'i Press. doi.org/10.21313/hawaii/9780824835149.001.0001.

Lasslett, K. (2018). *Uncovering the crimes of urbanisation: Researching corruption, violence and urban conflict.* Routledge. doi.org/10.4324/9781315651798.

May, R. J. (2004). *State and society in Papua New Guinea: The first twenty-five years.* ANU Press. doi.org/10.22459/SSPNG.05.2004.

McKenzie, N., Baker, R. and Garnaut, J. (2015, 24 June). Steering corrupt cash into Australia from PNG: A how-to guide. *Sydney Morning Herald.* www.smh.com.au/national/steering-corrupt-cash-into-australia-from-png-a-howto-guide-20150623-ghv1sx.html.

Noonan, J. T. (1984). *Bribes.* Macmillan.

Otto, T. and Thomas, N. (1997). Introduction. In T. Otto and N. Thomas (Eds), *Narratives of nation in the South Pacific* (pp. 1–13). Harwood Academic Publishers.

Peake, G. and Dinnen, S. (2014). Police development in Papua New Guinea: The need for innovation. *Security Challenges, 10*(2), 33–51.

Pieper, L. (2004). *Deterioration of public administration in Papua New Guinea – Views of eminent public servants.* AusAID.

Post-Courier. (2021, 15 October). Court acquits O'Neill. postcourier.com.pg/court-acquits-oneill/.

Pupu, N. and Wiessner, P. (2018). *The challenge of village courts and Operation Mekim Save among the Enga of Papua New Guinea today: A view from the inside.* Discussion Paper, 2018/1. bellschool.anu.edu.au/sites/default/files/publications/attachments/2018-06/dpa_dp2018_1_pupu_and_wiessner_to_publish.pdf.

Reilly, B., Brown, M. and Flower, S. (2014). *Political governance and service delivery in Papua New Guinea: A strategic review of current and alternative governance systems*. Discussion Paper, no. 143. PNG National Research Institute.

Security Industries Authority. (2020). *Current status of the security business in PNG*. www.sia.gov.pg/security-companies-information/.

Standish, B. (1999). *Papua New Guinea 1999: Crisis of governance*. Research Paper, 4 1999–2000. www.aph.gov.au/About_Parliament/Parliamentary_Departments/Parliamentary_Library/pubs/rp/rp9900/2000RP04.

The National. (2020, 17 August). 11 shot dead in jailbreak. www.thenational.com.pg/11-shot-dead-in-jailbreak/.

Transparency International. (2022). *2021 Corruption perceptions index*. www.transparency.org/en/cpi#.

Transparency International Papua New Guinea. (2016). *Public opinion survey in five provinces on levels and consequences of corruption in Papua New Guinea and state and society response, 2015*. TI PNG.

Transparency International Papua New Guinea. (2017). *Lest we forget: A review of 20 unresolved issues of national concern 2007–2017*. TI PNG. s3-eu-west-1.amazonaws.com/downloads.pngiportal.org/documents/TIPNG2017.pdf.

Walton, G. W. (2015). Defining corruption where the state is weak: The case of Papua New Guinea. *The Journal of Development Studies*, *51*(1), 15–31. doi.org/10.1080/00220388.2014.925541.

Walton, G. W. (2016). Gramsci's activists: How local civil society is shaped by the anti-corruption industry, political society and translocal encounters. *Political Geography*, *53*, 10–19. doi.org/10.1016/j.polgeo.2016.01.009.

Walton, G. W. (2018). *Anti-corruption and its discontents: Local, national and international perspectives on corruption in Papua New Guinea*. Routledge. doi.org/10.4324/9781315506012.

Walton, G. W. (2019). *Governance and corruption in PNG's public service: Insights from four subnational administrations*. Development Policy Centre Discussion Paper, 81. doi.org/10.2139/ssrn.3365319.

Walton, G. W. and Dinnen, S. (2020, 16 January). Regulating the growth of private security in PNG. *Devpolicy Blog*. devpolicy.org/regulating-the-growth-of-private-security-in-png-20200116/.

Walton, G. W. and Hushang, H. (2020). Boom and bust? Political will and anti-corruption in Papua New Guinea. *Asia & the Pacific Policy Studies*, *7*(2), 1–17. doi.org/10.1002/app5.306.

Walton, G. W. and Jackson, D. (2020). *Reciprocity networks, service delivery, and corruption: The* wantok *system in Papua New Guinea*. U4 Anti-Corruption Resource Centre. U4 Issue 2020:1.

Walton, G. W. and Peiffer, C. (2017). The impacts of education and institutional trust on citizens' willingness to report corruption: Lessons from Papua New Guinea. *Australian Journal of Political Science*, *52*(4), 517–36. doi.org/10.1080/10361146.2017.1374346.

Watson, A. H. and Wiltshire, C. (2016). *Reporting corruption from within Papua New Guinea's public financial management system*. SSGM Discussion Paper, 2016/5. dpa.bellschool.anu.edu.au/sites/default/files/publications/attachments/2016-09/dp_2016_5_watson_and_wiltshire.pdf.

World Bank. (2020). Worldwide governance indictors. info.worldbank.org/governance/wgi/Home/Reports.

Yakam, L. T. (2019). Police officers' perceptions of the people's complaints regarding police use of excessive force in Port Moresby, Papua New Guinea. *Contemporary PNG Studies: DWU Research Journal*, *30*, 21–41.

Zvekic, U. and Wedderburn, D. J. (1994). *Papua New Guinea crime and criminal justice information*. United Nations Interregional Crime and Justice Research Institute.

Part II:
The Economy

5

PNG's economic trajectory: The long view

Stephen Howes, Rohan Fox, Maholopa Laveil, Luke McKenzie, Albert Prabhakar Gudapati and Dek Sum

Abstract

The absence of good time series data makes it difficult to analyse the economic history of Papua New Guinea (PNG). This chapter aims to fill this gap by providing time series for various important economic indicators since independence in 1975 or as close as possible thereafter. The data are available online for researchers as the PNG Economic Database at devpolicy.org/pngeconomic. The 36 graphs in this chapter are all sourced from the PNG Economic Database. The chapter also contains some analysis to tie the data together and begin to realise their value, and includes a summary of 15 findings of particular interest.

Introduction

Anyone who seeks to work on the economic history of Papua New Guinea (PNG) is disadvantaged by the paucity of time series data. The most comprehensive source of historical data is the 2007 Bank of Papua New Guinea (BPNG) book *Money and Banking*, but its tables only run from the early days of independence (1975) to about 2000. Current BPNG (and other) contemporary national data sources typically go back in time only for a decade or two.

The International Monetary Fund (IMF) and World Bank have some PNG economic variables with long time series, but many missing variables as well, and even the series that are complete are not necessarily consistent. For example, the World Bank's current price GDP series shows an increase of 60 per cent in a single year (2006) in which not much happened. That does not inspire confidence and makes a mockery of any efforts to compare commonly used ratios, such as debt-to-GDP, over time.

The absence of good time series data makes it difficult if not impossible to analyse the economic history of PNG. This itself is a pressing need since the last economic histories of the country were published over a decade ago: the above-mentioned BPNG (2007) and Webster and Duncan (2010). PNG is too young to suffer the fate of losing data from more than 20 years ago in the sands of time. Surely such data are not only of intrinsic interest, but relevant to an understanding of contemporary challenges.

This chapter aims to fill the data gap by providing time series for various important economic indicators since independence in 1975 or as close as possible thereafter. The methods used are documented in this chapter, mainly in the data notes in the Appendix. The data themselves are available online for researchers as the PNG Economic Database at devpolicy.org/pngeconomic. The series in the database are by no means comprehensive but are at least a start. Most of the time series used in this chapter run to 2019, but the database will be updated periodically to keep it current.

The 36 graphs that follow are all sourced from the PNG Economic Database. The chapter also contains some analysis to tie the data together and begin to realise their value. The discussion begins with population, then goes to economic activity (GDP, commodity exports and employment), the balance of payments, fiscal data and, finally, financial sector and monetary data. Some 15 findings of particular interest are summarised at the end.

Population

PNG has conducted decadal censuses since 1961, but the 2011 census is considered unreliable (Allen, 2014; Bourke and Allen, 2021). Bourke and Allen (2021) have constructed a time series using an earlier population growth rate (2.7 per cent, the average from 1980 to 2000, is their mid-range estimate) to estimate the national population from 2000 to 2020. This gives a 2020 population estimate of 8.8 million (Figure 5.1), close to the United Nations estimate for that year.

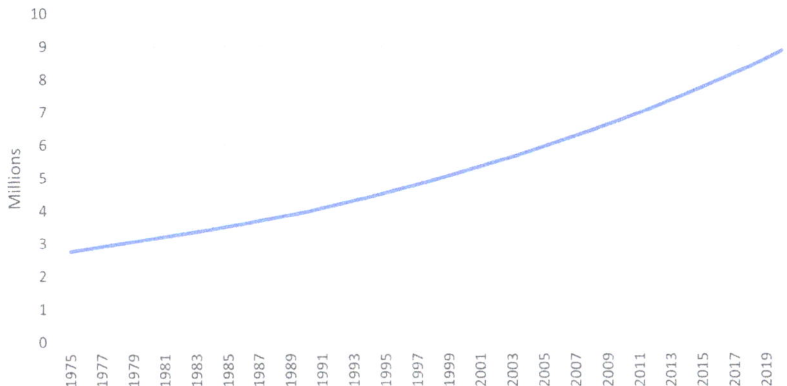

Figure 5.1: Population, 1975–2020.

Source: Annual figures interpolated from Bourke and Allen's (2021) decadal estimates.

PNG's population in 2020 is some three times its population at independence. This is one of the biggest changes between PNG then and PNG now. Every year now, PNG gains 230,000 citizens – 8 per cent of the population at the time of independence, and more than three times the annual increment at independence.

The World Bank estimates PNG's urban population share to be 13 per cent, only slightly above the 12 per cent at the time of independence. Bourke and Allen (2021) estimate a higher urban population share of about 15 per cent. Either way, PNG remains a predominantly rural country. According to World Bank data, PNG is the most rural country in the world (see Chapter 7, this volume).

GDP and non-resource GDP

For any country, gross domestic product or GDP is one of the most important economic variables. However, PNG has become over time one of the most resource-dependent economies in the world. For resource-dependent economies, GDP can be a misleading indicator of national economic activity, since a large proportion of the benefits from large resource projects typically flows offshore. Ideally, one would measure gross national income (GNI) – that is, the economic activity of PNG nationals. However, GNI is no longer reliably measured in PNG. An alternative is to measure non-resource GDP, which is GDP minus the output of the resources sector. The rationale for this is not that the resources sector should be ignored, but rather that its benefits to PNG largely accrue in the stimulus it provides to the non-resource sector via tax and royalty payments, and other linkages.

Our GDP current price series starts in 1976. It includes total GDP and, from 1980, value added in the resources, agriculture and manufacturing sectors. Non-resource GDP is simply GDP minus value added in the resources sector (the latter we sometimes refer to as 'resource GDP'). The constant price or real series covers the same variables, measured in 2013 prices, but sectoral data in constant prices are only available from 1983.

The GDP series from 2006 onwards was rebased in 2016 (National Statistical Office [NSO], 2020). The new series puts GDP some 50 per cent bigger in 2006 than in the old series. No explanation was ever provided for this massive increase. A comparison of the old and the new data reveals large increases in: mining value added (an increase of 72 per cent in 2006); wholesale and retail trade (186 per cent); transport, storage and construction (172 per cent); finance, real estate and business services (419 per cent); and community social and personal services (135 per cent). Agriculture (which includes forestry and fishing) and construction are virtually unchanged (–2 per cent), and petroleum (–16 per cent), manufacturing (–38 per cent) and utilities (–24 per cent) fall. We have integrated the two series to develop a single series from 1976.

PNG has become increasingly resource dependent over time (Figure 5.2). The ratio of resource to total GDP increased from around 10 per cent in 1980 to 15 per cent in the late 1980s. Although it fell back to 10 per cent with the closure of the Panguna mine on Bougainville in 1989, it grew over the 1990s with the commencement of oil production and the opening of a number of mines. Subsequently, the ratio has moved up and down with resource prices among other factors. With the commencement of PNG liquefied natural gas (LNG) exports in 2014, the country's resource dependency reached an all-time high of 28 per cent in 2018.

Figure 5.3 shows the share of agriculture, forestry and fishing as well as manufacturing in non-resource GDP, again at current prices. The share of the former rises and that of the latter falls, both mildly. Agriculture includes the production of commodities (discussed in the next section), the production of crops for domestic sale and subsistence production. The latter two variables are not measured, but rather increased annually in the national accounts in line with population growth, which is surely inaccurate.

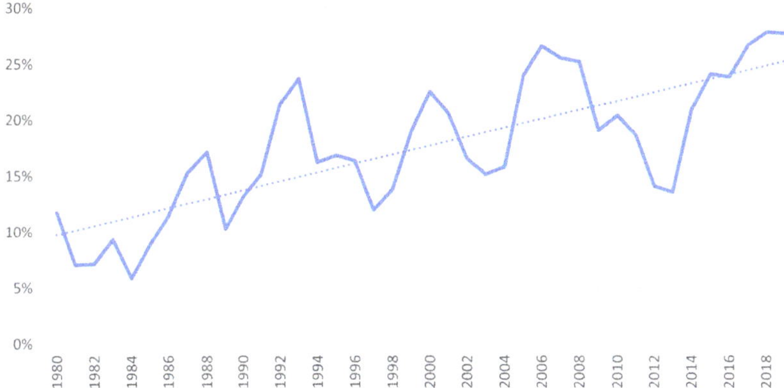

Figure 5.2: Resource dependency, 1980–2019.

Note: The percentage share of resources in total GDP, both measured in current prices; trendline added.

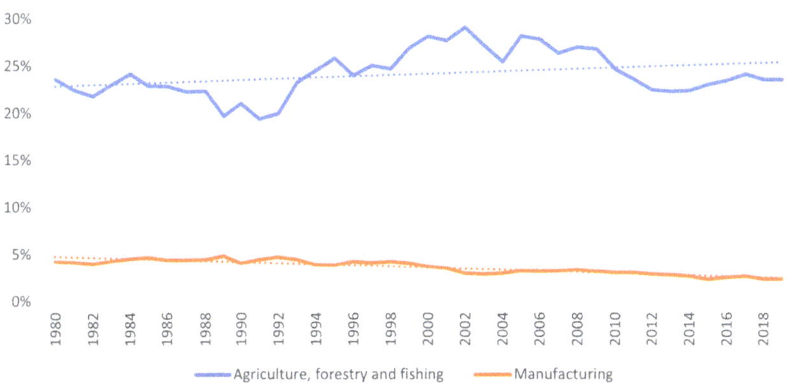

Figure 5.3: Agriculture and manufacturing as a share of non-resource GDP, 1980–2019.

Note: All variables measured in current prices; trendline added.

The deflators that convert from current to constant price GDP are shown in Figure 5.4, which, for convenience, sets them all equal to one (unity) in 1983. The resource deflator lies above the non-resource deflator with the GDP deflator by definition in the middle. The consumer price index (CPI) is also shown. It grows far more quickly, ending 60 per cent above the GDP deflator. As we will see, the choice of deflator is significant when assessing PNG's economic performance over time.

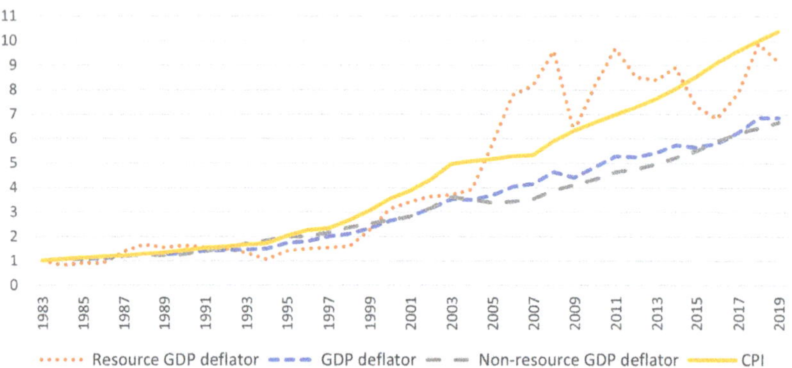

Figure 5.4: GDP deflators and CPI index, 1983–2019.

Note: All indices set to unity in 1983.

This separation of the CPI and the non-resource deflator mainly occurs between 1994 and 2004 (Figure 5.5), a period of rapid depreciation. This separation in the 1990s may reflect that, during this period, internationally tradeable goods (such as food) experienced more inflation than non-tradeable goods, which is what one would expect given the real wage flexibility that was evident in the PNG economy from the early 1990s onwards (see Figure 5.21) and the high rate of depreciation in that decade (see Figure 5.23). A report from the mid-1990s commented that 'the recent devaluation of the exchange rate has produced a substantial reduction in real wages' (AusAID, 1996, p. 41). It is also plausible that the CPI puts a higher weight on tradeable goods than the GDP deflator. For example, government services, which are largely non-tradeable, are an important part of GDP but do not feature in the CPI. This combination of factors would explain why CPI increased more than the GDP deflator in the 1990s.

This discrepancy between the GDP deflator and the CPI index raises the question of which deflator to use when. To get a consistent measure of output over time, we should use the GDP deflator. However, if we want to use GDP as a proxy for average living standards, then we should utilise the CPI index. We indicate in the notes to each relevant figure which deflator is used.

Figure 5.6 shows real GDP growth from 1977 onwards, using the GDP deflator. Key moments in the country's economic history are indicated on the figure.

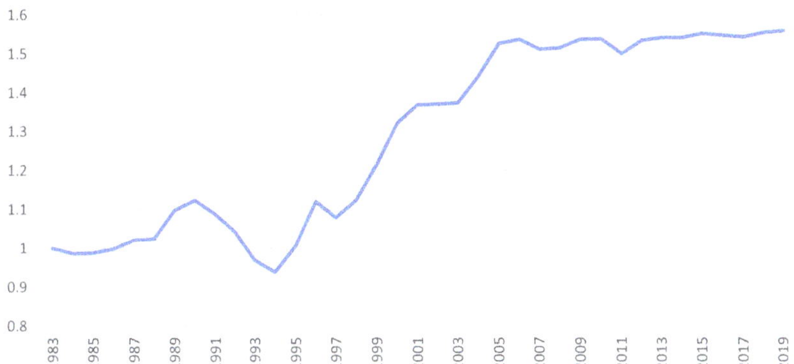

Figure 5.5: Ratio of CPI to non-resource GDP deflator, 1983–2019.

Note: Ratio set to unity in 1983.

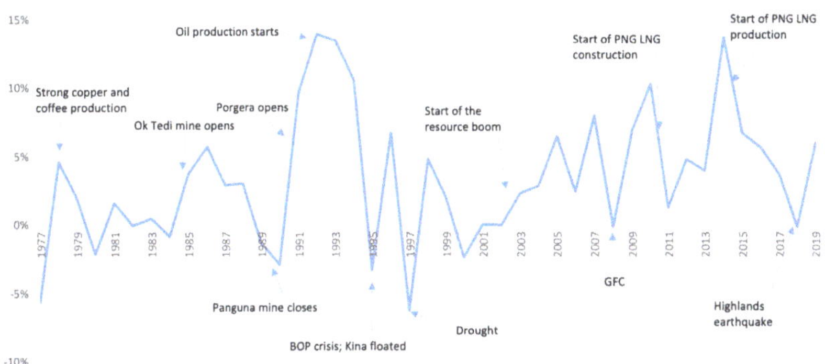

Figure 5.6: Annual real GDP growth, 1977–2019.

Note: GDP deflator used. GDP data in the early years of independence are generally regarded as less reliable.

Figure 5.7 shows GDP per capita and non-resource GDP per capita, using both the relevant GDP deflator and the CPI index. Both variables show an overall positive trend using the GDP and non-resource GDP deflator, respectively, but both show a decline if CPI is used as the deflator. Using the GDP deflators, average growth rates for the period 1983–2019 are 1.1 per cent and 0.4 per cent for GDP and non-resource GDP per capita, respectively; using CPI, annual average growth for the same period is –0.1 per cent and –0.6 per cent, respectively.[1]

1 These are end-to-end growth rates. For 1977–2019, the average growth rates for GDP per capita are 0.7 per cent (using the GDP deflator) and –0.2 per cent using the CPI.

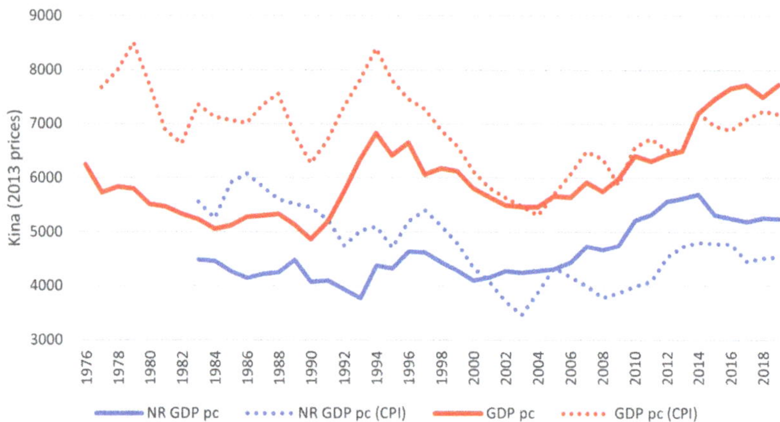

Figure 5.7: GDP (from 1976) and non-resource GDP (from 1983) per capita, with different deflators, to 2019.

Note: Variables denoted 'CPI' are deflated using the CPI. Other variables shown are deflated using the relevant GDP deflator. 'NR' is non-resource. All variables expressed in 2013 prices.

Whether PNG is better off today in terms of GDP or non-resource GDP per capita depends most of all on an assessment of inflation in the 1990s. Using the non-resource GDP deflator, PNG ended the decade with a non-resource GDP per capita the same as when it started. Using the CPI, PNG ended that period about 20 per cent worse off by the same measure.

The trajectory of non-resource GDP per capita can be used to demarcate four distinct periods in PNG's post-independence economic history (Figure 5.8).[2] The first to 1988 is a period of stability but also stagnation (with average growth from 1983 of –1.0 per cent per annum).[3] The second, from 1989 to 2003, is a period of economic instability – with interspersed periods of positive and negative growth cancelling themselves out (average of 0.0 per cent). The third is a long boom from 2004 to 2013, briefly interrupted by the global financial crisis (average of 2.8 per cent). Finally, the current period from 2014 is one of negative per capita growth, a bust following the boom (average of –1.1 per cent).

2 For convenience, each sub-period is defined to the (end of the) year before the next one starts.

3 Years prior to 1983 are missing, but other evidence suggests a similar conclusion: real GDP per capita growth for 1976–88 is –1.3 per cent; also see Figure 5.19 on employment.

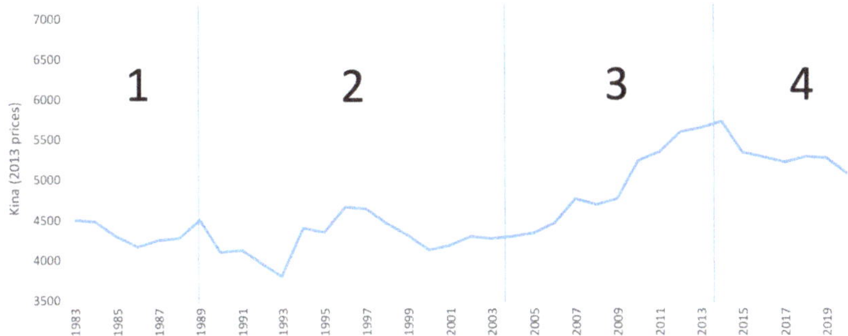

Figure 5.8: Non-resource GDP per capita and the four sub-periods of PNG's economic history post-independence, 1983–2019.

Note: Non-resource GDP deflator used.

Commodity production

The PNG economy is heavily reliant on the production of resource and agricultural commodities. Because these commodities are exported, they are well measured.

As Figure 5.9 shows, the value of commodity exports to GDP increased from about 25 per cent at the time of independence to almost 50 per cent at the height of the resource boom, and, after falling to as low as 25 per cent just before PNG LNG production began, recovered to almost 40 per cent by 2018.[4]

Adjusted by CPI, commodity exports have grown on average by 3.7 per cent between 1977 and 2019. This overall fairly rapid growth masks a radical shift in the composition of commodity exports, shown in Figure 5.10. At the time of independence, about half of commodities exported by value were agricultural. Now they are 10 per cent. Timber and marine exports have both grown to about 4 per cent of the total. Resource exports have grown from half to over 80 per cent.

4 The share of commodity exports in GDP exceeds the share of the resources sector in GDP (Figure 5.2) for two reasons. First, the latter compares the value added of the resources sector with total value added, and the former the output of the resources sector with total value added. Second, the former includes non-resource commodity exports as well.

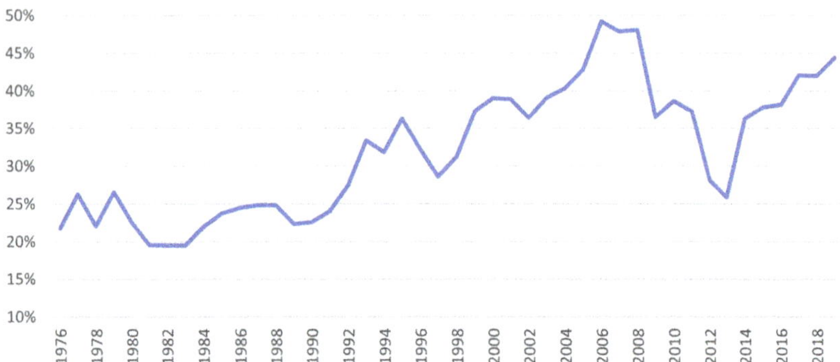

Figure 5.9: Commodity exports as a percentage of GDP, 1976–2019.

Note: Both variables measured in current prices. Commodity exports include resource exports, agricultural cash crops and other agricultural products, timber and other forest products, and marine products.

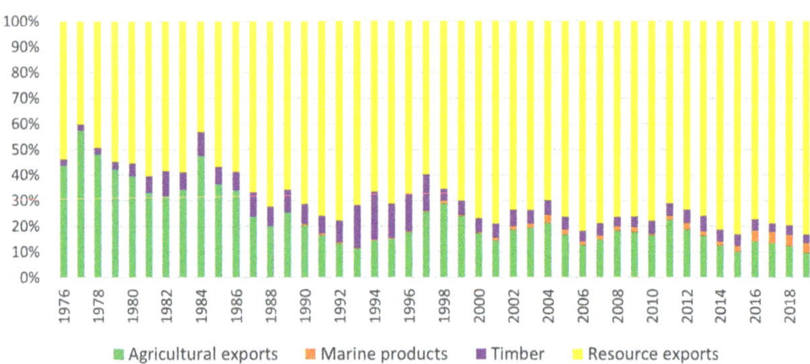

Figure 5.10: The composition of commodity exports by value, 1976–2019.

Note: All variables measured in current prices. Timber exports are logs and other forest products.

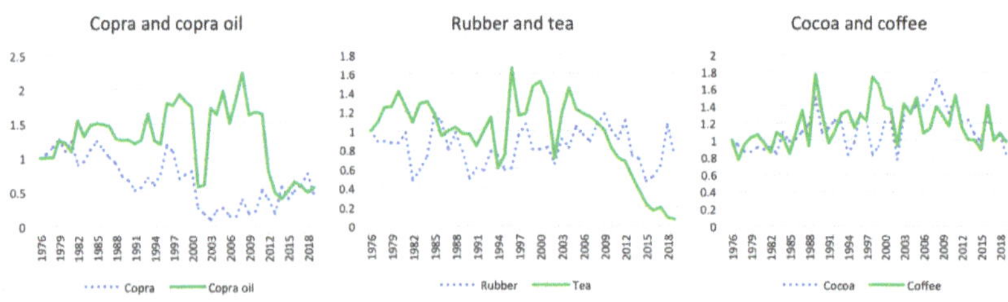

Figure 5.11: Export volume indices of copra, copra oil, rubber, tea, cocoa and coffee, 1976–2019.

Note: Indices set equal to unity in 1976.

In fact, most agricultural exports show either a decline or no growth in volume since independence. As shown in Figure 5.11, this is the case for copra, copra oil, rubber, tea, cocoa and coffee.

Unfortunately, the earlier claim by Bourke and Allen (2009) that cash crop export volumes are at a higher level than at independence is now only true for palm oil, shown in Figure 5.12. Twenty times as much palm oil is now produced as at independence (an annual average growth of 7.5 per cent). Marine product and log exports have also grown rapidly. The latter had a mini-boom in the mid-1990s, and overall have grown at an annual average rate of 4.5 per cent. Marine products are even more successful than palm oil. They were first counted in 1990 but have since grown at an annual average rate of 18.9 per cent. There is no volume index for the category of other (non-traditional) agricultural products, but, since 1990 (the first year in which it was recorded), its value, adjusted for inflation, has grown by an annual average of 6.1 per cent. As a result of these very different trends, the composition of the non-resource export bundle has changed completely (Figure 5.13). At independence, coffee was by far the most important crop by value, followed by cocoa. Together, these two made up two-thirds of non-resource exports. Now, they make up just over 10 per cent. Palm oil and timber now each make up just over 20 per cent: palm oil volumes have grown faster, but, as discussed below, timber prices have risen more. Marine product exports have become even more important, and now make up 28 per cent. Other (non-traditional) agricultural products at 10 per cent are more important than coffee (9 per cent) and other traditional agricultural exports.

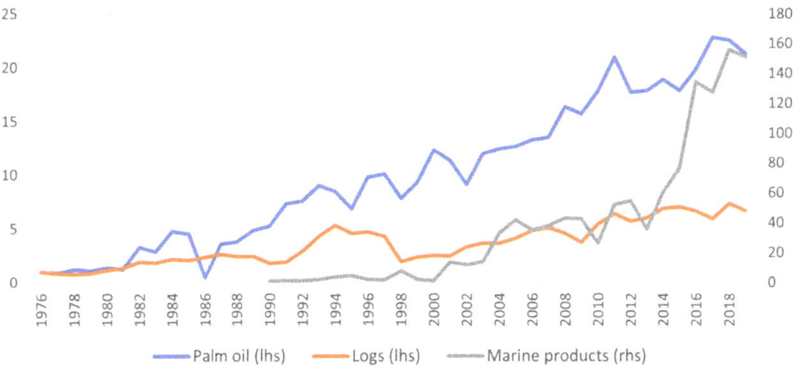

Figure 5.12: Export volume indices of marine products, palm oil and logs, 1976–2019.

Note: Indices set equal to unity in 1976 for palm oil and logs, and in 1990 for marine products.

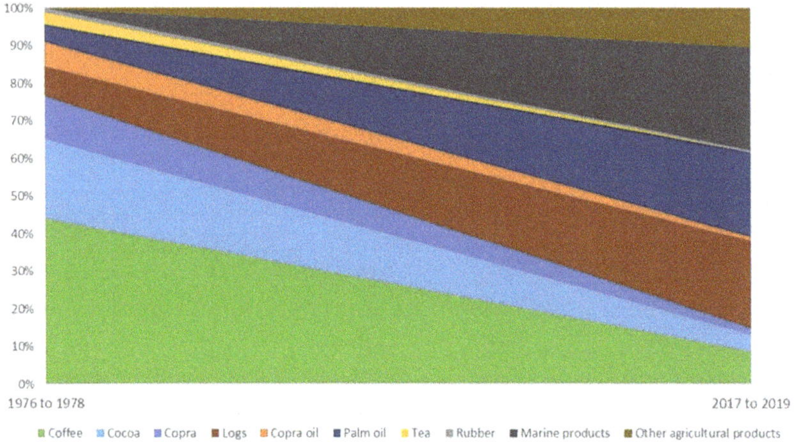

Figure 5.13: Composition of non-resource commodity exports by value, 1976–78 and 2017–19.

Note: Three-year averages taken to minimise year-to-year volatility. Current prices used for all variables. Timber exports are logs and other forest products.

We turn now to resource exports (Figure 5.14). Gold and copper have been exported since independence. Gold is the stand-out performer, with production more than tripling by volume since independence. Copper production is now only at half the level of independence. Oil exports began in 1992, peaked by volume the following year and have fallen ever since. Cobalt and nickel started in 2012 and LNG in 2014. It is striking that there is no significant increase in the volume of resources exported during the resource boom years of the 2000s. We shall see that the boom of this period was rather driven by resource prices.

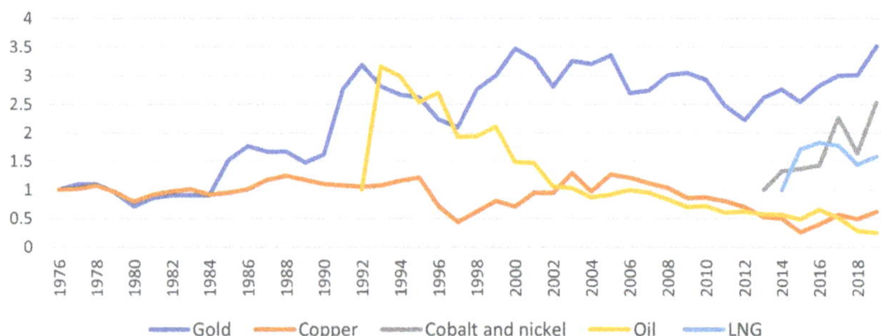

Figure 5.14: Resource export volume indices, 1976–2019.

Note: Indices set equal to unity in 1976 for copper and gold and in the first year of production for other commodities.

Turning now to the value of resource exports, copper dominated at independence. Now LNG does, followed by gold (Figure 5.15).

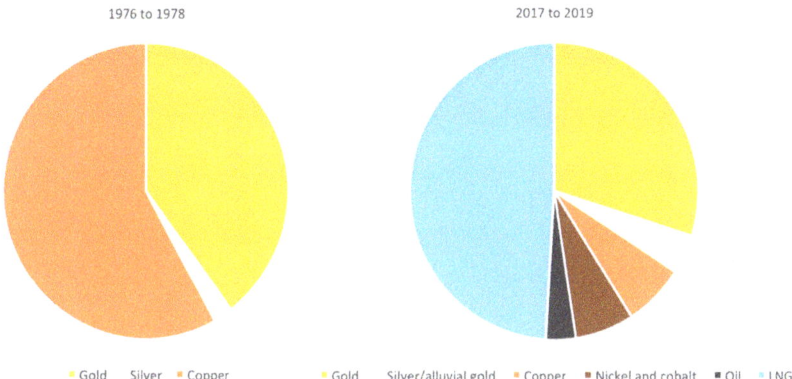

Figure 5.15: Composition of resource commodity exports by value, 1976–78 and 2017–19.

Note: Three-year averages used to minimise year-to-year volatility. Current prices used for all variables.

Figure 5.16 shows aggregate export terms of trade for PNG from the IMF. The series uses exports as a share of GDP as weights, adjusting them over time, which means that the index can be interpreted as a measure of the windfall gain associated with commodity price increases (Gruss and Kebhaj, 2019).[5] Figure 5.16 is indispensable for an understanding of PNG's economic history. Apart from a minor rise in commodity prices immediately after independence, the 1980s and 1990s were a period of commodity price decline. Then, everything changed. Commodity prices rocketed upwards and, despite a mild decline in recent years, are still above their level at independence. PNG's economic turnaround in the 2000s finds a clear explanation in this trajectory.

Resource commodity prices have increased much more than non-resource prices. Figure 5.17 shows USD price indices over time relative to 1976 for PNG's three most important non-resource commodities for which data are available (palm oil, logs and coffee) and for gold and copper, the two resource commodities exported since independence. Cocoa, coffee and

5 'Variations in the commodity terms-of-trade index provide an estimate of the windfall gains and losses of income associated with changes in international prices. That is, a one percentage point change in the commodity terms-of-trade index can be interpreted as a change in aggregate disposable income equivalent to one percentage point of GDP' (Gruss and Kebhaj, 2019, p. 10).

palm oil show only moderate price growth. By contrast, the price of logs is now four times as high as it was in 1976. This no doubt reflects the fact that PNG is one of the few suppliers of tropical woods; in coffee and palm oil, by contrast, there has been massive growth in global supply, pushing prices down. Resource prices have done even better, with the copper price more than six times as high, and the gold price more than ten times as high in the 2010s as in 1976.

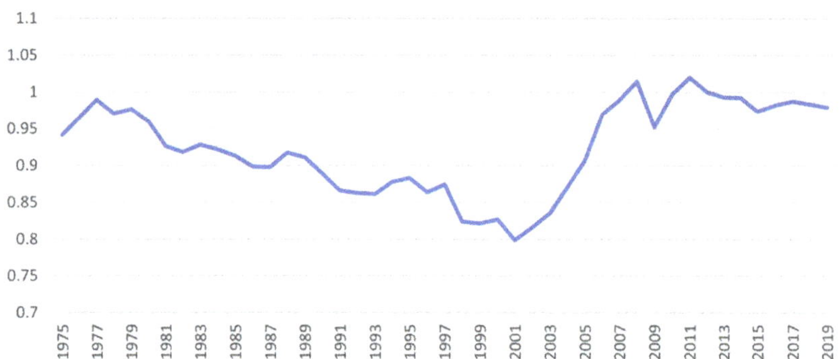

Figure 5.16: PNG's commodity export terms of trade, 1975–2019.

Note: Annual data; index set equal to unity in 2012; exports as shares of GDP used as weights.

Source: IMF (2021).

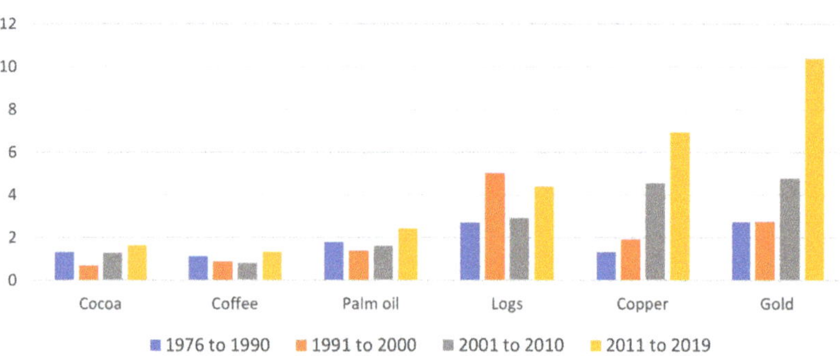

Figure 5.17: USD price indices of some important commodities, 1976–2019.

Note: Indices derived from unit value data calculated by dividing commodity export values by commodity export volumes and then by that year's USD–PGK exchange rate. Indices set equal to unity in 1976.

We close the discussion by returning to Figure 5.10, but now showing absolute growth in value rather than changes of shares. Figure 5.18 shows the growth in the value of exports from the four major commodity sectors: resources, agriculture, marine products and timber. We deflate nominal values by CPI. The real value of agricultural commodity production has declined, with the rapid growth in palm oil volumes and other agricultural products unable to offset the lack of growth in other sectors, and the lack of price improvement. Timber values have gone up but have never recovered their importance of the mid-1990s, when they briefly exceeded agricultural exports in value. Marine products have shown rapid growth in recent years. Resource commodity exports have performed strongly for most of the post-independence period, with an annual average growth of 5.1 per cent.

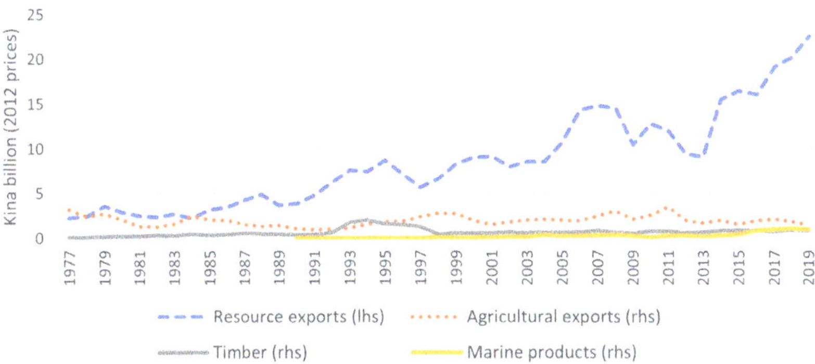

Figure 5.18: The value of resource, agricultural, timber and marine exports (Kina billion in 2012 prices), 1977–2019.

Employment

Employment is another key measure of economic activity. BPNG surveys formal sector employment in the private and state-owned enterprise (SOE) sectors. Ironically, the public service time series is incomplete. Formal sector employment, both private and public, is mainly flat until the end of the 1990s (Figure 5.19). Private sector/SOE employment increased rapidly in the 2000s, but has fallen since the boom ended. Overall, one sees a decline in the employment/population ratio, from 6 per cent just after independence to 4.5 per cent today. The share of formal employment in the public sector has grown only slightly, from 26 per cent at independence to 28 per cent in 2019.

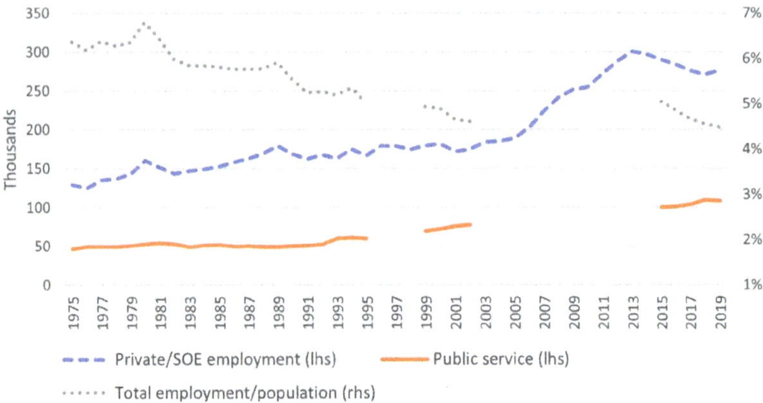

Figure 5.19: Formal sector employment, totals and population percentage, 1975–2019.

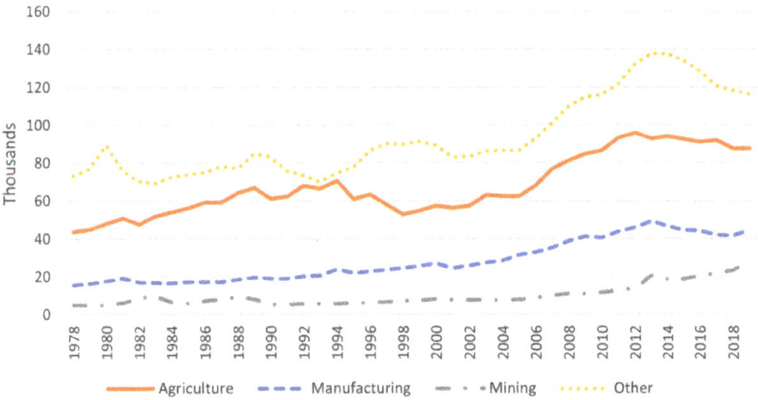

Figure 5.20: Formal employment by sector, 1978–2019.

Note: Only private sector and SOE employment shown, so 'other' excludes public servants.

Employment numbers by major sector are shown in Figure 5.20. The resources workforce has grown in importance over time but is still only 7 per cent of total employment (including the public service). Based on the latest data, the agriculture sector contributes 23 per cent of total employment, and the manufacturing sector 12 per cent. All sectors show strong employment growth in the 2000s, until the end of the resource boom. It would have been expected that agriculture and manufacturing would have suffered as a result of the real appreciation of the resource boom period (see Figure 5.24). On the other hand, this was a period of great confidence in the PNG economy, and presumably the expansion was on that basis.

Minimum wages were an important policy issue in the years after independence, when it was widely believed that the urban minimum wage was too high given the country's exchange rate. As Figure 5.21 shows, there was then a policy of partial indexation that resulted in a gradual decline in the real value of the urban minimum wage from independence to 1991. Then, during PNG's first structural adjustment program, the urban and rural wage were unified in 1992. There is no evidence that nominal wages were reduced, but the minimum wage was not increased for a decade. Nevertheless, there was little growth in formal sector employment until the boom years, suggesting that other constraints were holding back formal sector employment. Even today, in real terms, the minimum urban wage is less than the minimum rural wage at independence, and less than half of the minimum urban wage at that time.

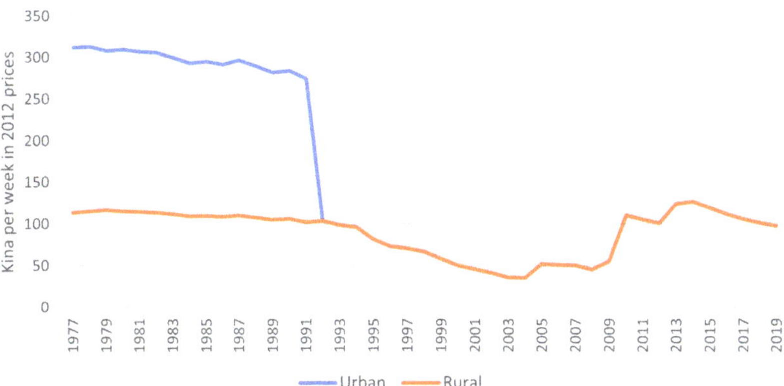

Figure 5.21: Urban and rural minimum weekly wage (Kina per week in 2012 prices), 1977–2019.

Note: CPI used to convert from current to constant prices.

Balance of payments and the exchange rate

Figure 5.22 shows exports and imports (of goods and services) as a percentage of GDP, along with the current account balance. Exports of services are small, but imports of services consequential. Imports outpaced exports until the early 1990s, when oil exports commenced. For the next two decades, PNG mainly ran current account surpluses. During the early boom years, both exports and imports grew rapidly. Exports fell briefly with the global financial crisis, but imports remained strong due to the PNG LNG construction, and PNG returned to a sustained current account deficit for several years. Then, from 2014, PNG entered a new era with strong export growth due to the PNG LNG project coming on line. However, imports fell sharply in part due to foreign exchange rationing, discussed further below. The current account balance is now in excess of 20 per cent of GDP, and imports that had been on a rising trend fell from 47 per cent of GDP in 2013 to 28 per cent in 2014 and 16 per cent in 2016. They recovered slightly to 25 per cent in 2019, but are still at one of the lowest levels seen since independence. The previous lowest (before the last few years) was 28 per cent in 1994, another time of foreign exchange crisis.

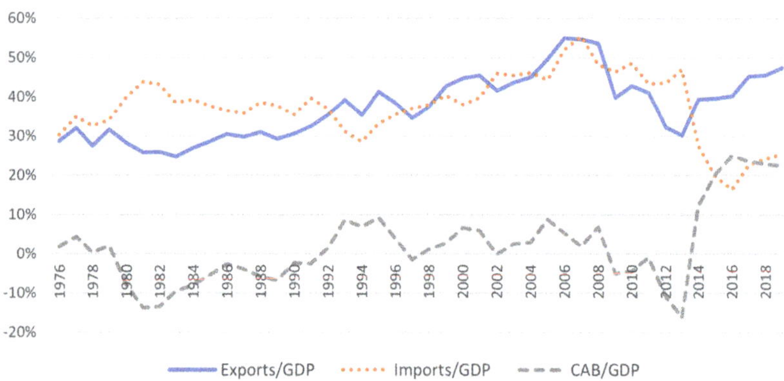

Figure 5.22: Exports, imports and the current account balance (% GDP), 1976–2019.

Note: CAB is the current account balance.

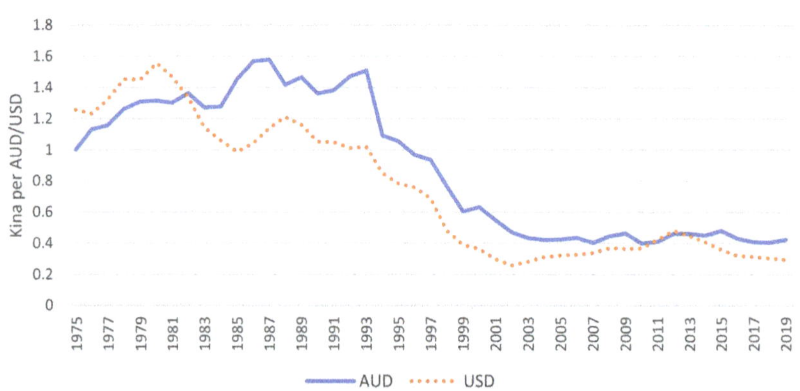

Figure 5.23: The PGK–AUD and PGK–USD exchange rates, 1975–2019.

PNG went into independence with a 'hard kina' policy, which was essentially a commitment not to engage in nominal depreciation. The kina was originally pegged to the Australian dollar, but after a couple of years the peg was changed to a basket of currencies. As the Australian dollar weakened over this period, the kina appreciated against it. The hard kina policy was softened over the course of the 1980s (Goodman et al., 1987), but the peg remained. With the closure of the Panguna mine in 1989, the government depreciated the kina by 10 per cent in response to the loss of foreign exchange. There was then a period of expansionary fiscal policy, leading to the depletion of foreign exchange reserves and a balance of payments crisis in 1994. In response, the kina was again depreciated, and then floated, and it began a period of rapid depreciation (Figure 5.23). The kina fell against the USD every year to 2002, with major falls in 1994 (17 per cent), 1998 (30 per cent), 1999 (19 per cent), 2001 (18 per cent) and 2002 (14 per cent), at which stage the kina was only one-quarter of its pre-float 1993 value.

Then, in 2003, with the start of the resource boom, the kina began to appreciate again, reaching a high of USD0.48 in 2012. The end of the resource boom and LNG construction in 2013 saw the resumption of depreciation, but after a couple of years, the government introduced exchange rate rationing and brought the kina back under a de facto crawling peg to limit further depreciation. The shift from a floating to a pegged exchange rate sounds like a return to the hard kina policy of independence; however, the crucial difference is that now, with queueing to obtain foreign exchange to purchase imports, the kina is no longer convertible. There is little support for depreciation; at the same time, the shortage of foreign exchange is the primary complaint of business.[6]

Figure 5.24 shows the value of the kina in real terms, using data from the World Bank on PNG's real effective exchange rate. The figure shows that the kina is almost back at its pre-float hard kina level, once inflation is taken account of in both PNG and its trading partners. The fact that commodity prices are significantly above their value at independence, and that the resources sector as a whole is much bigger than at independence might support this as a reasonable outcome. However, the PNG kina was widely regarded as overvalued in the early years of independence

6 According to a survey of CEOs conducted between 2012 and 2018, from 2014, foreign exchange shortages have been one of the top four concerns of CEOs, and, since 2016, it has been their major concern (Howes, 2018).

(see e.g. Goodman et al., 1987, p. 65). Extensive import rationing implies that currently the currency is certainly overvalued. This is linked to the fact that, as we discuss below, a declining share of resource sector revenue (and thus foreign exchange) is finding its way into the rest of the economy.

Figure 5.25 shows foreign exchange reserves. A prerequisite of the hard kina policy was to have sufficient reserves to meet demand for the kina at the exchange rate set. In fact, however, foreign exchange reserves fell over time as a ratio of months of imports most years starting in the late 1970s. In this sense, the balance of payments crisis of 1994 was a long time coming. Despite the macroeconomic reform program mounted in response to that crisis, there was a second balance of payments crisis in 1988–99, also evident from the graph.

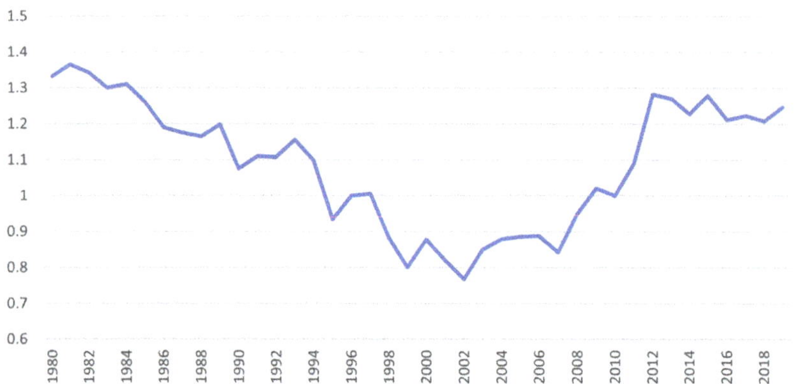

Figure 5.24: Real effective exchange rate index, 1980–2019.

Note: Index set equal to unity in 2010.

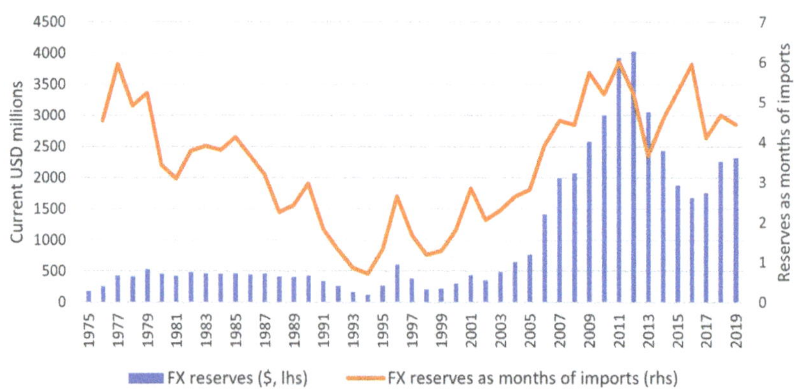

Figure 5.25: Foreign exchange (FX) reserves, 1975–2019.

Fiscal data

Fiscal data have been collated from successive budgets and from BPNG (2007) for earlier years. In the boom years, a significant amount of funds were allocated to trust funds for later spending. From 2005 to 2011, these funds were counted as expended when they were placed in a trust fund, rather than when they were actually spent. We have adjusted official expenditure figures to correct this.

Government expenditure and revenue as a share of GDP are shown in Figure 5.26. Both are highly volatile. Revenue is on a downward trend.

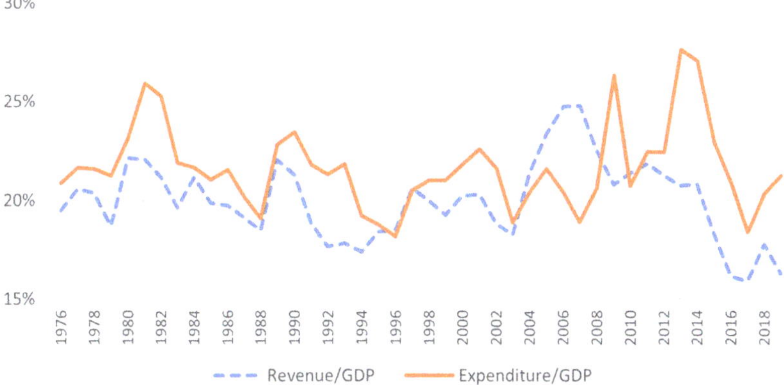

Figure 5.26: Government revenue and expenditure (% GDP), 1976–2019.

The weak revenue growth can be explained by the poor revenue performance of the resources sector and by declining foreign aid, both shown in Figure 5.27. The reduction in aid/GDP is hardly surprising, though it should also be noted that there was a shift from budget support to project aid over the 1990s, which means that the decline in total aid underestimates the fiscal shock from the change in aid policy over this period.

Resource revenue to GDP was about 3 per cent for most of the 1990s. Resource revenue exploded in the 2000s reaching almost 10 per cent of GDP, as high copper prices coincided with high copper exports. This is the primary explanation of the economic boom of the 2000s. However, copper production declined, and commodity prices fell with the global financial crisis. While some fall in resource revenues was expected, their almost complete disappearance was a surprise, especially given high gold prices.

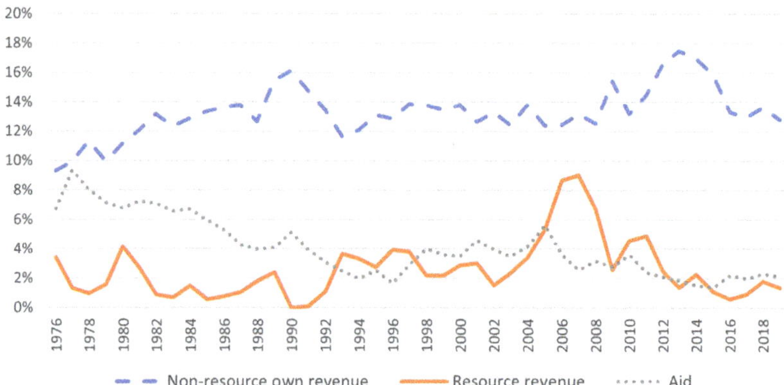

Figure 5.27: Non-resource revenue, resource revenue and aid (% GDP), 1976–2019.

Note: Own revenue is revenue excluding foreign aid.

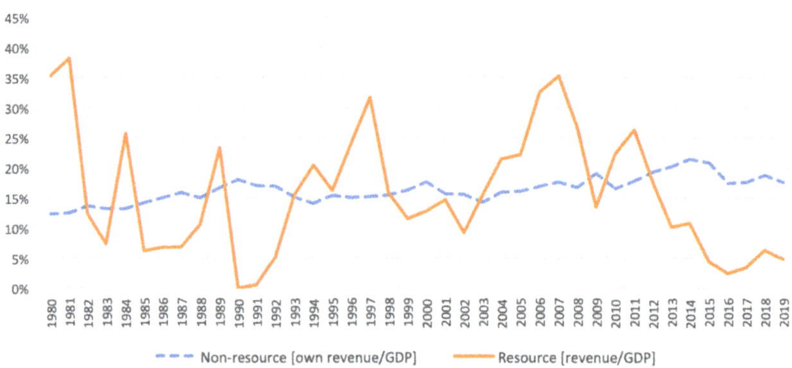

Figure 5.28: (Non) resource revenue as a percentage of (non) resource GDP, 1980–2019.

Note: Own revenue is revenue excluding foreign aid.

The picture is even starker if we show resource revenue as a percentage of resource value added or GDP, and non-resource (own) revenue as a percentage of non-resource GDP (Figure 5.28). The former, albeit volatile, is on a declining trend and the latter is on an increasing trend. Whatever the reason, PNG has become less effective at raising revenue from the resources sector and, therefore, is having to tax the non-resource sector more to meet expenditure needs.

Poor revenue performance has no doubt been a factor behind PNG's tendency to run deficits: as seen from Figure 5.29, they are observed in 36 of the 44 years for which we have data. However, the deficits have mainly been mild: 19 of the 36 have been below 2 per cent of GDP, and only eight have been above 4 per cent. Most of the surpluses (six of the eight) were in the boom years, between 2004 and 2010. However, these surpluses were modest, just 2.6 per cent on average. In hindsight, PNG should have run much larger surpluses in the boom period to avoid the fiscal squeeze it is currently experiencing. In more recent years, we have seen record high deficits: of the eight above 4 per cent of GDP, five have been after 2012.

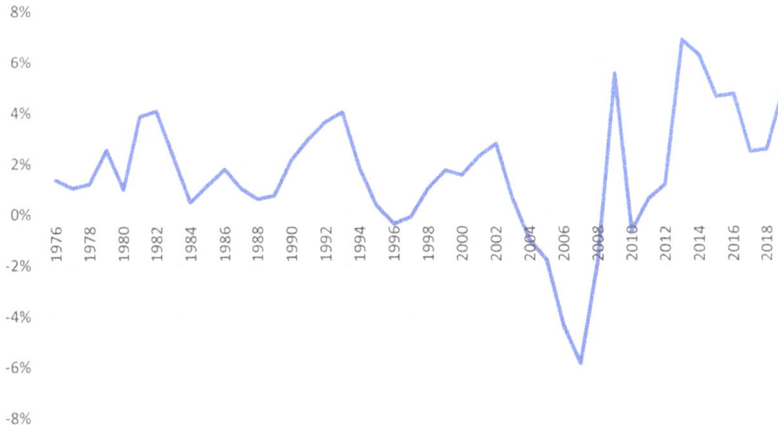

Figure 5.29: Deficits/GDP (%), 1976–2019.

Note: A negative deficit is a surplus.

As a result of large recent deficits, debt/GDP is now almost back at its record pre-boom level. However, since revenue is falling, it is more useful to measure either debt/revenue or interest/revenue, which are also shown in Figure 5.30. Debt/revenue is back at a record level, while interest/revenue is at its second highest level ever.

Not only has government debt doubled as a share of GDP since independence, but also its composition has greatly changed (Figure 5.31). For the first decade of independence, only about 20 per cent of PNG's government debt was domestic. By the mid-1990s that figure had reached 50 per cent, and, by 2012, around 70 per cent. That shift reflected major changes in the PNG banking sector, as discussed in the next section.

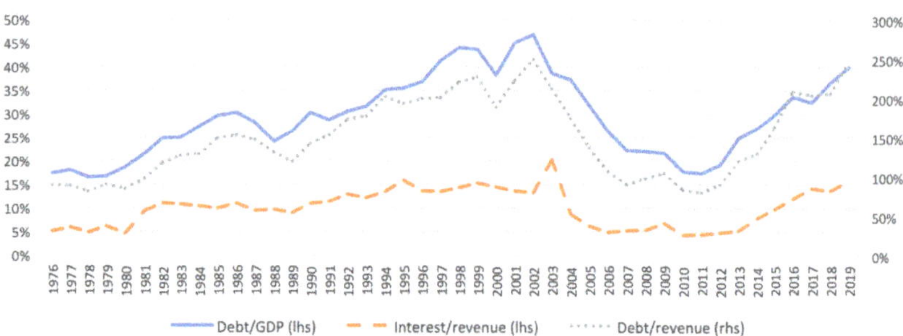

Figure 5.30: Debt/GDP, debt/revenue and interest/revenue (%), 1976–2019.

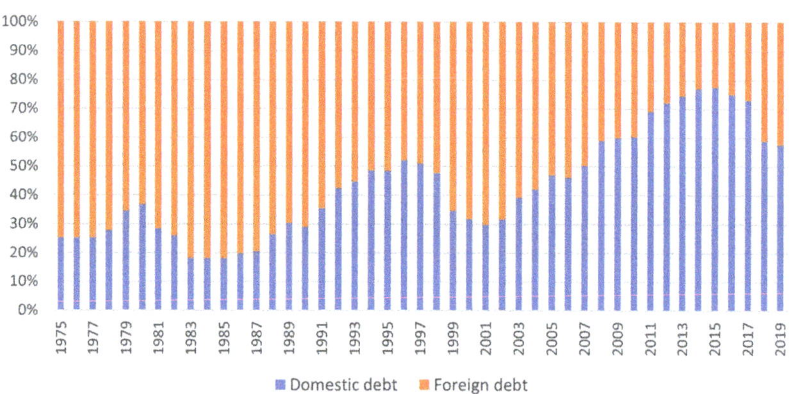

Figure 5.31: Domestic and foreign debt as percentages of total, 1975–2019.

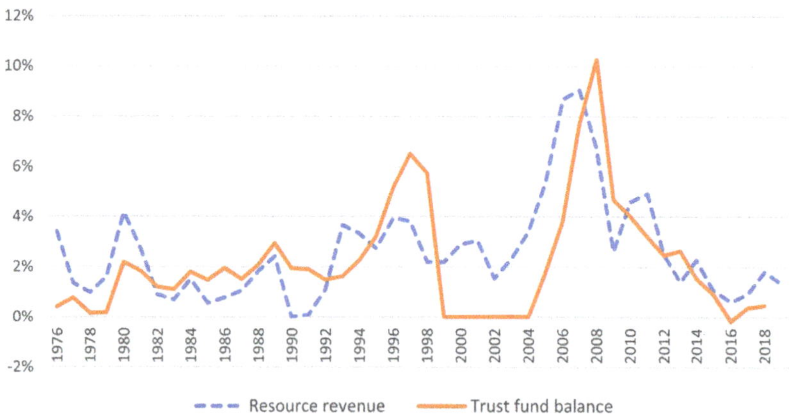

Figure 5.32: Resource revenues and trust fund balances (% GDP), 1976–2019.

Note: Trust fund balance only to 2018.

One of the policy challenges confronting PNG is the management of volatile resource revenue, and the need to save revenue in good times to spend in bad. From independence through to 1999, PNG used the Mineral Resources Stabilisation Fund (MRSF) to stabilise resource revenue. However, the MRSF came to be seen as ineffective in preventing macroeconomic and fiscal crises, and was abolished in 1999. Then, a few years later, when the resources boom began, PNG started using a system of trust funds to park surplus revenue. Figure 5.32 summarises PNG's experience with trust funds (including the MRSF) from independence onwards. The MRSF (the orange line up to 1999) accumulated a positive balance that increased from 2 per cent in the 1980s to 6 per cent in the late 1990s. However, this was a period of acute fiscal stress and, as mentioned, the MRSF was abolished, and the proceeds used to pay off domestic debt. The new trust funds quickly accumulated significant value, reaching 10 per cent of GDP in 2008, but those balances were spent down very quickly, and exhausted just a few years after the boom ended. Not enough was saved during the boom period. Expenditure increased from around 20 per cent pre-boom to 25 per cent of GDP in 2012–14, just a few years after revenue hit this rare high (2006 and 2007). By this time, however, revenue had already retreated to below 20 per cent. The result has been large deficits and the accumulation of arrears.

It is fair to say that stabilisation of resource revenue remains an elusive goal. While there is a new sovereign wealth fund in place, it is not active. In hindsight, the abolition of the MRSF just before the boom began was incredibly bad timing.

Monetary policy and banking

Inflation has generally been moderate in PNG. Average annual CPI growth from 1977 to 2019 is 7 per cent. However, inflation did increase in the 1990s in the context of rapid currency depreciation (Figure 5.33).

In terms of deposits, the banking sector is close to twice the size it was at independence relative to GDP (Figure 5.34). Around independence, deposits were about 15 per cent of GDP. They reached 24 per cent in 1997 but fell back to 15 per cent in 2003. Then, with the resource boom, deposits reached 39 per cent of GDP in 2013, before falling to their current level of 25 per cent of GDP. The main beneficiary of this growth in deposits has been the government. Bank government debt has increased from 2 per cent in 1980 to 10 per cent in 2019. The outstanding stock of debt to the private sector is little changed relative to GDP: 10 per cent in 1980 and 11 per cent in 2019. State-owned enterprises have become significant debtors in recent years with outstanding bank debt (and resultant significant debt distress) of some 4 per cent of GDP, up from zero prior to 2012.

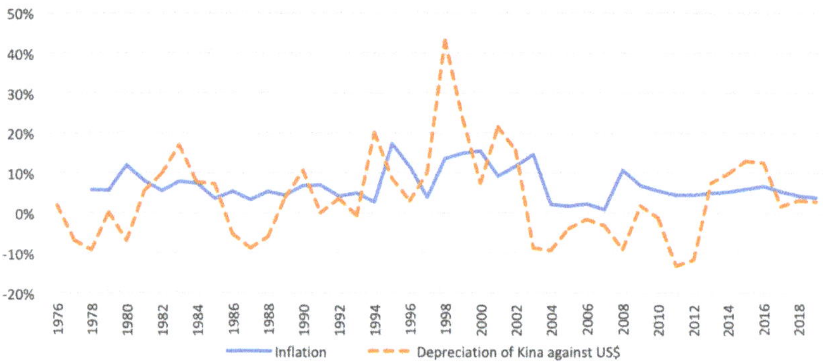

Figure 5.33: Inflation and currency depreciation, 1976–2019.

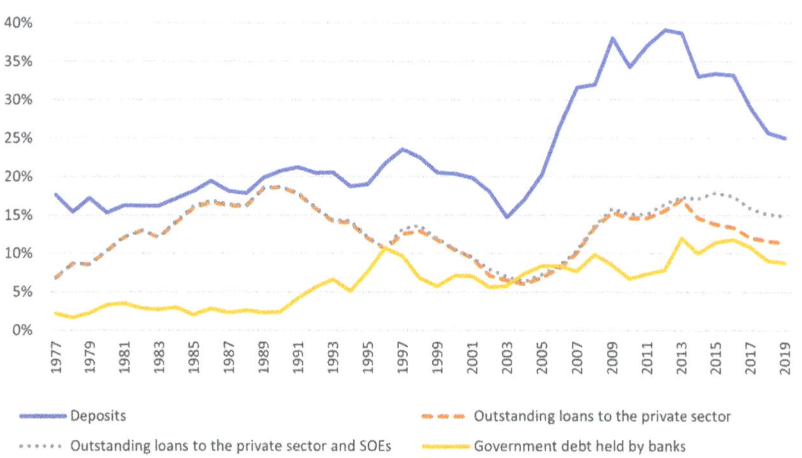

Figure 5.34: Deposits and lending ratios (% GDP), 1976–2019.

As a result of this shift in lending behaviour, the banks' average liquid asset ratio has grown above 50 per cent (government securities are counted as liquid assets, even though they are not actually very liquid). In the 1980s, BPNG used the minimum liquid asset ratio as a regulatory instrument to influence bank behaviour, and, as Figure 5.35 shows, for much of this period it was binding. However, that is no longer the case, and the ratio is no longer targeted by the authorities. There is still a cash reserve requirement, but that is also not binding. BPNG uses the kina facility rate as its primary monetary policy lever, but it seems to have limited sway over lending rates, since banks fund their loans from their deposits.

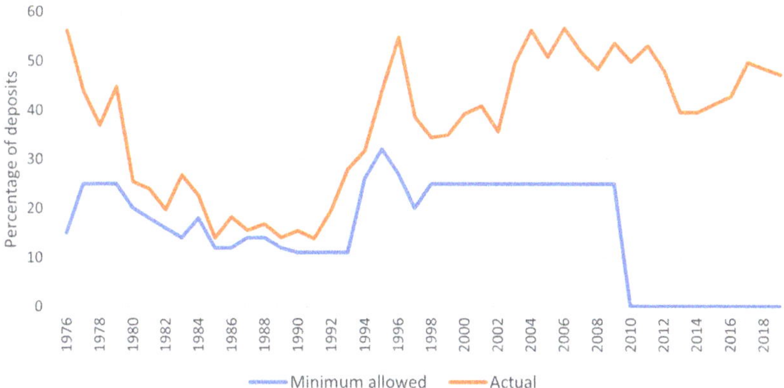

Figure 5.35: Banks' liquid asset ratios: Actual and statutory minimum, 1976–2019.

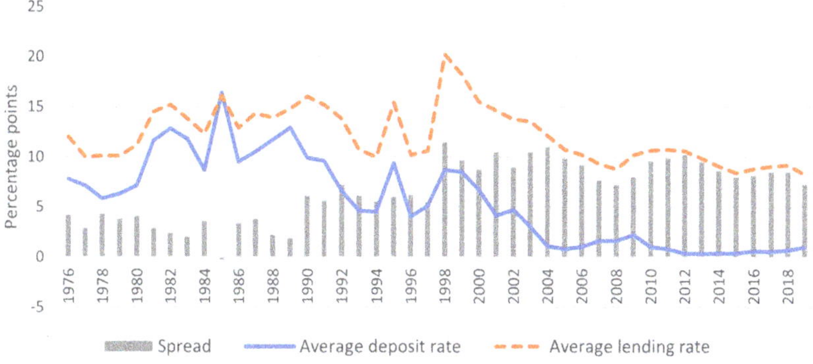

Figure 5.36: Weighted average lending and deposit rates and spreads, 1976–2019.

At independence, the banking sector was highly regulated. The main effect of deregulation seems to have been a decline in deposit rates to virtually zero (Figure 5.36). The spread between deposit and lending rates has risen from well under 5 per cent to well above it, meaning that lending rates have not fallen by nearly as much as deposit rates. PNG's banks have become among the most profitable in the world. That they are able to maintain such a spread is testimony to their monopoly power.[7]

Conclusion

The purpose of this chapter has been to introduce a new data set, the PNG Economic Database, with basic time series for PNG since independence. The data notes at the end of the chapter provide additional information on the data compiled, which are available online.

To conclude, we highlight 15 findings from the chapter:

1. Every year PNG's population now increases by 230,000, three times the annual absolute increase at independence.
2. PNG has become more resource dependent over time; the share of the resources sector in the economy has grown from about 10 per cent in 1980 to nearly 30 per cent.
3. Using the official GDP deflator, GDP per capita has grown at an average rate of 1.1 per cent since 1983, and the more useful indicator of non-resource GDP per capita has grown at an average rate of 0.4 per cent. CPI has grown significantly faster than the GDP deflators, and, if used as a deflator for nominal GDP, gives a result of overall negative GDP per capita growth.
4. Non-resource GDP per capita can be used to divide PNG's post-independence history into four periods: stability but stagnation (1983–88), instability (1989–2003), the resource boom (2004–13) and the subsequent bust (2014 to the current time).
5. At independence, PNG's commodity exports were divided fairly evenly between resources and agricultural commodities. Now 80 per cent are from the resources sector.

7 PNG's biggest bank, the Bank of the South Pacific, estimates that it has a 65 per cent market share (*Post-Courier*, 2020).

6. Outside of the resources sector, palm oil, non-traditional agricultural products, logging and marine products have shown significant growth. With the exception of palm oil, production of traditional export cash crops is lower than at independence.
7. With the exception of the boom period, formal sector employment has overall grown slowly, and the ratio of formal sector employment to population has fallen since independence.
8. Adjusting for inflation, the minimum wage paid to urban workers is half of its independence level. (The declining absolute level of formal sector employment suggests, however, that now is not the time to raise the minimum wage.)
9. The nominal PGK–USD exchange rate is only one-quarter of its value at independence, but the real effective exchange rate is back at close to its independence level, when the kina was thought to be overvalued.
10. The import/GDP ratio is at its lowest level in the independence era, in part due to foreign exchange rationing.
11. The revenue/GDP ratio is on a downward trend. This reflects declining aid and a declining share of resource sector value added captured by the government.
12. Debt/GDP, debt/revenue and interest/revenue ratios all indicate that government debt levels are at historically high levels in PNG, following the record deficits of recent years.
13. Efforts to stabilise resource revenues have not been sustained or successful.
14. At independence, government debt was mainly financed offshore; now it is mainly financed onshore.
15. Banks have shifted away from lending to the private sector towards the role of government financiers. And lending spreads have increased. These two trends have resulted in a highly profitable banking sector.

We leave it to the reader to draw out the policy recommendations that follow from these results. We conclude by noting that, despite our best efforts, we are still far from having a comprehensive set of economic data for PNG. There are many variables – GNI, investment, savings and others – that would enrich our analysis. We also need to extend the GDP series to, or at least closer to, 1975. Nevertheless, we hope that our PNG Economic Database makes a useful contribution towards a better understanding of PNG's economic history and prospects.

Acknowledgements

The authors acknowledge with thanks the excellent research assistance of Rubayat Chowdhury, Ephraim Feto, Lyanne Gewageu and Kingtau Mambon. They also thank their colleagues at The Australian National University and University of Papua New Guinea for their insights and comments, and the participants of the October 2020 workshop, in particular Professor Satish Chand and Dr Osborne Sanida for their excellent comments.

References

Allen, B. (2014). *Papua New Guinea national census 2011: Rates of population change in local level government areas*. SSGM In Brief 2014/44. dpa.bellschool.anu.edu.au/experts-publications/publications/1279/papua-new-guinea-national-census-2011-rates-population-change.

AusAID. (1996). *The economy of Papua New Guinea, 1996 report*. International Development Issues No. 46. Australian Agency for International Development.

Bank of Papua New Guinea. (2007). *Money and banking in Papua New Guinea*. Melbourne University Press.

Batten, A. (n.d.). *Asian Development Bank – PNG macroeconomic modelling* [Data set]. devpolicy.org/pngeconomic/wp-content/uploads/ADB-PNG-dataset-modelling.xlsx.

Bourke, R. M. and Allen, B. (2009). Twenty myths about Papua New Guinea agriculture. In R. M. Bourke and T. Harwood (Eds), *Food and agriculture in Papua New Guinea*. ANU Press. doi.org/10.22459/FAPNG.08.2009.

Bourke, R. M. and Allen, B. (2021). *Estimating the population of Papua New Guinea in 2020*. Development Policy Centre Discussion Paper 90. doi.org/10.2139/ssrn.3770356.

Connell, J. (1997). *Papua New Guinea: The struggle for development*. Routledge.

Department of Foreign Affairs and Trade. (2004). *Papua New Guinea: The road ahead*. Australian Government.

Department of National Planning and Monitoring. (1999). *Papua New Guinea National Population Policy 2000–2010*. Department of National Planning and Monitoring.

Goodman, R., Lepani, C. and Morawitz D. (1987). *The economy of Papua New Guinea: An independent review*. National Centre for Development Studies, The Australian National University.

Gruss, B. and Kebhaj, S. (2019). *Commodity terms of trade: A new database*. International Monetary Fund. Working Paper 19/21. doi.org/10.5089/9781484393857.001.

Howes, S. (2018, 22 June). Private sector perspectives on the PNG economy. *Devpolicy Blog*. devpolicy.org/private-sector-perspectives-png-economy-20180622/.

International Monetary Fund. (2021). *Commodity terms of trade* [Data set]. data.imf.org/?sk=2CDDCCB8-0B59-43E9-B6A0-59210D5605D2.

Jones, L. T. and McGavin, P. A. (2015). *Grappling afresh with labour resource challenges in Papua New Guinea: A framework for moving forward*. Institute of National Affairs.

McGavin, P. A. (1997). Labour absorption in Papua New Guinea. In Ila Temu (Ed.), *Papua New Guinea: A 20/20 vision* (pp. 65–97). National Research Institute and National Centre for Development Studies.

National Statistical Office. (2002). *Papua New Guinea 2000 Census: Final figures*. National Statistical Office of Papua New Guinea.

National Statistical Office. (2020). *PNG GDP 2006–2018* [Data set]. www.nso.gov.pg/download/86/national-accounts-gdp/2999/png-national-accounts-key-aggregates-2006-2018.xlsx.

Post-Courier. (2020, 25 August). Competition needs a broader commitment to PNG, BSP. postcourier.com.pg/competition-needs-a-broader-commitment-to-png-bsp/.

Treasury. (2020). *2019 final budget outcomes*. Government of Papua New Guinea.

Webster, T. and Duncan, L. (Eds). 2010. *Papua New Guinea's development performance*. PNG National Research Institute.

Appendix: Data notes

Population

Annual values are interpolated from decadal population figures from the Department of National Planning and Monitoring (1999) to 1990 and NSO (2002) for 2000 and projections from 2001 are based on the 1980–2000 growth rate (2.7 per cent), the mid-range estimate of Bourke and Allen (2021).

GDP: Current prices

For GDP data in current prices, 1976–80 data are available from Goodman et al. (1987), and 1980–2002 from BPNG (2007). From 1989 to 2006 we take information from the PNG Budget Database (devpolicy.crawford.anu.edu.au/png-project/png-budget-database) from successive budget volumes (Table 1 of Volume 1). Agricultural data 1980–2006 are taken from historical Asian Development Bank (ADB) PNG Key Indicators spreadsheets. In 2006, a new GDP series was created by NSO, increasing the 2006 GDP by 50 per cent relative to the old estimates. Data are available from NSO for the years 2006–18 in the new series. Data for 2019 use Treasury figures from the 2021 National Budget (Volume 1) GDP estimates, which are consistent with the new series. We create two series: the first using nominal growth rates from 2006 onwards to extend the pre-2007 series forwards (GDPoldc) and the second using nominal growth rates from 2006 back to 1980 (and then from 1980 to 1976) to extend the post-2005 series backwards (GDPnewc). The same method is used for GDP by sector with the same sources (sectoral data available from 1980, whereas GDP available from 1976). BPNG (2007) notes a break in the series from 1994; it also notes that, for the years 1994–2002, GDP excludes the imputed value for bank service charges. Unless specified otherwise, GDPnewc is used in the analysis. Note that earlier GDP data (from 1975–76 and earlier) are available from BPNG (2007). However, these show high real growth (11 per cent) in 1983, which we are unable to find other evidence for. Therefore, we use Goodman et al.'s (1987) current and constant price GDP growth data for the earlier years.

GDP: Constant prices

GDP data in constant prices are available from Goodman et al. (1987) for 1976–83; BPNG (2007) from 1983 to 2002; Budget Volume 1, 2003–2006; NSO (2020), 2006–2018; and the 2021 Budget Volume 1 for 2019. Data for GDP, non-resource GDP, agriculture and manufacturing are available (for GDP from 1976; for others from 1983). These series have different bases: 1976–83 are in 1977 prices; 1983–93 are in 1983 prices; 1994–2002 from BPNG (2007) and 2003–06 from the Budget are in 1998 prices; and 2006 onwards are in 2013 prices. The earlier years are rebased so that all GDP data are in 2013 prices (GDPnewk). To rebase, we need data for the cut-off years calculated in both old and new base prices. Goodman et al.'s (1987) constant price growth rates up to 1984 are applied to the BPNG 1983 baseline (i.e. converted from 1977 to 1983 prices). ADB statistical indictors were located that report GDP for 1994 in both 1983 and 1998 prices. This allows conversion of the entire series up to 2006 into 1998 prices. Budget documents report 2006 at 1998 prices, while NSO reports 2006 at 2013 prices. This allows for calculation of 2006 in both 1998 and 2013 prices, and thus conversion of the whole series to 2013 prices. Note that the rebasing in 2006 adjusts both for a different price base year and for the rebasing of current price GDP. The GDP deflator is the constant price GDP over the current price GDP (GDPnewc).

Commodities

Data on commodity volumes are available from BPNG (2007) from 1976 to 2005, and the BPNG's *Quarterly Economic Bulletin* (QEB) Table 8.4 for agricultural products, and Table 8.5 for logs, marine products and minerals/metals from 2006. The following commodities are covered: copra, copra oil, cocoa, coffee, palm oil, rubber, tea, marine products, logs, gold, silver, copper, nickel, cobalt, oil and condensate/LNG. Data on commodity values are available from BPNG (2007) from 1976 to 2005, and QEB Table 8.3 for agricultural exports, and Table 8.2 for logs, marine products and minerals/metals from 2006. The same commodities are covered as for quantities, except that 'other agricultural produce' and 'other forest products' are added, with data beginning in 1990. Marine products value data also begin in 1990. The total commodities value figure is the sum of all commodities covered in this database, which is equivalent to the total exports figure in QEB Table 8.2 after removing the value of refined petroleum products in QEB Table 8.3 from the total.

Other agricultural products and other forest products do not appear in BPNG (2007); they are relatively small in early years but larger in later years. Data on other agricultural products and other forest products appear in QEB Tables 8.3 and 8.2, respectively, and go back to 1990. Condensate and LNG figures are added together to attain the combined condensate/LNG figure. In BPNG (2007), alluvial gold is included in the total gold figure, but from 1990 the figure for silver and alluvial gold is calculated by taking the 'total' minerals figure and subtracting the value of the other mineral resources, as per notes in QEB Table 8.2. Other agricultural products includes a very small proportion of manufactured goods as per note (f) in QEB Table 8.3.

There is a break in series in commodity data from 2001, which reflects a reconciliation between BPNG and the commodity boards' export figures. A comparison of the two volume series in 2001 shows that copra and copra oil volume figures are around half of what they were in the old series. Other commodity volumes have differences between series in 2001 ranging from –15 per cent to 27 per cent. There are also differences in export prices series; a comparison (in 2001) between the two series shows that copra prices are around 45 per cent higher in the new series. Copra values are around 40 per cent smaller in the new series, and 50 per cent smaller for copra oil. Other value differences range between –20 per cent and 1 per cent. Metals and oil volumes and values are unchanged across series.

Commodity export terms of trade are from the IMF (2021), using shares of exports in GDP as weights.

Employment

Annual formal employment data are sourced via an index from BPNG (2007) from 1978 to 2005 and BPNG QEB Table 9.7 from 2006. Employment figures are averages for the year. Where annual QEB estimates are not available or are unreliable, the geometric mean of quarterly estimates are used.

Total employment as defined by this index excludes the public service but includes SOE employment. The indices are provided by sector (retail, wholesale, manufacturing, construction, transport, agriculture, financial and mineral) as well as total.

The series was rebased in 2002 to Q1 2002 (= 100) (from Q2 1989 = 100); therefore, the earlier data required rebasing.

Employment numbers are available for 1968–91 in Connell (1997) Table 8.2 for the public sector (total, public service and SOEs) and the private sector (total, mining, agriculture from 1976 and manufacturing from 1979). These data are combined with the indices to provide numbers for these series throughout the period, except for the public service. More recent public service data are available from McGavin (1997) for 1992–95, Department of Foreign Affairs and Trade (2004) for 1999–2002 and Treasury (2020) for 2015–19.

Minimum wage

Data on the weekly rural and urban minimum wage for 1972–2014 are provided in Jones and McGavin (2015, Annex 7.1, which runs from 1972 to 2014). This is updated from 2015 using QEB Table 9.1. There are some minor discrepancies between BPNG (2007) and Jones and McGavin (2015). The latter suggests that the minimum urban and rural wages were unified in 1992, while data from the former suggests that unification occurred first in 1993. Minimum wage data are for the end of the year.

CPI

BPNG reports CPI (headline and by expenditure group) for 1977–2013 with 1977 as the base year (QEB Table 9.2) and for 2010–19 with 2012 Q1 as the base quarter (QEB Table 9.4). We rebase the earlier series (up to 2010, which uses an older consumer basket), using 2012 Q1 as the base quarter to align with the QEB Table 9.4 data. As a result, we have CPI from 1977 at a single base year, 2012.

The World Bank also reports annual headline CPI inflation rates from 1971 onwards as variable FP.CPI.TOTL.ZG, which are reported with 2010 as the base year. The constructed series is consistent with the World Bank figures.

Exchange rates and foreign exchange reserves

Nominal exchange rates (USD, AUD, Yen, UKP, Euro) are available from 1975. Up to 1990, we use data from BPNG (2007); post-1990, from QEB Table 8.11. Exchange rates are averages for the year (from 1995).

The real effective exchange rate is available from World Development Indicators (WDI) as variable WDI PX.REX.REER. It is an index with 2010 = 100. The variable is defined as follows:

> [The r]eal effective exchange rate is the nominal effective exchange rate (a measure of the value of a currency against a weighted average of several foreign currencies) divided by a price deflator or index of costs.

Foreign exchange reserves are taken from WDI up to 2002 as variable WDI FI.RES.TOTL.CD (in USD and converted to PGK using annual exchange rates). From 2002, they are taken from the 'total international reserves' column in QEB Table 8.10, which presents end of year data (in PGK and converted to USD using annual exchange rates). 2012 data is missing from QEB, and so WDI data are used for that year.

Foreign exchange reserves in months of imports is calculated using import figures; see below.

Balance of payments

Merchandise exports and imports, service exports and imports ('invisible credits' and 'debits'), net transfers and the current account balance are available from 1976 to 2005 in BPNG (2007) and from QEB Table 8.1B from 2002 onwards. We use the QEB data from 2002. 'Invisible credits' and 'invisible debits' are equal to the sum of services credits/debits and income credits/debits in the QEB tables, respectively. 'Net transfers' are equivalent to 'transfers balance' in the QEB tables. Provisional balance of payments data are not used because they are subject to large revisions.

Fiscal data

Data on government revenue, expenses and borrowing comes from BPNG (2007) Table A27 for 1975–88, and from the PNG Budget Database from 1989 onwards. Resource revenue equals mining and petroleum taxes plus mining and petroleum dividends.

Two expenditure variables are provided: (a) and (b). PNG switched its Government Financial Statistics (GFS) system for fiscal accounts from the 1986 to the 2014 GFS in 2016. Transfers into trust funds (see below) were included in the old GFS as spending from 2005 to 2011. Definition (a) uses the old GFS data for as long as they are recorded, that is, until 2015. Definition (b) uses the new GFS data from when they are available (2012) and adjusts spending from 2005 to 2011 to exclude from spending net transfers into trust funds. The deficit variable is revenue minus expenditure (b). Expenditure includes net lending.

Resource revenue data are from BPNG (2007) from 1975 to 1999 and PNG Budget Database from 2000 on. These do not include interest earned in the MRSF (see below) but capture the sum of company tax and dividend withholding tax paid by mining and petroleum firms, other mining and petroleum taxes, and mining and petroleum related dividends received by the government.

Trust fund balances are the MRSF from 1975 to 1998 (the last year with a non-zero balance) from BPNG (2007). From 2005 onwards, trust fund balances are obtained from the 2018 final budget outcomes document. 2019 trust fund figures cannot be reconciled with 2018, and are small, so the series is discontinued in 2018.

The stock of government debt (total, domestic and foreign) is extracted from Batten (n.d.) up to 1989, QEB Table 7.3 for 1990 to 1998, and the PNG Budget Database for 1999 onwards.

Other than as detailed for the two expenditure measures, figures using the 2014 GFS are used when both are available. Only actuals are included.

Monetary and financial data

Data on the liquid asset ratio ('total approved liquid assets' over 'total deposits and other prescribed liabilities') and minimum liquid asset requirement or MLAR are available from BPNG (2007) for 1976–2005 and from QEB Table 3.13 for later years. We use QEB data from 2002 onwards. (There is a discrepancy in 2002.) From June 1999, the liquid asset ratio excludes cash reserve requirement deposits held at BPNG, and in October 2010 the MLAR was reduced to zero (see the notes to QEB Table 3.13).

The lending rate ('weighted average advances') and deposit rate ('weighted average deposits') are available from BPNG (2007) for 1976–2005 and from QEB Table 6.1 from 1990 onwards. There are a few years in which the data do not match. We use BPNG (2007) up to 2005, and thereafter QEB.

Deposits, loans to the private sector (domestic), foreign currency loans to the private sector, and loans to the private sector and SOEs (domestic) are available from BPNG (2007) and QEB Table 3.6 (deposits) and Table 3.7 (loans). Monetary deposits equal 'all deposits' plus 'central government liabilities'. Loans to SOEs include a small amount of loans to the central government and provincial and local governments, but are mainly loans to public non-financial corporations. Government debt held by banks is from BPNG (2007) Table A12 and QEB Table 3.3 (sum of Treasury bills and inscribed stocks). Foreign loans to the private sector are shown separately and are not included in the 'domestic' variables.

Fiscal/calendar year

The calendar year is used unless specified here. PNG changed its accounting period in 1978. From 1 January 1978, the calendar year was used. Prior to this, the July to June financial year was used. Flows from the 1975–76 and 1976–77 years are reported as 1976 and 1977, respectively. (This method slightly exaggerates growth in 1978 since it compares January to December 1978 with July 1976 to June 1977.) Stocks at the end of 1975–76 and 1976–77 are reported as 1975 and 1976, respectively, and the end of December 1977 is used for 1977. This is used for fiscal and GDP data. It is also assumed that this is the way that commodity and balance of payments data are calculated. Monetary stocks and minimum wages are generally end of year (December) figures.

6

Have living standards improved in PNG over the last two decades? Evidence from Demographic and Health Surveys

Manoj K. Pandey and Stephen Howes

Abstract

Did living standards improve in Papua New Guinea (PNG) over the last two decades, and especially as a result of the resource boom of the 2000s? This question remains unanswered to date. The best source to answer it is the three PNG Demographic and Health Surveys for 1996, 2006 and 2016–18. Analysis of these three surveys leads to three types of results. First, there are clearly some ways in which living standards have improved: more households have rainwater tanks; more children are at school, albeit from a low base; and childhood mortality rates have fallen. Second, there are areas of regress: less access to traditional media and worse health services. Third, there are areas of stagnation: no growth in the importance of non-agricultural jobs, and little sign of improved status for women. Overall, the results show some benefits from economic growth, but also areas of real concern, and little sign of the structural transformation needed for sustained and successful development. Interestingly, the analysis also reveals a trend to convergence between urban and rural living standards.

Introduction

The lack of consistent, reliable and up-to-date data remains a major obstacle to assessing progress in living standards in Papua New Guinea (PNG). There are only two Household Income and Expenditure Surveys, for 1996 and 2009–10 (World Bank, 2013), and they used different methods (Gibson, 2012). The 2011 census is widely regarded to be unreliable (Bourke and Allen, 2021). This chapter draws upon three PNG Demographic and Health Surveys (DHSs) for 1996, 2006 and 2016–18 to examine whether the standard of living in PNG has improved over the last two decades.

The two most recent DHSs are of particular value because they were fielded roughly on either side of PNG's biggest boom, which ran from 2003 to 2013. High commodity prices and the construction of the large PNG liquefied natural gas project led to the strongest period of economic growth seen in PNG post-independence. As argued in Chapter 5, non-resource GDP (excluding the largely foreign-owned resources sector) is the best indicator of national economic activity for PNG. Adjusting for inflation, non-resource GDP grew at an average of 2.8 per cent between 1983 and 2003, and only 1.5 per cent between 2013 and 2019, but at a much higher average of 5.6 per cent between 2003 and 2013 (see Chapter 5, this volume, for sources).

This raises many questions. Did the boom make a difference? Are households better off as a result? Do they have more durables? Do they have better access to clean water? Are they in better health? Are their children more likely to be in school? Are the women of PNG having fewer children and are their births safer? Are they marrying later and do they have better access to contraception?

The findings of this chapter can be divided into three groups.

First, there are clearly some ways in which living standards have improved over the last two decades: many more households have a rainwater tank; more children are at school, albeit from a low base; and childhood mortality rates have fallen. These positive results reflect the positive impact of economic growth on household income, as well as on government revenue and therefore spending in the case of education.

The second group of results are the areas of regress. Vaccination rates and access to traditional media have both plummeted over the last decade. These would seem to be cases of worsening governance leading to poorer service delivery despite economic growth.

Finally, there are areas of stagnation. There is no growth in the share of non-agricultural jobs post-2006, a key indicator of economic transformation. There is also little sign of improved status for women. Women are more likely to be heads of households, but they are hardly marrying later, or having children later, or having fewer children. While access to contraception has improved, it remains very low, and women are no more likely to receive antenatal care than they were 20 years ago, and hardly more likely to give birth in a health facility.

This third group of results is perhaps the most worrying, as it suggests that, despite some short-term benefits from growth, there is little sign of the structural transformation needed for sustained and successful development.

Interestingly, the analysis also shows that urban areas are less likely to show improvements in living standards and are more likely to show declines than rural areas. We interpret this as being due to the growth of urban settlements. The result is a tendency towards convergence between urban and rural living standards.

The next section provides a summary of the DHS data. Subsequent sections evaluate: employment outcomes; trends in household durables, quality and infrastructure; changes in schooling and exposure to the media; trends in mortality and health; and household gender roles. The final section concludes the chapter.

DHS data

Demographic and Health Surveys are conducted worldwide and provide comprehensive socio-economic and demographic information through household and individual surveys. The household questionnaire (answered by the self-identified household head) typically collects information on characteristics of household members (age, sex, education) and of housing (access to drinking water, sanitation facilities, housing quality, durable ownership). The supplementary questionnaire for eligible women (aged 15–49) typically collects information on fertility, marriage, family planning, breastfeeding practices, nutrition, childhood and adult mortality, and maternal and child health. That for eligible men (aged 15–49 years) typically collects information on employment and gender roles, awareness and behaviour regarding HIV/AIDS and other sexually transmissible infections.

The 1996 PNG DHS surveyed 4,319 households and 4,917 women (National Statistical Office [NSO], 1997). The 2006 DHS surveyed 9,017 households, 10,352 women and 10,077 men, and the 2016–18 DHS surveyed 16,021 households, 15,198 women and 7,333 men (NSO, 2009, 2019).[1]

There are some differences between the three surveys. First, the 2016–18 survey but not the earlier two surveys stratified provinces into rural and urban areas. The three surveys actually show a declining urban share of the population (Table 6.1), which is not credible. Care must be taken when comparing aggregates as a result, and we normally show results separately for urban and rural areas.

Table 6.1: Share of urban and rural population according to the three DHSs (1996–2018, %).

	1996		2006		2016–18	
	Urban	Rural	Urban	Rural	Urban	Rural
Population share	18.1	81.9	14.1	85.9	11.6	88.4

Source: NSO (1997, 2009, 2019).

Second, the 2006 and 2016–18 DHSs included a male and female questionnaire (in addition to the household survey), but the 1996 one only had an additional female questionnaire. Third, whereas the 1996 and 2006 surveys were collected over a single year, the 2016–18 DHS was collected over three years. Fourth, the definition of some indicators and reference periods changed over time.

In summary, while the three surveys are not identical to each other, many estimates are comparable, and only those that are comparable are used in this chapter. Definitions of indicators and associated explanations are provided in Table A.1 in the Appendix at the end of the chapter.

1 Fewer men were surveyed in 2016–18 because they were selected only from every second household rather than every household as in previous surveys.

Estimates in the chapter for the first two surveys are from the relevant DHS reports (NSO, 1997, 2009). For the third survey, where available, we use estimates published in NSO (2019). We have the micro data for the 2016–18 survey, and so for that round, where required for the sake of comparability, we are able to calculate estimates ourselves, using appropriate sampling weights.

Employment

The most direct way in which an economic boom would be expected to affect household living standards would be through improved employment prospects. All three DHS surveys provide information on economic activity in the week preceding the survey, though the 1996 DHS only has information regarding women. A change in the classification of economic activities reduces comparability with 2016–18, but still allows for comparison of the proportion engaged in non-agricultural activity (Table 6.2).

The share of women engaged in non-agricultural activity rose significantly between 1996 and 2006, but has not increased since, nor has the share of men. This suggests an improvement relative to the crisis years of the mid-1990s, but not a sustained structural transformation in the pattern of employment.

Table 6.2: Engagement in non-agricultural economic activity (1996–2018, %).

	1996			2006			2016–18		
	Urban	**Rural**	**Total**	**Urban**	**Rural**	**Total**	**Urban**	**Rural**	**Total**
Male	–	–	–	51.1	19.8	25.1	48.7	17.9	22.1
Female	30.1	5.6	10.6	41.5	13.0	17.5	36.9	13.0	16.1
All	–	–	–	46.4	16.3	21.2	40.9	14.6	18.1

For sources and notes, see Appendix Table A.1. Dash (–) indicates estimates not available as data on men not available for 1996.

Household durables, quality and infrastructure

One would also expect an economic boom to lift the ownership of economic durables, to result in improved housing quality and to lead to better housing infrastructure (water, sanitation and electricity), though much of the latter is dependent on government action.

Mobile phone ownership, which was not asked about in earlier surveys, but would have been zero or close to it if it had been, is at 56 per cent of households in 2016–18 (Table 6.3). Computers have also emerged in PNG in recent years, and in 2016–18 as many households had a computer as a refrigerator (about 10 per cent). The percentage of households with a radio has fallen (from 31 per cent in 1996 to 24 per cent in 2016–18). That is partly offset by a similar increase in the share with a television (from 8 per cent to 13 per cent).

Table 6.3: Household durable goods (1996–2018, %).

	1996			2006			2016–18		
	Urban	**Rural**	**Total**	**Urban**	**Rural**	**Total**	**Urban**	**Rural**	**Total**
Durable goods									
Radio	59.6	24.9	30.6	63.9	29.4	33.1	49.4	21.0	23.7
TV	40.0	1.4	7.7	46.2	4.3	8.8	47.8	8.9	12.6
Refrigerator	49.4	1.5	9.3	42.9	4.3	6.6	45.1	6.3	10.0
Non-mobile telephone	14.1	0.4	2.6	26.3	1.2	3.9	8.3	1.6	2.2
Mobile phone	–	–	–	–	–	–	87.8	53.0	56.3
Computer	–	–	–	–	–	–	42.7	7.3	10.6

For sources and notes, see Appendix Table A.1. Dash (–) indicates estimates not available.

Housing quality has worsened, with the share of dwellings with a finished floor falling from 21 per cent in 1996 to 15 per cent in 2016–18 (Table 6.4). This reflects worsening housing quality in urban areas, presumably due to the growth of urban settlements. House crowding, on the other hand, has become slightly less of a problem over time, reflecting the slightly smaller average household size discussed later in the chapter (see Table 6.12).

Table 6.4: Household floor quality and crowding (1996–2018).

	1996			2006			2016–18		
	Urban	Rural	Total	Urban	Rural	Total	Urban	Rural	Total
Types of floor material (%)									
Natural floor	1.5	19.7	16.7	5.5	25.7	23.5	5.5	20.3	18.9
Rudimentary floor	32.4	67.9	62.1	29.7	62.2	58.6	44.2	67.2	65.0
Finished floor	66.0	12.4	21.2	62.4	9.0	14.8	49.9	11.4	15.1
Mean persons per sleeping room	2.8	2.9	2.9	3.4	3.3	3.3	2.5	2.5	2.5

For sources and notes, see Appendix Table A.1. Percentages may not add up to 100 due to small share of missing/'do not know' responses.

We turn now to housing infrastructure and the extent to which households have access to electricity, clean water and sanitation (Table 6.5). There is a vast disparity between urban and rural households in relation to all these indicators, but in many cases the urban–rural gap is falling. Electricity access via the grid improved in rural areas from 3 per cent in 1996 to 10 per cent in 2016, and fell in urban areas from 59 per cent to 55 per cent, reflecting perhaps the growth of new, unelectrified settlements.[2]

There is no improvement in the share of households with access to piped water, but more households have access to a dug well or a rainwater tank than before (30 per cent in 2016–18 compared to 19 per cent in 2006). Significantly, this is a solution to their domestic water needs that households can arrange for themselves, rather than having to rely on the government. In 2016–18, 51 per cent of households still had to rely on an unimproved water source (surface water or spring), a decline from 59 per cent in 1996. The share of rural households reliant on unimproved water sources fell from 70 per cent in 2006 to 55 per cent in 2016–18, but the share of urban households thus reliant rose over the same period from 7 per cent to 16 per cent. There was little change overall in sanitation arrangements. Comparing 1996 and 2016–18, fewer urban households have flush toilets and more use pit latrines.

2 Solar lighting was asked about separately in the most recent round. In 2016–18, 16 per cent of urban, 33.9 per cent of rural and 33.2 per cent of all households used solar as a lighting source.

Table 6.5: Household electrification, drinking water and sanitation (1996–2018, %).

	1996			2006			2016–18		
	Urban	**Rural**	**Total**	**Urban**	**Rural**	**Total**	**Urban**	**Rural**	**Total**
Electricity from a grid	59.2	3.2	12.3	61.3	6.5	12.4	54.6	10.4	14.6
Sources of drinking water									
Piped water	71.7	8.5	18.8	70.0	9.9	16.4	55.2	14.3	18.1
Dug well	1.9	8.7	7.5	6.0	7.4	7.3	4.6	13.5	12.7
Rainwater and tank	19.5	12.3	13.4	14.4	11.1	11.6	24.0	16.9	17.6
Surface water and spring	5.4	69.2	58.8	7.4	70.2	63.5	15.7	54.9	51.1
Other	1.6	1.4	1.4	1.6	0.9	1.0	0.4	0.1	0.2
Access to sanitation									
Flush toilets (1)	58.3	2.5	11.6	46.7	1.8	6.8	44.8	8.1	11.6
Pit latrine (2)	34.9	77.9	70.9	43.2	76.6	72.9	44.6	72.3	69.5
Others (3)	3.5	3.3	3.3	4.4	3.5	3.6	2.8	1.7	1.9
Open defecation	3.1	16.3	14.1	4.8	17.7	16.3	7.4	17.6	16.7
Access to sanitation facility (1+2+3)	96.9	83.7	85.9	95.2	82.3	83.7	92.6	82.4	83.3

For sources and notes, see Appendix Table A.1.

Education and exposure to mass media

In PNG, as in many other countries, educational attainment is negatively associated with poverty (Gibson, 2012; Gibson and Rozelle, 2003) and vulnerability (Jha and Dang, 2010). To the extent that a resource boom increases government revenue and the demand for education, one would expect it to lead to more widespread schooling. The PNG Government abolished tuition fees in 2012, which led to a spurt in enrolment (though tuition fees were partially reintroduced in 2019).

Table 6.6 shows rapid growth in school attendance across the period examined, from 37 per cent of all 6–20-year-olds in 1996 to 65 per cent in 2016–18. There is a closing of both the gender and urban–rural gap.

Table 6.6: School attendance (1996–2018, %).

Residence/ age group (years)	1996			2006			2016–18		
	Male	Female	All	Male	Female	All	Male	Female	All
Urban									
6–10	50.8	47.2	49.0	61.9	58.4	60.3	64.9	67.4	66.1
11–15	79.5	75.7	77.8	76.6	76.9	76.6	85.5	87.4	86.4
16–20	34.1	28.6	31.6	50.9	39.6	45.4	61.0	58.0	59.6
6–20	54.8	50.5	52.8	63.1	58.3	60.8	70.5	70.9	70.7
Rural									
6–10	28.1	28.2	28.1	39.4	37.8	38.6	50.3	49.2	49.8
11–15	55.4	57.1	56.2	69.1	69.5	69.2	79.8	79.7	79.8
16–20	16.8	11.3	14.2	41.2	32.0	36.7	63.2	52.0	58.0
6–20	33.4	32.2	32.8	49.9	46.4	48.2	64.4	60.3	62.5
All									
6–10	31.7	31.3	31.5	41.9	40.0	41.0	54.5	54.5	54.5
11–15	59.7	60.2	59.9	70.0	70.3	70.2	81.9	81.4	81.7
16–20	20.5	14.9	18.0	42.8	33.2	38.0	64.5	54.1	59.3
6–20	37.3	35.5	36.5	51.6	47.8	49.7	67.0	63.3	65.2

For sources and notes, see Appendix Table A.1.

With improvements in school attendance, the share of those without education fell from 42 per cent in 1996 to 32 per cent in 2016–18 for males and from 50 per cent to 40 per cent for females in the same period (Table 6.7). We also see convergence across regional areas and to some extent between urban and rural areas, and between men and women.

Table 6.7: Highest educational attainment (1996–2018, %).

	1996				2006				2016–18			
	No education	Grades 1–5	Grade 6	Grade 7+	No education	Grades 1–5	Grade 6	Grade 7+	No education	Grades 1–5	Grade 6	Grade 7+
Gender												
Male	41.5	24.5	17.2	16.8	34.9	27.6	14.5	23.0	32.2	25.2	12.0	30.6
Female	50.2	24.2	15.9	9.7	44.5	24.5	14.3	16.7	40.0	24.4	11.2	24.4
Residence												
Urban	24.4	21.1	19.4	35.1	23.1	20.1	14.3	42.5	19.6	21.7	10.5	48.3
Rural	50.5	25.1	15.9	8.6	42.3	27.0	14.5	16.2	38.1	25.2	11.8	24.9
Region												
Southern	28.7	25.4	23.8	22.1	29.4	26.7	18.2	25.8	29.4	25.1	13.4	32.1
Highlands	62.3	21.5	9.0	7.2	48.6	26.6	9.9	14.9	44.6	23.6	7.7	24.1
Momase	44.2	24.9	19.4	11.5	41.6	24.3	16.2	17.8	33.4	25.6	13.9	27.1
Islands	30.3	30.1	19.4	20.2	25.4	26.6	18.5	29.5	25.0	26.0	16.3	32.6
All	45.7	24.4	16.5	13.4	39.6	26.0	14.4	19.9	36.0	24.8	11.7	27.6

For sources and notes, see Appendix Table A.1.

Better funded government services and higher household incomes should also lead to greater media access. In fact, however, there is a sharp reduction in access to traditional media (Table 6.8). Data for men is unavailable for the full period. The share of women watching TV remained steady, while shares of those reading a newspaper and especially listening to a radio fell sharply; for example, the share of women reading a paper at least once a week fell from 25 per cent in 1996 to 18 per cent in 2016–18. Men and those living in urban areas have greater exposure to all forms of mass media. It is not obvious what is driving these results. It may be that radio and TV broadcasting networks have not been well maintained. Papers may be less widely distributed if roads have worsened in quality and law and order problems have intensified.

Table 6.8: Access to mass media (1996–2018, %).

	1996			2006			2016–18		
	Urban	Rural	Total	Urban	Rural	Total	Urban	Rural	Total
Women									
Read newspaper at least once a week	60.8	16.3	25.4	63.7	22.9	29.3	41.1	14.0	17.6
Listen to radio at least once a week	71.1	36.6	43.7	83.2	41.7	48.2	41.5	15.0	18.5
Watch television at least once a week	54.5	4.2	14.5	71.6	13.3	22.4	46.1	10.5	15.2
Men									
Read newspaper at least once a week	–	–	–	82.3	36.6	44.4	65.7	27.6	32.7
Listen to radio at least once a week	–	–	–	92.3	56.4	62.5	63.2	27.1	31.9
Watch television at least once a week	–	–	–	81.1	20.1	30.5	57.1	16.4	21.8

For sources and notes, see Appendix Table A.1. Dash (–) indicates estimates not available as data on men not available for 1996.

Mortality and health

Cross-country empirical evidence suggest that poverty reduction is closely linked with reductions in mortality rates (e.g. Anand and Bärnighausen, 2004; Anand and Ravallion, 1993; Harttgen and Misselhorn, 2006; Pritchett and Summers, 1996). Certainly, one would expect a resource boom to lead to declining mortality and improved health services due to growing household income and government revenue.

Table 6.9 depicts declining trends in different childhood mortality rates between 1996 and 2016–18. These mortality rates have substantially fallen for both sexes, across regions and for children in rural areas. They have not, however, uniformly declined in urban areas. In fact, between 1996 and 2016–18 the urban neonatal mortality rate increased from 21 to 25 per 1,000 live births while the urban infant mortality rate remained stagnant at 34 per 1,000 live births.

Table 6.9: Childhood mortality rates (1996–2018, per 1,000).

	1996					2006					2016–18				
	NN	PNN	I	C	U5	NN	PNN	I	C	U5	NN	PNN	I	C	U5
Sex															
Male	37	46	82	28	108	29	30	60	18	77	26	13	39	15	53
Female	33	39	72	21	91	29	28	57	15	71	21	15	36	14	50
Residence															
Urban	21	12	34	13	46	20	11	31	12	42	25	8	34	11	45
Rural	38	49	87	27	112	31	32	62	18	79	24	15	38	15	53
Region															
Southern	27	14	41	26	66	25	20	45	13	58	23	7	29	11	40
Highlands	42	72	114	28	139	32	41	72	19	90	23	24	47	20	66
Momase	37	39	76	22	96	30	25	55	18	71	25	9	34	15	48
Islands	23	26	49	18	67	29	21	50	15	64	26	6	31	5	36
All	35	43	77	25	100	29	29	58	17	74	24	14	38	15	52

For sources and notes, see Appendix Table A.1. NN: neonatal mortality rate; PNN: post-neonatal mortality rate; I: infant mortality rate; C: child mortality rate; U5: under-five mortality rate. All mortality rates are expressed per 1,000 live births except for child mortality, which is expressed per 1,000 children surviving to age 12 months.

These reductions in childhood mortality are certainly welcome (and are observed worldwide), but they are not matched in PNG by commensurate improvements in health services or practices. Table 6.10 shows results relating to vaccination coverage and breastfeeding. In 2009, the pentavalent vaccine was introduced in PNG, replacing the DPT (diphtheria, pertussis and tetanus) vaccine. The pentavalent vaccine is more effective since it protects from diphtheria, whooping cough and tetanus (as does DPT), but also hepatitis B and haemophilus influenzae type b. The introduction of the pentavalent vaccine may have helped reduce child mortality, but the level of basic vaccine coverage actually fell sharply between 2006 and 2016, from 52 per cent to 35 per cent. The share of children not vaccinated at all increased from 7 per cent in 2006 to 24 per cent in 2016–18.

Table 6.10: Child health (1996–2018).

	1996			2006			2016–18		
	Urban	**Rural**	**Total**	**Urban**	**Rural**	**Total**	**Urban**	**Rural**	**Total**
Child vaccinations (% of children aged 12–23 months)									
All basic vaccinations (%)	69.7	32.4	38.7	63.8	50.2	52.0	48.8	33.4	35.3
Not vaccinated (%)	0.0	9.5	7.9	1.1	7.9	6.9	7.2	26.7	23.7
Breastfeeding									
Median breastfeeding duration (months)	20.4	25.8	25.4	23.5	26.6	26.0	23.9	24.1	23.9
No initial breastfeeding (%)	3.9	2.8	3.0	6.5	3.5	3.8	7.0	3.7	4.1

For sources and notes, see Appendix Table A.1.

The duration and intensity of breastfeeding provides children protection against a variety of acute and chronic disorders (Fewtrell, 2004; León-Cava et al., 2002; NSO, 2019; World Health Organization, 2007). There was no change in median breastfeeding duration, and an increase, especially in urban areas, of children who were never breastfed (likely to result in worse nutrition outcomes for children; see Hurney, 2017).

Gender and the household

With economic development comes a reduction in fertility and household size, and empowerment for women, reflected in improved contraceptive rates, later ages of marrying and giving birth, and great support during pregnancy and birth. We see few such signs of progress in the DHS data.

Table 6.11: Fertility rates and preferences (1996–2018).

	1996			2006			2016–18		
	Urban	Rural	Total	Urban	Rural	Total	Urban	Rural	Total
ASFR (per 1,000 women per year)									
15–19	91	73	77	55	67	65	57.1	80.1	76.7
20–24	207	235	229	172	216	209	159.2	206.3	200.5
25–29	209	240	234	200	209	208	178.9	217.1	212.1
30–34	176	192	189	155	181	177	143.9	178.3	174.0
35–39	86	131	122	82	135	127	107.9	127.6	124.9
40–44	22	94	82	41	63	60	38.4	62.2	59.2
45–49	9	38	35	13	33	31	5.7	28.6	25.7
TFR 15–49 (per woman)	4	5	4.8	3.6	4.5	4.4	3.5	4.5	4.4
GFR (per 1,000 women)	147	171	166	125	153	148	112.2	146.2	141.7
CBR (per 1,000 population)	33.6	33.9	33.9	31.0	32.6	32.4	27.6	30.3	30.0
Women's fertility preferences									
Want no more children (%)	45.6	46.1	46.0	37.0	39.0	38.7	51.4	45.5	46.2
Ideal number of children	3.3	3.6	3.5	3.2	3.7	3.6	2.8	3.1	3.0
Men's fertility preferences									
Want no more children (%)	–	–	–	32.7	34.2	34.0	37.7	40.2	39.9
Ideal number of children	–	–	–	3.5	4.1	4.0	3.1	3.7	3.6

For sources and notes, see Appendix Table A.1. Dash (–) indicates estimates not available. ASFR: age-specific fertility rates; TFR: total fertility rates; GFR: general fertility rates; CBR: crude birth rates.

PNG's fertility rates have not changed substantially since 1996 and remain high (Table 6.11). For example, the total fertility rate (TFR) fell from 4.8 to 4.4 between 1996 and 2006, but then remained at 4.4 in 2016–18. The general fertility rate (GFR, the weighted average of the age-specific fertility rates) fell, but only from 148 per 1,000 in 2006 to 142 per 1,000 in 2016–18. Age-specific fertility rates hardly fell, and some increased, confirming that the fall in the GFR is due to the changing demographic composition of the adult female population not a reduction in the number of children PNG's women are having.

Consistent with the slight fall in the GFR, the crude birth rate fell slightly from 34 per 1,000 in 1996 to 32 in 2006 to 30 in 2016–18. Fertility remains higher in rural areas, but by less than it used to be. The ideal number of children both women and men want is falling, but women now have 50 per cent more children than they want on average (4.4 versus 3).

Table 6.12 shows a range of characteristics related to household composition, size and headship. Average household size in PNG is 5.0 – higher than the global average of 4.0 (United Nations, 2017), and only slightly lower since 1996 (5.7 persons). This reflects the slow change in the fertility rate, discussed earlier. Surprisingly perhaps, but reflecting the higher cost of land in urban areas, urban households are larger than rural, by about one person on average, and the gap between average urban and rural household size is growing. Related to this, the proportion of households with three or more related adults has increased in urban PNG but declined in rural areas.

The population comprises 51 per cent males and 49 per cent females, with no change since 1996. PNG households are still predominantly headed by males. However, the share of female-headed households has more than doubled since 1996 to reach 18 per cent. The largest increase was in urban areas, where the share of female-headed households tripled from 7 per cent to 21 per cent between 1996 and 2016–18. What lies behind this increase requires further analysis. Gibson (2012) established that the incidence of poverty in PNG was lower for female-headed households.

Table 6.12: Household composition (1996–2018).

	1996			2006			2016–18		
	Urban	Rural	Total	Urban	Rural	Total	Urban	Rural	Total
Gender: household head (%) and mean family size									
Male	92.7	91.4	91.6	85.4	83.1	83.3	79.4	82.9	82.5
Female	7.3	8.6	8.4	14.6	16.9	16.7	20.6	17.1	17.5
Mean family size	6.3	5.6	5.7	6.8	5.0	5.2	6.0	4.9	5.0
Relationship structure: household members (%)									
One adult	5.1	7.5	7.1	6.5	13.9	13.1	7.8	12.4	12.0
Two related opposite sex	28.3	36.4	35.1	18.8	36.1	34.3	21.9	37.3	35.8
Two related same sex	2.1	1.9	1.9	3.2	4.1	4.0	3.5	3.8	3.8
3+ related adults	49.9	49.1	49.3	63.8	44.5	46.6	56.1	42.0	43.3
Other	14.5	5.1	6.6	7.8	1.4	2.1	10.8	4.5	5.1
Gender: household members (%)									
Male	18.9	81.1	51.7	14.6	85.4	51.1	11.7	88.3	51.4
Female	17.2	85.4	48.3	13.5	86.5	48.9	11.6	88.4	48.6
All	18.1	81.9	100.0	14.1	85.9	100.0	11.6	88.4	100.0
Age groups: household members (%) and other statistics									
Less than 15	41.5	44.3	43.8	37.5	44.1	43.2	36.6	42.3	41.7
15–64	57.8	53.8	54.6	61.0	53.4	54.4	60.7	54.6	55.2
65+	0.7	1.9	1.6	1.4	2.5	2.4	2.5	2.9	2.9
Median age (years)	–	–	18.3	–	–	21.2	20.0	18.0	19.0
Dependency ratio (%)	73.0	85.9	83.2	63.8	87.3	83.9	64.4	82.8	80.8

For sources and notes, see Appendix Table A.1. Dash (–) indicates estimates not available.

The age structure of PNG's population has changed little since 1996, including the median age and the dependency ratio (i.e. the ratio of those aged less than 15 or more than 65 divided by those in the economically active 15–65 age range). However, the urban dependency ratio fell more (from 73 per cent in 1996 to 64 per cent in 2016–18), indicating some degree of urban ageing, and resulting in a growing gap between the urban and rural dependency ratio, from 13 to 17 percentage points. A higher dependency ratio is often associated with chronic poverty (Lawson et al., 2006) and vulnerability to poverty and malnutrition (Anríquez and Stloukal, 2008).

Data relating to women's marital status, childbearing and fertility preferences are shown in Table 6.13.

Consistent with the rise in the share of female-headed households between 1996 and 2016–18, the proportion of women who are married decreased from 73 per cent to 66 per cent. However, the median age of marriage is unchanged at 20 since 1996. Polygyny (the practice of having more than one wife) has become more common, with the share of women in polygynous relationships increasing from 14 per cent to 18 per cent.

Table 6.13: Marriage and childbearing (1996–2018).

	1996			2006			2016–18		
	Urban	Rural	Total	Urban	Rural	Total	Urban	Rural	Total
Women's marital status (%) and age at marriage									
Polygynous	10.3	15.2	14.2	18.7	18.2	18.3	18.8	18.1	18.2
Unmarried	–	–	20.9	–	–	23.7	–	–	26.1
Married/living together	–	–	72.6	–	–	69.7	–	–	66.1
Widowed/divorced/separated	–	–	6.3	–	–	6.6	–	–	7.9
Median age at marriage among women 25–49	20.3	19.7	19.9	20.5	19.7	19.8	20.8	20.3	20.4
Age at first birth (%) and related statistics									
No birth	–	–	29.4	–	–	31.6	37.4	31.0	31.8
<18	–	–	15.7	–	–	15.9	11.1	15.2	14.7
18–21	–	–	33.1	–	–	28.8	26.4	28.3	28.0
22+	–	–	21.9	–	–	23.6	25.1	25.5	25.5
Median age at first birth among women 25–49	20.9	21.1	21.0	20.8	20.9	20.8	22.2	21.8	21.9
Teenage childbearing (%)	13.8	13.9	13.8	12.5	13.7	12.9	9.8	12.5	12.1
Median birth interval (months)	32.7	32.4	32.5	28.2	28.8	28.7	37.4	32.9	33.2

For sources and notes, see Appendix Table A.1. Dash (–) indicates estimates not available. Percentages may not add up to 100 due to small share of missing/'do not know' responses.

Women's median age at first birth increased marginally from 21 in 1996 and 2006 to 22 in 2016–18. The share of teenage mothers also fell marginally overall, but more in urban areas (14 per cent in 1996 to 10 per cent in 2016–18). The median birth interval remained the same (33 months).

Table 6.14 shows a range of reproductive health indicators relating to contraceptive use, and the provision of antenatal care and care at birth.

Table 6.14: Women's reproductive health and care (1996–2018).

	1996			2006			2016–18		
	Urban	Rural	Total	Urban	Rural	Total	Urban	Rural	Total
Contraceptive use (%)									
Knowledge of any method	85.7	74.2	76.4	94.1	80.9	82.8	98.4	86.1	87.6
Contraceptive prevalence rate	35.8	23.5	25.9	44.1	30.5	32.4	50.2	34.9	36.7
Antenatal care provision (%)									
Skilled provider	94.8	73.7	77.5	93.6	77.0	79.3	87.4	74.2	75.7
Unskilled provider	0.5	2.8	2.5	1.2	2.9	2.5	0.2	0.3	0.3
No antenatal care	4.7	23.5	20.0	3.4	18.2	16.2	12.4	25.5	24.0
% mothers who received tetanus toxoid injection during pregnancy	85.6	65.0	68.8	83.1	67.6	69.6	80.0	61.3	63.5
Place of birth (%)									
Baby delivered in health facility	87.4	42.9	51.0	88.8	47.3	52.0	86.7	51.9	55.8

For sources and notes, see Appendix Table A.1. Percentages may not add up to 100 due to small share of missing/'do not know' responses.

The share of the female population with an awareness of contraceptive methods has increased from 76 per cent in 1996 to 88 per cent in 2016–18. However, actual use of contraceptive methods remains much lower, though has also risen over the same period, from 26 per cent to 37 per cent.

There was no increase in the share of women who received antenatal care from a skilled provider. A quarter of women did not receive any antenatal care in 2016–18, a slight increase from 1996. Tetanus toxoid injections are given to mothers during pregnancy to prevent neonatal tetanus, a major cause of early infant death in many developing countries. Again, there was no increase in the share of women who received such an injection, which remained at around two-thirds.

Access to proper medical attention and hygienic conditions during delivery can reduce the risk of death or serious illness to both the mother and the baby (NSO, 2009). There was a small increase in the share of rural women who delivered birth in a health facility: from 43 per cent in 1996 to 52 per cent in 2016–18.

Conclusion

This chapter has used the PNG 1996, 2006 and 2016–18 DHSs to examine whether living standards have improved in PNG over the last two decades. The results obtained can be divided into three groups.

First, there are clearly some ways in which living standards have improved over the last two decades. Many more households have rainwater tanks; more children are at school, albeit from a low base; and childhood mortality rates have continued to fall. These positive results reflect the positive impact of economic growth on household income, and on increased government revenue and therefore spending in the case of education. It is striking that childhood mortality rates have improved despite worsening vaccination rates.

The second group of results are the areas of regress. The clearest examples of this are plummeting vaccination rates and levels of access to traditional media. These would seem to be cases of worsening governance leading to poorer service delivery despite economic growth.

Finally, there are areas of stagnation. For example, there is no growth in the share of non-agricultural jobs post-2006, a key indicator of economic transformation. There is also little sign of improved status for women. Although women are more likely to be heads of households, they are hardly marrying later, or having children later, and they are hardly having fewer children. Access to contraception has improved, but remains low, and women are no more likely to receive antenatal care than they were 20 years ago.

This third group of results is perhaps the most worrying, as it suggests that, despite some short-term gains from growth, there is little sign of the structural transformation needed for sustained and successful development. Clearly, shifting employment away from agriculture is a critical part of the development process. The link from empowerment of women to economic development is also now widely accepted. For example, the World Bank argues that gender equality 'not only guarantees basic rights but also plays a vital role in promoting the robust, shared growth needed to end extreme poverty' (World Bank, 2014, p. xi; see also Duflo, 2012).

Interestingly, the analysis also shows that urban areas are less likely to show improvements in living standards and are more likely to show declines than rural areas. We interpret this as being due to the growth of urban settlements. The result is a tendency towards convergence between urban and rural living standards. This in turn is consistent with the low rate of urbanisation in PNG. If the superiority of living standards in urban areas becomes less obvious, then fewer households will migrate from the countryside to the towns and cities.

This is the first study to make use of the three DHS surveys to ask this very basic question about whether living standards have improved or not in PNG. Much more analysis could and should be done, ideally with the raw data, though this seems no longer to be publicly available (despite the donor funding that all DHS surveys have received), except for the most recent round. The lack of interest in movement in basic economic, social and health indicators over time speaks to the political economy of PNG. Until politicians are held accountable for improvements or stagnation in household welfare across the country, any resource boom is likely only to bring temporary and superficial improvements in living standards, rather than the structural change needed to transform the daily life of everyday Papua New Guineans.

Acknowledgements

The authors thank their colleagues at The Australian National University and University of Papua New Guinea for their insights and comments, and the participants of the October 2020 workshop to discuss draft chapters, in particular Dr Cate Rogers and Dr Eugene Ezebilo for their excellent comments.

References

Anand, S. and Bärnighausen, T. (2004). Human resource and health outcomes: Cross-country econometric study. *The Lancet, 364*, 1603–09. doi.org/10.1016/S0140-6736(04)17313-3.

Anand, S. and Ravallion. M. (1993). Human development in poor countries: On the role of private incomes and public services. *Journal of Economic Perspectives, 7*, 133–50. doi.org/10.1257/jep.7.1.133.

Anríquez, G. and Stloukal, L. (2008). Rural population change in developing countries: Lessons for policymaking. *European View, 7*, 309–17. doi.org/10.1007/s12290-008-0045-7.

Bourke, M. and Allen, B. (2021). *Estimating the population of Papua New Guinea in 2020*. Development Policy Centre Discussion Paper, 90. doi.org/10.2139/ssrn.3770356.

Duflo, E. (2012). Women empowerment and economic development. *Journal of Economic Literature, 50*(4), 1051–79. doi.org/10.1257/jel.50.4.1051.

Fewtrell, M. S. (2004). The long-term benefits of having been breast-fed. *Current Paediatrics, 14*, 97–103. doi.org/10.1016/j.cupe.2003.11.010.

Gibson, J. (2012). *Papua New Guinea poverty profile: Based on the household income and expenditure survey*. Technical report.

Gibson, J. and Rozelle, S. (2003). Poverty and access to roads in Papua New Guinea. *Economic Development and Cultural Change, 52*(1), 159–85. doi.org/10.1086/380424.

Harttgen, K. and Misselhorn, M. (2006). *A multilevel approach to explain child mortality and undernutrition in South Asia and Sub-Saharan Africa*. University of Göttingen.

Hurney, M. (2017). *Short changed: The human and economic cost of child undernutrition in Papua New Guinea*. Save the children Australia. www.savethechildren.org.au/getmedia/565e0352-6a4f-46c1-bea8-331acd1b4c8c/png-nutrition-report.pdf.aspx.

Jha, R. and Dang, T. (2010). Vulnerability to poverty in Papua New Guinea in 1996. *Asian Economic Journal, 24*(3), 235–51. doi.org/10.1111/j.1467-8381.2010.02038.x.

Lawson, D., Mckay, A. and Okidi, J. (2006). Poverty persistence and transitions in Uganda: A combined qualitative and quantitative analysis. *The Journal of Development Studies, 42*(7), 1225–51. doi.org/10.1080/00220380600884191.

León-Cava, N., Lutter, C., Ross, J. and Martin, L. (2002). *Quantifying the benefits of breast-feeding: A summary of the evidence*. Pan American Health Organization.

National Statistical Office. (1997). *Papua New Guinea demographic and health survey 1996 national report*. National Statistical Office. tinyurl.com/NSOdemographichealthsurvey1996.

National Statistical Office. (2009). *Papua New Guinea demographic and health survey 2006 national report*. National Statistical Office. www.nso.gov.pg/wpfd_file/demographic-health-survey-2006-report/.

National Statistical Office. (2019). *Papua New Guinea demographic and health survey 2016–18 national report*. National Statistical Office and ICF. dhsprogram.com/pubs/pdf/FR364/FR364.pdf.

Pritchett, L. and Summers, L. (1996). Wealthier is healthier. *Journal of Human Resources, 31*, 841–68. doi.org/10.2307/146149.

United Nations. (2017). *Household size and composition around the world*. United Nations Department of Economic and Social Affairs. www.un.org/en/development/desa/population/publications/pdf/popfacts/PopFacts_2017-2.pdf.

World Bank. (2013). *Navigating turbulent waters: Addressing looming policy challenges for revived growth and improved living standards*. documents1.worldbank.org/curated/en/916051468145186292/pdf/832420BRI0PNG000Box379886B00PUBLIC0.pdf.

World Bank. (2014). *Voice and agency: Empowering women and girls for shared prosperity*. World Bank.

World Health Organization. (2007). *Evidence on the long-term effects of breast-feeding: Systematic reviews and meta-analyses*. World Health Organization.

Appendix: Definitions and data notes

Table A.1: Definitions and data notes.

Variable	Table	Household, male or female individual questionnaire	Raw and/or published data used for 2016–18	Definitions and data notes
Eligible women/men	Various	Male and female individual	Raw and published	All women or men aged 15–49 years in the selected households. For some specific characteristics, only currently married women are treated as eligible.
Non-agricultural economic activity	6.2	Household for 1996 and 2006; male and female individual for 2016–18	Raw	Women and men aged 15–49 who were currently employed or had worked in non-agricultural economic activity or activities in the last seven days before the survey. The denominator is all women or all men or all persons.
Household durable goods	6.3	Household	Published	Information on mobile phones and computers was collected for the first time in 2016–18 DHS. Percentages are calculated out of total households.
Floor type	6.4	Household	Raw and published	Natural floor includes earth and sand. Rudimentary floor materials include wood planks and palm/bamboo. Finished floor includes polished wood, vinyl/asphalt strips, ceramic tiles, cement, carpet and unpolished floor. Mean persons per sleeping room is the total household size divided by number of rooms used for sleeping.

Variable	Table	Household, male or female individual questionnaire	Raw and/or published data used for 2016–18	Definitions and data notes
Sanitation facilities	6.5	Household	Published	Flush toilet includes own and shared flush/pour flush to piped sewer system, septic tank, pit latrine or other places. Pit latrine includes all types of traditional and improved pit latrines. Other includes composting toilet, bucket system, hanging toilet/hanging latrine, etc.
Sources of water				Sources of water are reclassified to compare across 1996, 2006 and 2016–18 DHS. Piped water includes piped into dwelling, own or neighbour's yard/plot, public tap or standpipe, tube well or borehole. Dug well includes water well in yard as well as public well. Rainwater and tank include rainwater, communal tank and tanker truck. Surface water includes water sourced from river, dam, lake, pond, stream, canal, irrigation channel or spring.
School attendance	6.6	Household	Raw and published	School attendance is defined in relation to the school-going population, aged five years and above for 1996 and 2006 DHS and aged 5–24 years in 2016–18 DHS. For the sake of analysis, only 6–20-year-olds were covered for all years. All estimates for 1996 and 2006 for each age group (6–10, 11–15 and 16–20) are used from NSO (1997, 2009). Due to non-availability of population data for each relevant subgroup for 1996 and 2006, all estimates for combined age group 6–20 for all the years are simple averages of estimates for individual age groups (6–10, 11–15 and 16–20). Comparison of 1996 (rural + urban combined), 2006 (rural + urban combined) and 2016–18 estimates show that the difference in weighted average and simple averages are not substantial.

Variable	Table	Household, male or female individual questionnaire	Raw and/or published data used for 2016–18	Definitions and data notes
Educational attainment	6.7	Household	Raw and published	Educational attainment was recorded for population aged five years and above. Population with no education include those who were currently in school but had not completed Grade 1 at the time of the survey.
Access to mass media	6.8	Male and female individual	Published	Traditional mass media includes newspaper, radio or television. 1996 estimates for men were not available.
Child mortality rate (C)	6.9	Female individual	Raw; all 2016–18 estimates were recomputed with a reference period of ten years preceding interview to make them comparable to 1996 and 2006 DHS estimates	The probability of children dying between first and fifth birthday, expressed per 1,000 children surviving to age 12 months.
Infant mortality rate (I)				The probability of newly born babies dying between birth and the first birthday, expressed per 1,000 live births.
Neonatal mortality rate (NN)				The probability of newly born babies dying within the first month of life, expressed per 1,000 live births.
Post-neonatal mortality rate (PNN)				The probability of infant deaths between one month and one year, expressed per 1,000 live births.
Under-five mortality rate (U5)				The probability of children dying between birth and the fifth birthday, expressed per 1,000 live births.

Variable	Table	Household, male or female individual questionnaire	Raw and/or published data used for 2016–18	Definitions and data notes
Basic vaccinations	6.10	Female individual	Published	The basic vaccine bundle included DPT in 1996 and 2006 DHS, and the pentavalent vaccine in 2016–18 DHS.
Median breastfeeding duration (months)			Published	Number of months of breastfeeding that half of the children born in the three years preceding the survey experienced.
No initial breastfeeding (%)			Raw; the 2016–18 estimates were recomputed with a three-year reference period to make them comparable to 1996 and 2006 DHS estimates.	Proportion of children who were born in the three years preceding the surveys but never breastfed.
Age-specific fertility rate (ASFR)	6.11	Female individual	Raw; all 2016–18 estimates were recomputed with reference period five years preceding interview to make them comparable to 1996 and 2006 DHS estimates	The number of live births to women in a particular age group divided by the number of women in that age group five years preceding the interview.
Total fertility rate (TFR)				The average number of children a woman in the age group 15–49 would have by the end of her childbearing years if she passes through those years bearing children at the currently observed ASFR.
General fertility rate (GFR)				The number of births occurring during a specific period divided by the number of women in the reproductive age 15–44 years.
Crude birth rate (CBR)				The number of live births per 1,000 population in a given year.
Fertility preferences		Male and female individual	Raw and published	Fertility preferences constitute whether currently married women and men aged 15–49 want more children and expected ideal number of children.

Variable	Table	Household, male or female individual questionnaire	Raw and/or published data used for 2016–18	Definitions and data notes
Median age (years)	6.12	Household	Raw	Age that divides a population such that half of the population is below and the rest is above median age.
Dependency ratio				The number of persons in the 'dependent ages' (less than 15 years and 65 years and over) divided by the 'economically active' persons in the population (aged 15–64) multiplied by 100.
Median age at first marriage	6.13	Female individual	Published	Age by which half of ever married women aged 25–49 years have had their first marriage.
Age at first birth (shares)				Shares by the age at which women aged 15–49 years had their first child.
Median age at first birth				Age by which half of women currently aged 25–49 years had their first child.
Teenage childbearing				Share of women aged 15–19 years who had given birth or are pregnant with their first child.
Median birth interval (months)				Number of months since the preceding birth by which half of children are born in the five years before the survey.

Variable	Table	Household, male or female individual questionnaire	Raw and/or published data used for 2016–18	Definitions and data notes
Awareness of contraceptive methods	6.14	Female individual	Published	Percentage of currently married women aged 15–49 years who had heard about at least one method of contraception.
Contraceptive prevalence rate				Percentage of currently married women aged 15–49 years who were currently using, or whose sexual partner was currently using, at least one method of contraception, regardless of the method used, at the time of the survey.
Skilled/unskilled provider			Raw; all 2016–18 estimates were recomputed with reference period three years preceding interview to make them comparable to 1996 and 2006 DHS estimates	Skilled providers include doctor, midwife, nurse (including trained community health workers) and trained village health volunteer. Unskilled providers include village birth attendant, female relative and others.
Health facility				Health facilities and personnel include government or church or private hospitals, health centres, mobile clinics, aid posts, community health workers, private doctors, chemists and others.
Tetanus toxoid injection				An injection given to women aged 15–49 during pregnancy to prevent newborn babies from neonatal tetanus. The percentage reported is out of all women aged 15–49 with a live birth in the three years before the survey.

Source: NSO (1997, 2009, 2019) and authors.

Part III: Society

7

Uneven development and its effects: Livelihoods and urban and rural spaces in Papua New Guinea

John Cox, Grant W. Walton, Joshua Goa and Dunstan Lawihin

Abstract

In this chapter, we examine the uneven nature of development within and between rural and urban spaces in Papua New Guinea (PNG). We focus on economic activities in urban and rural spaces and the ways these have shaped social and environmental outcomes. This analysis highlights three key issues. First, it shows the importance of thinking about development processes, networks and enclaves in addition to more traditional ways of framing development challenges and opportunities. Second, it points to the importance of PNG's rural spaces for policymaking and politics. Finally, it notes that while large-scale development projects, such as mining and liquified natural gas, have significantly shaped urban and rural spaces over the past two decades, due to economic shifts, it is becoming less likely PNG will reshape its urban and rural spaces as dramatically in the years to come.

Introduction

In this chapter, like others before us (e.g. Connell, 1997), we highlight the geographical diversity of economic opportunities across Papua New Guinea (PNG) and show that this diversity is not confined to national and subnational administrative boundaries. Indeed, we suggest PNG is a patchwork quilt of vastly different types of economic activity that shape social relations and the surrounding environment in very different ways. This includes resource enclaves that dramatically reshape the physical landscape, while also changing social and economic relations by attracting new concentrations of people who migrate to these areas for paid work, artisanal mining or to claim a share of royalty payments. Such projects often sit beside economic activities that can be traced back thousands of years. Other patches of our metaphorical quilt might be geographically small but provide an even greater economic diversity. Urban areas, for instance, provide many different types of legal and illegal economic opportunities. The patches of economic activity of our metaphorical quilt are sewn together by a complex network of people and things that move across districts and provinces and around the globe.

In focusing on the geographical diversity of economic activity, our analysis differs from studies that assess the nature of development through aggregated data tied to administrative scales; for example, analysis that compares levels of development between provincial and district governments (National Research Institute, 2010). We also move beyond analyses solely focused on the national scale, what some refer to as 'methodological nationalism' (Wimmer and Schiller, 2002). 'Methodological nationalism' includes economic and other analyses that draw on national-level data to describe the nature of PNG's development challenges. In addition, we push against the 'localised particularism' of some studies that focus on one community, town or location. Rather, we suggest that a broader and more fluid understanding of the processes and networks of PNG's patchwork quilt of economic activity can provide insights into the country's key social and environmental challenges.

Having said this, our analysis does not include all types of economic activities in PNG; for example, we do not focus on the important and often overlooked contribution of those providing unpaid housework and care. Including all types of economic activity would require another few chapters, perhaps a book. While colourful, we admit our patchwork quilt has some holes in it, which we will leave for others to sew together. The key takeaway from our analysis is that in PNG, economic opportunities and activities vary greatly between and within urban and rural spaces; and that, as the least urbanised country in the world, PNG is somewhat unique in the way its citizens have responded to this uneven development.

The chapter first provides a brief history of urban and rural development in PNG; in this section, we highlight some of the historical processes that have shaped economic and social development in the country. In the second section, we highlight the uneven nature of development in urban areas. The next section focuses on rural areas and the unique nature of development in these spaces. The fourth section reflects on the way PNG's uneven development has shaped social relations and the environment. Finally, we conclude by reflecting on what these findings mean for policymaking and research.

A (very) short history of urban and rural development

PNG's environmental, political, economic and social landscape has been significantly shaped by the long history of human settlement that dates back over 50,000 years. Over that time, Melanesian people established highly sophisticated social systems that involved extensive trade networks over land and sea, sometimes including large villages (Irwin et al., 2019). The movement of people and objects across what is now known as PNG changed the landscape in very different ways. For example, some areas in PNG have some of humanity's oldest records of agriculture. Archaeological evidence from Kuk in the upper Wahgi Valley in Western Highlands Province, suggests agricultural practices began around 10,000 years ago (Bourke, 2009). Pre-colonial trade also shaped the environment as well as economic and social systems. The introduction of sweet potato around 300 years ago helped to improve food security, and it continues to be a key staple for much of the current day population. Allen et al. (2005) make a convincing case that environmental factors, such as soil quality, reliable rainfall and topography, have been the long-term determinants of poverty in PNG even before the colonial period. They argue that subsequent investments in infrastructure and service delivery have largely followed the initial environmental endowments of areas such as the Gazelle Peninsula or the coffee growing areas of the Highlands.

The nature of the uneven development we see in PNG today can also be directly traced back to the country's colonial history. While Europeans and others made sporadic contact with Papua New Guineans from around the mid-1500s, colonial engagement from the late nineteenth century most significantly shaped the country's development infrastructure. As European economic and political interests expanded into the Pacific in the nineteenth century, colonial powers established small towns from which they extended their rule (urban centres were not a feature of pre-colonial Melanesia [Connell, 1997]). These towns were often set up in locations with access to natural harbours that could link the newly established colony to global markets. In 1873, the English Captain John Moresby claimed Port Moresby for Britain, naming the new settlement after his father. In part, Port Moresby prospered because colonial powers were able to ship goods in and out of Fairfax Harbour. In 1884, Germany annexed what was then known as New Guinea, the northern part of PNG, establishing their colonial capital at Rabaul, a township planned and built around the sheltered seaport of Simpson Harbour. The British and German halves of PNG came together following World War I when Australian troops occupied German New Guinea and subsequently administered both territories until PNG's independence in 1975.

Colonialism has also shaped rural development across PNG through the establishment of various enterprises, such as plantations, and through the introduction of systems of colonial governance, based at towns and district centres, as well as the reorganisation of rural life from dispersed hamlets to bigger villages that were more easily managed by colonial authorities. Some scholars have argued that the ongoing legacies of these colonial engagements could explain the different development trajectories of groups across the country (Bray, 1985; Connell, 1997; Errington and Gewertz, 1993; Walton, 2019). For example, Bray (1985) has argued that, because they were in contact with Europeans earlier than other Papua New Guineans, the Tolai and Duke of York islanders of East New Britain were provided with a 'head start' in education and economic development. Walton (2019) has suggested that the nature of colonial settlement – along with geographical, political and cultural factors – helps to explain the divergent development trajectories of Gulf and East New Britain Provinces.

Uneven development and urban Papua New Guinea

Broadly, urbanisation refers to a process of urban growth through citizens moving from rural to urban areas. Around the world, urbanisation is occurring. In 2018, 55 per cent of the world's population lived in urban areas, up from 30 per cent in 1950 (United Nations Department of Economic and Social Affairs [UN DESA], 2019, p. 1). With greater urbanisation and overall growth of the global population, urban areas across the globe could add another 2.5 billion people to their populations over the next three decades. By 2050, the proportion of people living in urban areas is set to increase to 68 per cent (UN DESA, 2019, p. 1). Papua New Guinea has also experienced urbanisation, though to a lesser extent than other countries in the region and around the world. Indeed, the World Bank (2022) calculates that PNG is the least urbanised country in the world in terms of the percentage of the population living in urban areas. Figure 7.1 shows that levels of urbanisation in PNG are lower than they are for the Melanesian region and Oceania (which includes Pacific Island countries and Australia and New Zealand).[1] In 1950, only 1.7 per cent of PNG's citizens lived in urban areas; by 2018, that figure had risen to 13.2 per cent. Census data from 2011 suggests that 40 per cent of people residing in urban areas were not born there (Pryke and Barker, 2017, p. 31). While predicting demographic trends in PNG is difficult due to uncertainties around the reliability of some of the underlying data and urban boundary definitions (see Allen, 2014; Pryke and Barker, 2017), the UN projects that, by 2050, a quarter of PNG's citizens will live in urban areas (UN DESA, 2019, p. 35).

It is important to note that 'urbanisation' differs from 'urbanism', which for our purposes – and reflecting our sociological backgrounds – refers to patterns of social life within urban populations (Scott, 2015). This interpretation can be traced back to Louis Wirth (1938), who coined the term urbanism and whose essay 'Urbanism as a Way of Life', which focuses on minority groups and mass media in the United States, is a seminal study in urban studies literature. Since this time, studies of urbanism have highlighted the social and environmental dynamics that shape cities and those living in them. Below we examine the nature of urbanism in PNG.

1 Oceania in Figure 7.1 includes Australia and New Zealand along with countries from Melanesia, Micronesia and Polynesia. Melanesia includes Fiji, New Caledonia, PNG, Solomon Islands and Vanuatu.

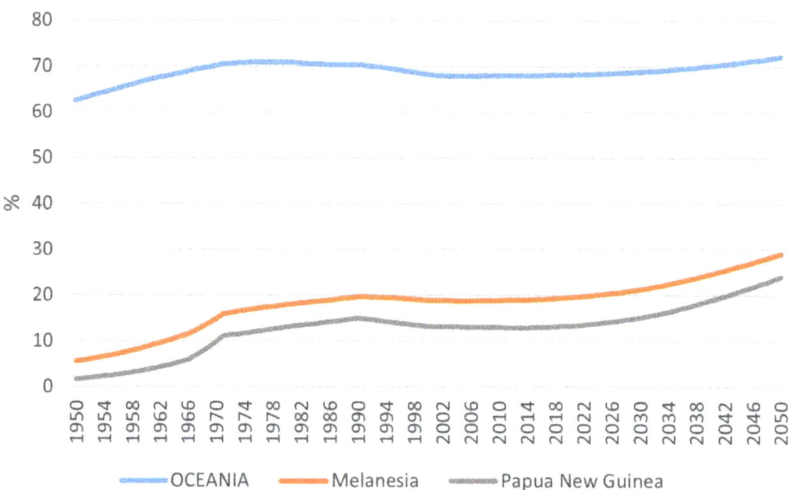

Figure 7.1: Percentage of urbanites: PNG, Melanesia and Oceania.
Source: Adapted from UN DESA (2019).

For many (particularly those outside of the country), PNG's urban landscape is riven with crime, conflict and dysfunction. Indeed, the Economist Intelligence Unit regularly ranks Port Moresby as one of the least liveable cities in the world; in 2019, it rated PNG's capital as the sixth least liveable city (Buckley, 2019), a slight improvement from 2004 when it was listed as the world's least liveable city (*Sydney Morning Herald*, 2010). However, such assessments are based on a narrow sample of wealthy expatriate businesspeople and so ignore the perceptions of the many Papua New Guineans who make cities their homes. As we highlight below, focusing on PNG's unique forms of urbanism reveals a more nuanced picture than such broadbrush assessments suggest.

The colonial experience shaped the development of urban areas in PNG. Port Moresby is built on the land of the Koita and Motu peoples. Their lives have been profoundly reshaped by the appropriation of land and subsequent urbanisation of Port Moresby (Goddard, 2010). In his history of Port Moresby, Oram argued that social problems – including poverty, high crime rates and social disorder – arose during the colonial period due to administrative institutions and policies that reflected 'Western needs and goals, unrelated to the needs and aspirations of the Papua New Guinean population' (Oram, 1976, p. x). Colonial towns were originally established as enclaves for European settlers, traders and administrators. The movement, residence and behaviour of Melanesian people in these towns were tightly regulated. Colonial administrations needed (mostly male) workers but envisaged their presence in town as only temporary and not as long term or permanent.

Goddard (2005) noted that the city's settlements grew quickly in the first decade after World War II due to the lifting of previous restrictions over indigenous urban migration, which allowed women to join their husbands and raise families in town. This trend has increased, particularly since independence. However, Port Moresby and other cities remain places where women tread carefully and work hard to make themselves feel 'at home in the city' (Demian, 2017; Spark, 2014b, 2019). Recent research conducted in Lae has highlighted the prevalence of family and sexual violence in urban areas and the lack of services for both men and women to address this problem (Rooney et al., 2019). Hayward-Jones (2016) noted that:

> Port Moresby, Lae, and Mount Hagen have high crime rates. Disturbingly, the physical features of the business centres and residential areas in those urban centres are security walls.[2]

For several decades, people from all areas of the country have been making their homes in Port Moresby, Lae and other towns. The size, geography and social fabric of these urban centres vary significantly. While Port Moresby is home to over 360,000 people, the population of Lae is less than half that number (150,000), with other towns such as Wewak, Madang and Mount Hagen smaller again. These towns are home to different types of economic activities and have different relationships to the people in their hinterlands, with some places, such as Madang, becoming home to large numbers of settlers from across the northern coastal provinces and the Highlands.

Most urban residents live in settlements. UN Habitat (2010, p. 9) estimated that around 45 per cent of Port Moresby's residents live in settlements, which 'are characterized by a lack of planning, poor infrastructure and a lack of urban services'. Koczberski et al. (2001) noted that every major town in PNG (including Port Moresby, Lae, Madang, Rabaul, Kokopo, Goroka and Kimbe) has attempted (sometimes violent) squatter clearances. Many urban residents 'return' to rural homelands to retire at the end of their careers, and the custom of sending bodies 'back

2 See also Chapter 4, this volume.

home' for burial remains strong, as do remittances to kin, even as these are becoming understood as 'development' (Cox, 2021; Dalsgaard, 2013; Rasmussen, 2015). However, new generations of people who have grown up in towns and who are not familiar with the day-to-day rhythms of village life are now growing in number. These people have made cities their permanent homes.

Nevertheless, the expectation that Melanesians do not rightly belong in urban areas and should see their true homes as being in 'the village' has largely been accepted as common sense, as even the urban elite feel some discomfort with their position within the nation (Foster, 2008; Golub, 2014; Martin, 2010). This sense of discomfort has a long history. Indeed, in 1973, PNG's first prime minister, Sir Michael Somare, argued against developing cities (Connell, 1997, p. 187). In some ways, the legitimacy of Melanesian urbanism is yet to be established, more than 40 years after Somare expressed concern about developing cities and Levine and Levine (1979) wrote their study of 'ambivalent townsmen'.

While urban areas are home to better government services than rural and remote locations (Brydon and Lawihin, 2016; Howes et al., 2014), urban investment often exacerbates urban inequalities. Because urban needs are imagined as elite – and because of the ways government investment has been co-opted by political patronage – spending on urban infrastructure is often directed to iconic projects (see below) that do little to improve the day-to-day lives of urban residents. Housing, water supply and sanitation remain pressing challenges in all PNG cities, but particularly in the 'settlements' that are home to the majority of urban residents. Settlements are found on both public and customary land and have a reputation for poverty and crime. This stereotype fails to consider the strong communities that are found in settlements (Craig and Porter, 2018; Rooney, 2017) and the increasing number of salaried wage earners from the lower middle classes who cannot afford to live elsewhere in town and have often made substantial investments in settlement housing, even without the security of land tenure (Rooney, 2017). Despite these changed circumstances and pressing needs, there are few signs of a developing urban political agenda, even among the emerging middle class (Barbara et al., 2015).

In many ways, large-scale infrastructure investment has been shaped by the aspirations of PNG elites to position Port Moresby as a global city and, in turn, position the country as a regional middle power. Examples of this includes investments in the Jackson's international airport, new roads, and sporting and conference facilities around Port Moresby in the lead up to hosting major international events such as the Pacific Games (2015), FIFA U-20 Women's World Cup (2016) and APEC (2018). Major events that are directed to an international audience typically neglect the needs of ordinary people and the urban poor and may even result in intensified policing of marginalised groups seen as undermining the modernist aesthetics of orderliness and prosperity. Many global cities forcibly relocate homeless people in advance of international events; in Port Moresby, people were evicted from settlements to make way for roads and accommodation (Rooney, 2017, p. 118). Informal economic systems are also regular targets of such measures aiming to 'modernise' urban spaces. In PNG's cities, betel nut sellers exemplify these tensions. Betel nut vendors sell a national commodity that represents Melanesian solidarity and sociality, yet they are also spoken of in popular debate as a criminal underclass whose activities undermine law and order and public health and have even been the target of the notorious 'buai ban' (see Busse and Sharp, 2019; Hukula, 2019; Rooney, 2019). While a few small- and medium-scale local entrepreneurs have emerged, they often struggle to sustain their businesses (Imbun, 2016).

Reminders of large-scale crime, dispossession and corruption are also etched into PNG's urban environments. According to Lasslett (2018), urbanisation includes anti-competitive practices, corruption and state-corporate violence, which have helped reduce costs associated with acquiring high-value real estate. His analysis, which focused on the dispossession of Paga Hill in Port Moresby and land grabs in Madang, is a reminder of the uneven outcomes associated with urbanisation shaped by global capitalism and political cronyism.

While urban areas face many challenges, in recent years there have been more sustained attempts to improve living standards in Port Moresby. These include the *National Urbanisation Policy 2010–2030* (Office of Urbanisation, 2010), which aims to address the social and economic challenges of urbanisation through better management of urban areas, *Papua New Guinea Vision 2050* (National Strategic Plan Taskforce, 2009) and the *National Strategy for Responsible Sustainable Development* (Department of National Planning and Monitoring, 2014). National Capital District Governor Powes Parkop has also been a strong supporter of creating better public spaces and nurturing a sense of belonging through the Yumi Lukautim Mosbi project. The National Housing Corporation has tried to address housing affordability but, as Ezebilo (2017) has argued, the beneficiaries of their programs have been the middle class, which already has the capacity for home ownership, not low-income households. In turn, the beneficiaries of urbanism in PNG are largely determined by social class.

Uneven development and rural Papua New Guinea

PNG's rural population still relies on subsistence horticulture for food and shelter, many using ancient cultivation, hunting and fishing techniques that have proved their worth over centuries, even in the face of more recently introduced technologies and systems of governance. Agriculture dominates the formal rural economy of PNG (Bourke and Harwood, 2009). Most of the rural population supplements subsistence production with other cash livelihoods, growing commodities for export, or fresh food or betel nut for domestic consumption (Sharp and Busse, 2019, p. 195). However, we should not assume a hearty 'subsistence affluence' to be the state of all or even most rural communities. There is considerable variation in rural livelihoods and incomes and, depending on local environmental conditions, seasonal and extreme weather and geological events, access to towns and markets, and proximity to mining operations or other major enterprises, many households struggle to meet basic needs and have little support from state services (Howes et al., 2014).

In the colonial period, much good agricultural land was used for plantations, growing coconuts for sale to an export market, with the profits accruing to Christian missions, settler expatriates or parent companies in Britain, Germany and Australia – all with little regard shown for the welfare of Melanesian labourers or customary landowners. In the 1960s, the Australian Government facilitated labour schemes that brought Sepik, Chimbu and Engan workers to oil palm plantations in West New Britain and Oro Provinces. These settlers were given leaseholds on 'blocks' of plantation land, giving rise to tensions between leaseholding migrant labourers and indigenous landowners (Koczberski and Curry, 2004). Smallholder blocks have mostly replaced the larger plantations in the production of coffee, cocoa, copra and other commodities (Sharp and Busse, 2019, p. 198).

As PNG moved towards independence in the 1970s, plans were made for localisation of agricultural and other enterprises. Ramu Sugar (now Ramu Agri-Industries) was initiated by the PNG Government in 1977, with a feasibility study by Booker Tate International, the British parent company that has managed the sugar operations since inception. Ramu Sugar was initially conceived as a new national industry that would supply sugar for domestic consumption (Errington and Gewertz, 2004). Today, while there is more Papua New Guinean ownership of oil palm, cocoa and coffee plantations, foreign management, capital and supply chains are still fundamental to these industries.

Allen et al. (2005) have argued that more fertile parts of the country provide a better or easier means of making a subsistence living for their inhabitants and that areas with poor soil, steep slopes, high altitude and/or high rainfall and flooding have been poor for generations, even before the introduction of colonial rule and capitalist enterprises. These environmental determinants remain relevant today, as people from these areas are more likely to migrate to more prosperous areas in search of work. Over time, the initial environmental advantages (good harbourage, fertile soil) have set in train and compounded the effects of other processes of accruing wealth and related advantages such as education, health services, shops, transportation and access to public service employment.

Rural areas with established plantations, harbours and other industries and infrastructure are relatively well serviced with commercial and public goods when compared to more remote areas and provide some indirect economic benefits for rural people living in their immediate hinterland, such as small-scale markets for garden produce. Marketing fresh vegetables for local markets has been primarily a livelihood for women that supports household needs. Men are more likely to work cultivating cash crops with their rewards often accruing to them as individuals (Curry et al., 2019). Transporting and selling garden produce over longer distances is often only marginally profitable. Over shorter distances, fresh garden produce may be combined with more profitable commodities such as betel nut. The betel nut trade has facilitated face-to-face networks between various producers and sellers along the commodity routes that link rural areas to towns (Sharp, 2016, 2019). In the Highlands, some communities close to major towns are scaling up fresh food production to a commercial scale (Sharp and Busse, 2019). Like larger towns, wealthier areas of rural PNG also become places that draw migration from other parts of the country, as those whose land does not produce a sufficient surplus for them to access education or employment from their own land – or those who do not have access to land – seek opportunities for better livelihoods (Allen et al., 2005; Bainton and Banks, 2018).

The contrast between the predominantly rural population dependent on agriculture and the national economy's reliance on resource extraction funded by international capital is stark. Indeed, PNG governments have come to depend on the resource sector to provide much-needed revenue; the figures from the World Bank (2022) show that PNG is five times more dependent on its natural resources (calculated as total natural resource rents as a percentage of GDP) than the global average. Mining, gas and oil operations provide dramatic examples of how remote places can be transformed into centres of economic activity and service provision at least during the active life of a mine. Mines are often located well away from major centres and require considerable investment in roads and other infrastructure during the construction period. Once a mine is established, modern mining companies provide a range of high-level services and facilities for their employees. These are usually better than anything the state is able to provide, particularly in remote locations and, indeed, allows the state to devolve service delivery to mining companies (Filer and Macintyre, 2006).

As Dwyer and Minnegal (1998, 2014) have shown, expectations of mineral wealth can travel ahead of the resource frontier to communities at some distance from actual resource project sites, even if they have no realistic basis for their hopes. These advantages (or anticipations of such) in turn generate in-migration of people from other areas, notably at Ok Tedi (Western Province) and Porgera (Enga Province). Over a short period, relatively sparsely populated places can become bustling towns (Bainton and Banks, 2018). As new arrivals come in search of work or to establish their claim to landowning benefits, social and administrative questions of who exactly can be recognised as 'local' become very complex (Bainton, 2017; Filer and Macintyre, 2006). Mining towns tend to be dominated by male workforces and have a reputation for social issues such as gambling, alcohol abuse and violence (Walton and Barnett, 2007). In some instances, mining sites have helped exacerbate violent conflicts between landowners, companies and the state – indeed, concerns about the local impacts of the Panguna Mine in Bougainville helped spark a long-running civil war (see Lasslett, 2014). Porgera has also had a history of violence, not least against women in the area (Johnson, 2011). Most mining companies have some commitment to creating work for local people through direct employment or through community development schemes and encouragement of small businesses (Bainton and Macintyre, 2013; Banks et al., 2013).

Extractive industries can also leave land and waterways degraded with little benefit flowing to communities. This is clearly the case in relation to the forestry industry in PNG, where 70 per cent of logging is estimated to be illegal (Lawson, 2014). Logging infrastructure, such as roads, is usually temporary and is not maintained once operations move on (Hanson et al., 2001, p. 221). Malaysian timber companies typically import their own labourers, so logging provides very limited opportunities for rural employment. However, royalties to landowners still act as an incentive, even if they flow to very few beneficiaries and cause considerable local conflict (Australian Conservation Foundation, 2006; Lattas, 2011). The forestry industry in PNG has been characterised by endemic corruption and, in recent years, has attempted to use Special Agricultural Business Leases as a means of alienating customary land (Filer, 2011; Filer and Numapo, 2017; Finau et al., 2019). Though PNG politicians have announced that these leases have been cancelled, in reality, the legal status of many Special Agricultural Business Lease agreements remain uncertain (Filer, 2019).

These findings provide a counter narrative to popular framings of the nature of rural life in the country. In public discourse, rural people in PNG are often spoken about (by development agencies or by the national middle class) as if they were frozen in a pre-colonial past, living on customary land according to the ways of their ancestors and providing for themselves without money (Cox, 2021; Tammisto, 2019). However, as the above discussion indicates, a range of capitalist enterprises interact with rural life in various ways and rural people actually move from place to place in significant numbers.

Climactic variability and geological volatility are also important factors in determining how and where rural Papua New Guineans live, and are likely to exacerbate these trends into the future. El Nino droughts and associated frosts have caused great hardship in the Highlands, disrupting essential subsistence food production and displacing thousands of people. Remittances from kinsfolk have often been more effective than large-scale relief efforts in meeting basic food needs in these disaster situations (Kanua et al., 2016). Volcanic eruptions, such as that on Manam Island, have forced thousands of people from their land and many have not been able to return (Connell and Lutkehaus, 2017). A serious earthquake in 2018 hit Hela Province, triggering landslides, death, destruction of property and mass displacement of affected people. Low-lying parts of PNG, notably the atolls of the Carteret Islands in Bougainville, have also experienced forced migration due to coastal erosion and saltwater incursions that are the effects of sinking landmasses (Connell, 2016). In the future, these areas will face further problems from rising sea levels driven by climate change.

Rural and community development

The challenges described above have been met with various attempts by governments, non-governmental organisations (NGOs), donors and others to improve rural development. While the term 'rural development' is used in a variety of ways, it can be defined as 'a sustained and sustainable process of economic, social, cultural and environmental change designed to enhance the long-term well-being of the rural community' (Moseley, 2003, p. 4). In PNG, there are signs that rural development has stagnated, particularly in terms of service delivery. Research examining changes to service delivery between 2002 and 2012 found that key services have become more difficult to access from primary schools in many provinces (Howes et al., 2014, pp. 33–35). While, over the decade, urbanites in Port Moresby had similar levels of access to banks and trade stores, access had declined in most of the provinces visited by researchers in 2012. For example, in 2012, it took respondents (head teachers) from Gulf Province 12 more hours to reach a bank and 11 more hours to reach a trade store compared to 2002 (Howes et al., 2014, pp. 34–35). By comparison, it took, on average, just one hour to reach a bank in Eastern Highlands and Enga.

Development outcomes also vary greatly across the country. For example, studies have found that primary schools in East New Britain are of higher quality than those in six other mostly rural provinces – West New Britain, Morobe, Sandaun, Eastern Highlands, Enga and Gulf (Howes et al., 2014). Likewise, East New Britain's primary health facilities are also of a higher quality. Over time, successive governments, international and local NGOs and private companies have all made attempts to address disadvantage through a range of rural development programs. In the years following independence, these were led by government policies such as the Less Developed Areas Strategy that sought to address inequality and poverty through provincial scaled Integrated Rural Development

Programs funded by the World Bank, Asian Development Bank and the Australian Aid program. Crittenden and Lea (1989) analysed a number of these programs and noted the variation in strategy and emphasis across provinces, including components of infrastructure, service improvement, and both large- and small-scale business development.

After the perceived failures of these large Integrated Rural Development Programs, rural development programs became more fragmented and focused on building smallholder production in specific industries (e.g. coffee or fisheries) or on mitigating environmental damage from logging and other industries by creating local livelihood projects as alternatives (West, 2006). Other community development initiatives led by NGOs or church agencies have focused on gender inequality and violence against women, including violence related to sorcery accusations. Given the limited scale of these programs, some have called for policymakers to draw on indigenous forms of social protection when designing social policies (Lawihin, 2017).

Changing rural politics and service delivery

Because PNG is populated by a much higher proportion of rural dwellers than urbanites, getting services out to rural and remote areas has been a key political issue. As discussed in other chapters, efforts by the PNG state to redistribute the nation's wealth have increasingly been channelled away from programs delivered by the responsible government departments to more direct disbursements by politicians through their constituency development funds. This is argued to be more effective as it bypasses cumbersome bureaucratic systems (Wiltshire, 2013). However, this kind of justification ignores worsening inequality and the weakening of accountability for public funds as development money, in many instances, becomes accessible only through political patronage (Walton et al., 2017). While constituency development funds lack the checks and balances associated with providing services through national and subnational bureaucracies, they can help cement votes in upcoming elections, though members of parliament are not always successful in securing the required number of votes (Wood, 2017).

The PNG Government works in partnership with a host of non-state actors – such as churches, NGOs, international donors and the private sector – to deliver services in rural and urban areas of PNG. However, in some sectors, the state plays a far more important role in delivering services than in others. For example, in 2012, in the education sector, the national government weakened the role of church schools in delivering the country's Tuition Fee Free (TFF) policy (Walton, 2019). Under this policy reform, the national government paid funding to both church and state schools directly, which meant that church administrators ceased directly distributing funds to their schools, although they continued to play a role in providing teachers and monitoring church schools. The policy also meant that church and state schools were, officially, unable to charge fees, leading church leaders to threaten legal action.

While the TFF policy applied to both urban and rural schools, rural and remote schools found accessing TFF funds difficult, with many head teachers having to travel for days to access a bank account to access TFF funding (Howes et al., 2014). Not allowing schools to charge fees most likely exacerbated these problems; this is particularly the case for church schools, which tend to perform better on a range of measures and operate in rural and remote areas (Howes et al., 2014). While the TFF policy initially led to increased enrolments (Howes et al., 2014), its longer-term impacts have been questioned, with research suggesting that, in some provinces, TFF reforms threatened school–community relations, undermined school quality and weakened conditions for effective service provision (Walton and Davda, 2019).

In 2020, the Marape government abolished the TFF policy, replacing it with the Government Tuition Fee Subsidy. This marks the fourth time in PNG's history that a fee-free education policy has been tried and then abolished. Under this new policy, parents initially paid 36.6 per cent of the maximum school fee limit, although political leaders from some districts and provinces promised to draw on subnational funds to continue to ensure parents would not have to pay school fees (*The National*, 2020; Rai, 2020). In turn, this likely exacerbated the uneven nature of educational service provision (and, in particular, access to schooling) across PNG. In late 2021, the Marape government announced that parents would again not have to pay primary and secondary school fees.

Uneven development, inequality and social aspiration

While the various regions of PNG have their own histories and environmental conditions that have determined their opportunities for development, several accelerating trends are increasing connections between people across the nation. These include rural to urban migration (often circular); developing domestic community chains, such as the betel nut trade (Sharp, 2016, 2019); and the emerging urban middle class with its so-called mixed marriages of people from different parts of the country. Women, in particular, are finding new modes of self-expression and new forms of community across the Pacific region through markets, church and fashion (Barnett-Naghshineh, 2019; Cox and Macintyre, 2014; Spark, 2014a). Moreover, new opportunities for communication through mobile telephones (Foster and Horst, 2018; Watson, Chapter 8, this volume) now mean that PNG is more connected as a nation than ever before. These interconnections, however, also make people more aware of socio-economic inequality and the privileges that others enjoy.

PNG's resource boom has had mixed results. The health sector faced a 'lost decade', with primary health services regressing between 2002 and 2012 (Howes et al., 2014). On the other hand, on a number of indicators – such as teacher numbers, student numbers and classroom quality – primary schools improved over the same period. Still, the expectations of great wealth from the PNG liquified natural gas project have failed to materialise in the way many hoped (Banks, 2014). Some argue that PNG would have been better off without these resource developments (Jubilee Australia, 2019).

Perhaps the most egregious example of national inequality was the building boom and purchase of luxury vehicles for dignitaries attending the 2018 APEC meeting. While the government made preparations for hosting international guests, building new infrastructure and conference facilities in Port Moresby, polio re-emerged after decades of suppression: a sign of a severely under-resourced health system under enormous pressure (Bainton and McDougall, 2021). Inequality in PNG has become far more acute than would be expected given the egalitarian aspirations outlined in the preamble to the nation's constitution. The failures of service delivery become particularly obvious along borderlands. Indeed, Moran and Curth-Bib's (2020) edited volume shows the disparity of service delivery between those living along the South Fly coast on the PNG side of the border compared to neighbours in Australia's Torres Strait Islands.

As elsewhere in the world, financial hardship and relative deprivation fuel both patronage politics (Cox, 2009; Wood, 2018) and a 'disparagement of elites' (Martin, 2013). However, some of those considered 'elite' belong to a middle class that is struggling, not only with redistributive expectations of contributing to a village 'home' (Rasmussen, 2015) or supporting '*wantoks*' in town (Monsell-Davis, 1993; Schram, 2015), but also with the cost of urban living itself (Cox, 2014, 2018; Gibson, 2019). Indeed, many urban salary earners have adopted various means of supplementing their income, both licit and illicit. These can include microenterprises such as reselling phone cards or betel nut as well as other means of accessing short-term cash through 'pay day loans' with very high interest rates, or gambling (Goddard, 2005; Pickles, 2019; Sharp et al., 2015).

While such 'popular economies' (Krige, 2011) can simply reflect the struggle to survive on very limited incomes, they often also have an aspirational element. Pyramid selling schemes, such as the Filipino scheme AIM Global and Questnet, have been popular in PNG (and many other countries in the region), promising their followers success in business while relying on an unsustainable pyramidal recruitment structure for returns. Many of these schemes market pseudoscientific health products, dietary supplements or overpriced cosmetics, and health workers are often the target of recruiters (Cox, 2019; Cox and Phillips, 2015). Participants are typically drawn into these schemes via a combination of financial need and aspiration for career or business advancement, and training focuses on the cultivation of an entrepreneurial disposition, a theme picked up in the PNG self-development scheme Personal Viability (Bainton, 2011).

In a similar vein, fraudulent Ponzi schemes – known as 'fast money schemes' – show a remarkable persistence in PNG and continue to attract 'investors' from both the grassroots and the middle class (Cox, 2018). Fast money schemes claim to be legitimate investments but promise unrealistically high returns (e.g. 100 per cent returns per month) and only pay early investors by recycling money deposited by those who join later. The anthropologists John and Jean Comaroff (1999) developed a theory of 'occult economies' whereby global trends in financialisation have created complex and often mystified means of generating wealth that seem detached from the 'real' economy. Drawing on their fieldwork in South Africa, the Comaroffs argued that pyramid schemes, zombie stories and pastors preaching 'prosperity gospels' were all reflections of these broader economic conditions and were driven by a sense that windfall gains were available to an elite and that unlocking the secret of their success was the way to transform one's circumstances.

Fast money schemes in Melanesia have played a similar role, articulating local concerns with inequality and underdevelopment as the fulfilment of the Pentecostal prosperity gospel (U-Vistract, an elaborate Bougainvillean scam that includes elements of Bougainvillean separatism, PNG nation-making and a fraudulent vision of a new global economic system); as compensation for past wrongs (the Papalain scheme claims to be compensation owed to Sepik labourers for redundancies at a colonial-era timber company); or as a form of development assistance (the Solomon Islands Family Charity Fund).[3]

Conclusion

This chapter has highlighted the nature of uneven development within and between rural and urban spaces in PNG. This approach stands in contrast to the methodological nationalism, and localised particularism, that shape some accounts of PNG. The chapter has shown that, in some cases, the uneven nature of development in the country can be traced back to the processes of colonialism and the decisions made by colonisers about where and what sort of development should take place in the country. While linked to the past, PNG's patchwork quilt of economic activity has dramatically changed in the years since independence. International, national and local actors and organisations drive this change. For example, mining companies decide to explore for minerals and open mine sites based on calculations tied to international markets (e.g. the price of gold) and the economic and political risks involved. PNG's government sets out regulations around mining leases, while local landowners both assist with mining operations and resist, sometimes through violence.

The processes we describe are apparent in other countries; however, we suggest that uneven development in the country features some uniquely Papua New Guinean characteristics. In particular, while urban centres feature more economic activities and opportunities, Papua New Guineans have mostly resisted the call of the city. Rates of urbanisation in the country are low by both global and regional standards. This highlights the importance of the cultural and social connection citizens have to their local communities – most of which are located in rural areas. It also reflects the poverty of opportunity for many migrants moving into towns. While uneven development can help to explain the rise of some types of crime and lead to frustrated aspirations – so prevalent in urban settings around

3 See Cox (2019) for an overview of money schemes. For a deeper investigation of the long-running U-Vistract scam, see Cox (2018).

the world – it has also led some Papua New Guineans to engage with more positive responses, such as through informal economic activities and small and medium-size enterprises.

There are three key implications emanating from this analysis. First, traditional ways of trying to capture the nature of development in PNG – through development indicators tied to national and subnational administrative scales – are important, though limited. As we have shown, livelihood opportunities are fluid and shift within and between administrative boundaries. For example, while PNG's urbanisation level has risen over the past 40 years, many urbanites continue to have strong relations with their rural communities and move back to rural areas to start businesses or look after family. The impacts of the economic activity we describe are often concentrated in very specific places. For example, mining and logging operations cover a small portion of the provincial or district land on which they operate (even though the materials they produce are exported around the world). Very often, these operations are shaped by the relations between the company and surrounding community, with limited engagement of state officials. What this means is that we need to think about uneven development as a phenomenon that does not always fit neatly onto artificial national and subnational administrative boundaries (Allen et al., 2005; Hanson et al., 2001). This requires us to think about development processes, networks and enclaves, as well as national and subnational administrative units.

Second, due to low urbanisation levels, rural poverty and a high proportion of the population living in rural areas, policies that seek to address PNG's development challenges will, for many years to come, need to focus on the unique issues facing rural communities. This brings with it additional difficulties, as providing services to rural citizens is more expensive than in urban areas. To overcome these difficulties, some have suggested that more needs to be done to reallocate resources to rural and remote areas (see Howes et al., 2014). Given that the majority of votes are in rural and remote locations, the pressures for politicians and others to decentralise administration and funding to local levels of government are likely to continue (see also Chapter 3, this volume). The localised politics of distribution, which over the past few years has intensified through, for example, the rise of constituency funds and increased autonomy of district administrations, is also likely to continue.

Third, the country is moving into a distinctly different era than the one that has shaped its development over the past decade. As Chapter 5 (this volume) shows, the country's revenue base has recently diminished. The optimism that came with higher levels of revenue and the promises of large-scale natural resource projects led to the country hosting a range of events that shaped its urban and rural spaces. For example, it led to the country hosting APEC, the FIFA U-20 Women's World Cup and the Pacific Games, which led to significant restructuring of urban spaces and, for a short time, opportunities for employment, particularly in the hospitality and security industries. For now, it is unlikely PNG will reshape its urban and rural spaces as dramatically. Still, the challenges associated with uneven development that operates beyond artificially constructed national and subnational boundaries will remain. In turn, PNG's development policies will need to be tailored to address the problems associated with the changing nature of uneven development in the country.

Acknowledgements

We would like to thank Kylie McKenna, Tim Sharp, Stephen Howes and workshop participants for their insightful comments on early drafts of this chapter.

References

Allen, B. (2014). *Papua New Guinea national census 2011: Rates of population change in local level government areas*. SSGM In Brief, 2014/44. dpa.bellschool.anu.edu.au/experts-publications/publications/1279/papua-new-guinea-national-census-2011-rates-population-change.

Allen, B., Bourke, R. M. and Gibson, J. (2005). Poor rural places in Papua New Guinea. *Asia Pacific Viewpoint*, *46*(2), 201–17. doi.org/10.1111/j.1467-8373.2005.00274.x.

Australian Conservation Foundation. (2006). *Bulldozing progress: Human rights abuses and corruption in Papua New Guinea's large scale logging industry*. Australian Conservation Foundation.

Bainton, N. A. (2011). Are you viable? Personal avarice, collective antagonism and grassroots development in Melanesia. In M. Patterson and M. Macintyre (Eds), *Managing modernity in the Western Pacific* (pp. 231–59). University of Queensland Press.

Bainton, N. A. (2017). Migrants, labourers and landowners at the Lihir Gold Mine, Papua New Guinea. In C. Filer and P.-Y. Le Meur (Eds), *Large-scale mines and local-level politics: Between New Caledonia and Papua New Guinea* (pp. 313–51). ANU Press. doi.org/10.22459/LMLP.10.2017.11.

Bainton, N. A. and Banks, G. (2018). Land and access: A framework for analysing mining, migration and development in Melanesia. *Sustainable Development, 26*(5), 450–60. doi.org/10.1002/sd.1890.

Bainton, N. A. and Macintyre, M. (2013). 'My land, my work': Business development and large-scale mining in Papua New Guinea. In F. McCormack and K. Barclay (Eds), *Engaging with capitalism: Cases from Oceania* (pp. 139–65). Emerald Group Publishing Limited. doi.org/10.1108/S0190-1281(2013)0000033008.

Bainton, N. A. and McDougall, D. (2021). Unequal lives in the Western Pacific. In N. Bainton, D. McDougall, K. Alexeyeff and J. Cox (Eds), *Unequal lives: Gender, race and class in the Western Pacific* (pp. 1–46). ANU Press. doi.org/10.22459/UE.2020.01.

Banks, G. (2014). *Papua New Guinea national human development report 2014: From wealth to wellbeing: Translating resource revenue into sustainable human development.* United Nations Development Program.

Banks, G., Kuir-Ayius, D., Kombako, D. and Sagir, B. (2013). Conceptualizing mining impacts, livelihoods and corporate community development in Melanesia. *Community Development Journal, 48*(3), 484–500. doi.org/10.1093/cdj/bst025.

Barbara, J., Cox, J. and Leach, M. (2015). *The emergent middle classes in Timor-Leste and Melanesia: Conceptual issues and developmental significance.* SSGM Discussion Paper, 2015/4. dpa.bellschool.anu.edu.au/experts-publications/publications/1361/emergent-middle-classes-timor-leste-and-melanesia-conceptual.

Barnett-Naghshineh, O. (2019). Shame and care: Masculinities in the Goroka marketplace. *Oceania, 89*(2), 220–36. doi.org/10.1002/ocea.5219.

Bourke, R. M. (2009). History of agriculture in Papua New Guinea. In R. M. Bourke and T. Harwood (Eds), *Food and agriculture in Papua New Guinea* (pp. 10–26). ANU Press. doi.org/10.22459/FAPNG.08.2009.

Bourke, R. M. and Harwood T. (2009). *Food and agriculture in Papua New Guinea.* ANU Press. doi.org/10.22459/FAPNG.08.2009.

Bray, M. (1985). Social stratification and disparities in access to education in East New Britain. In M. Bray and P. Smith (Eds), *Education and social stratification in Papua New Guinea* (182–93). Longman Cheshire.

Brydon, K. and Lawihin, D. (2016). Melanesian visions? Some preliminary thoughts about social work education and practice in Papua New Guinea. *International Social Work, 59*(2), 192–204. doi.org/10.1177/0020872813515012.

Buckley, J. (2019, 5 September). World's most livable city for 2019, according to the Economist Intelligence Unit. CNN. edition.cnn.com/travel/article/worlds-most-livable-cities-2019-trnd/index.html.

Busse, M. and Sharp, T. L. M. (2019). Marketplaces and morality in Papua New Guinea: Place, personhood and exchange. *Oceania, 89*(2), 126–53. doi.org/10.1002/ocea.5218.

Comaroff, J. and Comaroff, J. L. (1999). Occult economies and the violence of abstraction: Notes from the South African postcolony. *American Ethnologist, 26*(2), 279–303. doi.org/10.1525/ae.1999.26.2.279.

Connell, J. (1997). *Papua New Guinea: The struggle for development.* Routledge.

Connell, J. (2016). Nothing there atoll? 'Farewell to the Carteret Islands'. In T. Crook and P. Rudiak-Gould (Eds), *Appropriating climate change* (pp. 73–87). de Gruyter. doi.org/10.2478/9783110591415-007.

Connell, J. and Lutkehaus, N. (2017). Environmental refugees? A tale of two resettlement projects in coastal Papua New Guinea. *Australian Geographer, 48*(1), 79–95. doi.org/10.1080/00049182.2016.1267603.

Cox, J. (2009). Active citizenship or passive clientelism: Accountability and development in Solomon Islands. *Development in Practice, 19*(8), 964–80. doi.org/10.1080/09614520903220784.

Cox, J. (2014). *'Grassroots', 'elites' and the new 'working class' of Papua New Guinea.* SSGM In Brief, 2014/6. dpa.bellschool.anu.edu.au/experts-publications/publications/1611/grassroots-elites-and-new-working-class-papua-new-guinea.

Cox, J. (2018). *Fast money schemes: Hope and disillusionment in Papua New Guinea.* Indiana University Press. doi.org/10.2307/j.ctv6mtfjm.

Cox, J. (2019). Money schemes in contemporary Melanesia. In E. Hirsch and W. Rollason (Eds), *The Melanesian world* (pp. 180–93). Routledge. doi.org/10.4324/9781315529691-10.

Cox, J. (2021). Inequalities of aspiration: Class, cargo and the moral economy of development in Papua New Guinea. In N. Bainton, D. McDougall, K. Alexeyeff and J. Cox (Eds), *Unequal lives: Gender, race and class in the Western Pacific* (pp. 237–66). ANU Press. doi.org/10.22459/UE.2020.09.

Cox, J. and Macintyre, M. (2014). Christian marriage, money scams and Melanesian social imaginaries. *Oceania*, *84*(2), 138–157. doi.org/10.1002/ocea.5048.

Cox, J. and Phillips, G. (2015). Sorcery, Christianity and the decline of medical services. In M. Forsyth and R. Eves (Eds), *Talking it through: Responses to sorcery and witchcraft beliefs and practices in Melanesia* (pp. 37–54). ANU Press. doi.org/10.22459/TIT.05.2015.02.

Craig, D. and Porter, D. (2018). *Safety and security at the edges of the state: Local regulation in Papua New Guinea's urban settlements*. The World Bank. doi.org/10.1596/30260.

Crittenden, R. and Lea, D. A. M. (1989). *Integrated rural development programmes in Papua New Guinea: External aid and provincial planning*. Papua New Guinea Institute of Applied Social and Economic Research and the Department of Geography and Planning, University of New England.

Curry, G. N., Koczberski, G. and Inu, S. M. (2019). Women's and men's work: The production and marketing of fresh food and export crops in Papua New Guinea. *Oceania*, *89*(2), 237–54. doi.org/10.1002/ocea.5222.

Dalsgaard, S. (2013). The politics of remittance and the role of returning migrants: Localizing capitalism in Manus Province, Papua New Guinea. *Research in Economic Anthropology*, *33*, 277–302. doi.org/10.1108/S0190-1281(2013)0000033013.

Demian, M. (2017). Making women in the city: Notes from a Port Moresby boarding house. *Signs: Journal of Women in Culture and Society*, *42*(2), 403–25. doi.org/10.1086/688185.

Department of National Planning and Monitoring. (2014). *National Strategy for Responsible Development for Papua New Guinea*. Government of Papua New Guinea. png-data.sprep.org/dataset/national-strategy-responsible-sustainable-development-papua-new-guinea2014.

Dwyer, P. D. and Minnegal, M. (1998). Waiting for company: Ethos and environment among Kubo of Papua New Guinea. *Journal of the Royal Anthropological Institute*, *4*(1), 23–42. doi.org/10.2307/3034426.

Dwyer, P. D. and Minnegal, M. (2014). Where all the rivers flow west: Maps, abstraction and change in the Papua New Guinea lowlands. *The Australian Journal of Anthropology*, *25*(1), 37–53. doi.org/10.1111/taja.12071.

Errington, F. and Gewertz, D. (1993). The triumph of capitalism in East New Britain? A contemporary Papua New Guinean rhetoric of motives. *Oceania*, *64*(1), 1–17. doi.org/10.1002/j.1834-4461.1993.tb02444.x.

Errington, F. and Gewertz, D. (2004). *Yali's question: Sugar, culture, and history.* University of Chicago Press.

Ezebilo, E. E. (2017). Evaluation of affordable housing program in Papua New Guinea: A case of Port Moresby. *Buildings*, *7*(3), 73. doi.org/10.3390/buildings7030073.

Filer, C. (2011). *The political construction of a land grab in Papua New Guinea.* READ Pacific Discussion Paper, 1. Crawford School of Economics and Government, The Australian National University. hdl.handle.net/1885/9709.

Filer, C. (2019). *Two steps forward, two steps back: The mobilisation of customary land in Papua New Guinea.* Development Policy Centre Discussion Paper, 86. doi.org/10.2139/ssrn.3502585.

Filer, C. and Macintyre, M. (2006). Grass roots and deep holes: Community responses to mining in Melanesia. *The Contemporary Pacific*, *18*(2), 215–31. doi.org/10.1353/cp.2006.0012.

Filer, C. and Numapo, J. (2017). The political ramifications of Papua New Guinea's commission of inquiry. In S. McDonnell, M. G. Allen and C. Filer (Eds), *Kastom, property and ideology: Land transformations in Melanesia* (pp. 251–82). ANU Press. doi.org/10.22459/KPI.03.2017.08.

Finau, G., Jacobs, K. and Chand, S. (2019). Agents of alienation: Accountants and the land grab of Papua New Guinea. *Accounting, Auditing and Accountability Journal*, *32*(5), 1558–84. doi.org/10.1108/AAAJ-10-2017-3185.

Foster, R. (2008). *Coca-globalisation. Following soft drinks from New York to New Guinea.* Palgrave Macmillan.

Foster, R. and Horst, H. (Eds). (2018). *The moral economy of mobile phones: Pacific Islands perspectives.* ANU Press. doi.org/10.22459/MEMP.05.2018.

Gibson, L. (2019). Class, labour and consumption in urban Melanesia. In E. Hirsch and W. Rollason (Eds), *The Melanesian world* (pp. 164–79). Routledge. doi.org/10.4324/9781315529691-9.

Goddard, M. (2005). *The unseen city: Anthropological perspectives on Port Moresby, Papua New Guinea*. Pandanus Books.

Goddard, M. (2010). *Villagers and the city: Melanesian experiences of Port Moresby, Papua New Guinea*. Sean Kingston Press.

Golub, A. (2014). *Leviathans at the gold mine: Creating indigenous and corporate actors in Papua New Guinea*. Duke University Press. doi.org/10.1215/9780822377399.

Hanson, L. W., Allen, B. J., Bourke, R. M. and McCarthy, T. J. (2001). *Papua New Guinea rural development handbook*. The Australian National University.

Hayward-Jones, J. (2016). *The future of Papua New Guinea: Old challenges for new leaders*. Lowy Institute. www.lowyinstitute.org/publications/future-papua-new-guinea-old-challenges-new-leaders.

Howes, S., Mako, A. A., Swan, A., Walton, G., Webster, T. and Wiltshire, C. (2014). *A lost decade? Service delivery and reforms in Papua New Guinea 2002–2012*. NRI-ANU Promoting Effective Public Expenditure Project.

Hukula, F. (2019). Morality and a Mosbi market. *Oceania, 89*(2), 168–81. doi.org/10.1002/ocea.5216.

Imbun, Y. B. (2016). Papua New Guinea's mixed experiences of globalisation. *Policy Forum*. www.policyforum.net/papua-new-guinea-in-a-changing-world/.

Irwin, G., Shaw, B. and McAlister, A. (2019). The origins of the Kula Ring: Archaeological and maritime perspectives from the southern Massim and Mailu areas of Papua New Guinea. *Archaeology in Oceania, 54*(1), 1–16. doi.org/10.1002/arco.5167.

Johnson, P. (2011). *Social impact of the mining project on women in the Porgera area*. Porgera Environmental Advisory Komiti.

Jubilee Australia. (2019). *The river is not ours: The Frieda River mine and the threat to the Sepik*. jubileeaustralia.org/resources/publications/river-not-ours-2019.

Kanua, M., Jinks, B., Lowe, M. and Bourke, R. M. (2016). *Assessing village food needs following a natural disaster in Papua New Guinea*. Church Partnership Program, Australian Government Department of Foreign Affairs and Trade.

Koczberski, G. and Curry, G. N. (2004). Divided communities and contested landscapes: Mobility, development and shifting identities in migrant destination sites in Papua New Guinea. *Asia Pacific Viewpoint, 45*(3), 357–71. doi.org/10.1111/j.1467-8373.2004.00252.x.

Koczberski, G., Curry, G. N. and Connell, J. (2001). Full circle or spiralling out of control? State violence and the control of urbanisation in Papua New Guinea. *Urban Studies*, *38*(11), 2017–36. doi.org/10.1080/00420980120080916.

Krige, D. (2011). 'We are running for a living': Work, leisure and speculative accumulation in an underground numbers lottery in Johannesburg. *African Studies*, *70*(1), 3–24. doi.org/10.1080/00020184.2011.557571.

Lasslett, C. (2014). *State crime on the margins of empire: Rio Tinto, the war on Bougainville and resistance to mining*. Pluto Press. doi.org/10.2307/j.ctt183p781.

Lasslett, C. (2018). *Uncovering the crimes of urbanisation: Researching corruption, violence and urban conflict*. Routledge. doi.org/10.4324/9781315651798.

Lattas, A. (2011). Logging, violence and pleasure: Neoliberalism, civil society and corporate governance in West New Britain. *Oceania*, *81*(1), 88–107. doi.org/10.1002/j.1834-4461.2011.tb00095.x.

Lawihin, D. (2017). Building a culturally relevant social work curriculum in Papua New Guinea: Connecting the local and global in field education [Unpublished master's thesis]. Monash University.

Lawson, S. (2014). *Illegal logging in Papua New Guinea*. Chatham House.

Levine, H. and Levine, M. (1979). *Urbanization in Papua New Guinea: A study of ambivalent townsmen*. Cambridge University Press.

Martin, K. (2010). The death of the big men: Depreciation of elites in New Guinea, *Ethnos, 75*(1), 1–22. doi.org/10.1080/00141840903581576.

Martin, K. (2013). *The death of the big men and the rise of the big shots: Custom and conflict in East New Britain*. Berghahn.

Monsell-Davis, M. (1993). Urban exchange: Safety-net or disincentive? Wantoks and relatives in the urban Pacific. *Canberra Anthropology*, *16*(2), 45–66. doi.org/10.1080/03149099309508434.

Moran, M. and Curth-Bibb, J. (Eds). (2020). *Too close to ignore: Australia's borderland with PNG and Indonesia.* University of Melbourne Press.

Moseley, M. (2003). *Rural development principles and practice*. SAGE.

National Research Institute. (2010). *Papua New Guinea district and provincial profiles*. National Research Institute.

National Strategic Plan Taskforce. (2009). *Papua New Guinea Vision 2050.* Government of Papua New Guinea. treasury.gov.pg/html/publications/files/pub_files/2011/2011.png.vision.2050.pdf.

Office of Urbanisation. (2010). *National urbanisation policy 2010–2030.* Government of Papua New Guinea.

Oram, N. (1976). *Colonial town to Melanesian city: Port Moresby 1884–1974.* Australian National University Press. hdl.handle.net/1885/115035.

Pickles, A. J. (2019). *Money games: Gambling in a Papua New Guinea town.* Berghahn Books.

Pryke, J. and Barker, P. (2017). A bumpy road: Societal trends in Papua New Guinea. In J. Pryke (Ed.), *Papua New Guinea: Seven snapshots of a nation* (pp. 23–42). Lowy Institute. interactives.lowyinstitute.org/archive/png-in-2017/png-in-2017-society-a-bumpy-road-societal-trends-in-papua-new-guinea.html.

Rai, F. (2020, 19 March). K5 million school fees for SHP students paid. *Post-Courier*. postcourier.com.pg/k5-million-school-fees-for-shp-students-paid/.

Rasmussen, A. (2015). *In the absence of the gift: New forms of value and personhood in a Papua New Guinea community.* Berghahn. doi.org/10.2307/j.ctt9qdb0f.

Rooney, M. N. (2017). 'There's nothing better than land': A migrant group's strategies for accessing informal settlement land in Port Moresby. In S. McDonnell, M. Allen and C. Filer (Eds), *Kastom, property and ideology: Land transformations in Melanesia* (pp. 111–43). ANU Press. doi.org/10.22459/KPI.03.2017.04.

Rooney, M. N. (2019). Sharing what can be sold: Women *hausmaket* vendors in Port Moresby's settlements. *Oceania, 89*(2), 154–67. doi.org/10.1002/ocea.5217.

Rooney, M., Forsyth, M., Aisi, M., Kuir-Ayius, D., Lawihin, D. and Goa, J. (2019). Men and women's perspectives on options to address FSV in Lae, Morobe Province – PNG. *PNG Update*. University of Papua New Guinea.

Schram, R. (2015). Notes on the sociology of *wantoks* in Papua New Guinea. *Anthropological Forum, 25*(1), 3–20. doi.org/10.1080/00664677.2014.960795.

Scott, J. (2015). Urbanism. In *A Dictionary of Sociology* (4th ed.). Oxford University Press. www.oxfordreference.com/view/10.1093/acref/9780199683581.001.0001/acref-9780199683581-e-2436.

Sharp, T. L. M. (2016). Trade's value: Relational transactions in the Papua New Guinea betel nut trade. *Oceania, 86*(1), 75–91. doi.org/10.1002/ocea.5116.

Sharp, T. L. M. (2019). Haggling highlanders: Marketplaces, middlemen and moral economy in the Papua New Guinean betel nut trade. *Oceania, 89*(2), 182–204. doi.org/10.1002/ocea.5221.

Sharp, T. L. M. and Busse, M. (2019). Cash crops and markets. In E. Hirsch and W. Rollason (Eds), *The Melanesian world* (pp. 194–222). Routledge. doi.org/10.4324/9781315529691-11.

Sharp, T., Cox, J., Spark, C., Lusby, S. and Rooney, M. (2015). *The formal, the informal, and the precarious: Making a living in urban Papua New Guinea.* SSGM Discussion Paper, 2015/2. dpa.bellschool.anu.edu.au/experts-publications/publications/1292/formal-informal-and-precarious-making-living-urban-papua-new.

Spark, C. (2014a). An oceanic revolution? Stella and the construction of new femininities in Papua New Guinea and the Pacific. *The Australian Journal of Anthropology*, *25*(1), 54–72. doi.org/10.1111/taja.12066.

Spark, C. (2014b). 'We only get the daylight hours': Gender, fear and 'freedom' in urban Papua New Guinea. *Security Challenges*, *10*(2), 15–32. www.jstor.org/stable/26467879.

Spark, C. (2019). At home in the city: Educated women, housing and belonging in Port Moresby. In S. Pinto, S. Hannigan, B. Walker-Gibbs and E. Charlton (Eds), *Interdisciplinary unsettlings of place and space: Conversations, investigations and research* (pp. 183–95). Springer. doi.org/10.1007/978-981-13-6729-8_12.

Sydney Morning Herald. (2010, 11 February). Port Moresby on 'worst cities' list. www.smh.com.au/world/port-moresby-on-worst-cities-list-20100211-ntvx.html.

Tammisto, T. (2019). Life in the village is free: Socially reproductive work and alienated labour on an oil palm plantation in Pomio, Papua New Guinea. *Suomen Antropologi: Journal of the Finnish Anthropological Society*, *43*(4), 19–35. doi.org/10.30676/jfas.v43i4.79476.

The National. (2020, 13 February). Atiyafa subsidising parents' component of school fee. www.thenational.com.pg/atiyafa-subsidising-parents-component-of-school-fee/.

United Nations Department of Economic and Social Affairs. (2019). *World urbanisation prospects: The 2018 revision.* United Nations. population.un.org/wup/Publications/Files/WUP2018-Report.pdf.

United Nations Habitat. (2010). *Papua New Guinea: Port Moresby urban profile.* www.fukuoka.unhabitat.org/projects/papua_new_guinea/pdf/Port_Moresby_March_2010.pdf.

Walton, G. W. (2019). The micro-politics of implementing and resisting principal-agent relations in a weak state. *Australian Journal of Political Science, 54*(3), 355–71. doi.org/10.1080/10361146.2019.1616077.

Walton, G. W. and Barnett, J. (2007). The ambiguities of 'Environmental' conflict: Insights from the Tolukuma gold mine. *Society and Natural Resources, 21*(1), 1–16. doi.org/10.1080/08941920701655635.

Walton, G. W. and Davda, T. (2019). School–community relations and fee-free education policy in Papua New Guinea. *Pacific Affairs*, *92*(1), 71–94. doi.org/10.5509/201992171.

Walton, G. W., Davda, T. and Kanaparo, P. (2017). *The challenges of providing free education in Papua New Guinea.* Development Policy Centre Discussion Paper, 61. doi.org/10.2139/ssrn.3011101.

West, P. (2006). *Conservation is our government now: The politics of ecology in Papua New Guinea.* Duke University Press. doi.org/10.1215/9780822388067.

Wiltshire, C. (2013, 3 April). Reflections on the PNG budget forum: Can devolved funding be effectively utilized? *Devpolicy Blog*. devpolicy.org/reflections-on-the-png-budget-forum-can-devolved-funding-be-effectively-utilised-2013040/.

Wimmer, A. and Schiller, N. G. (2002). Methodological nationalism and beyond: Nation-state building, migration and the social sciences. *Global Networks, 2*(4), 301–34. doi.org/10.1111/1471-0374.00043.

Wirth, L. (1938). Urbanism as a way of life. *The American Journal of Sociology, 44*(1), 1–24. doi.org/10.1086/217913.

Wood, T. (2017, 4 August). Winners and losers in the 2017 PNG elections. *Devpolicy Blog*. devpolicy.org/winners-losers-2017-png-elections-20170804/.

Wood, T. (2018). The clientelism trap in Solomon Islands and Papua New Guinea, and its impact on aid policy. *Asia & the Pacific Policy Studies*, *5*(3), 481–94. doi.org/10.1002/app5.239.

World Bank. (2022). *Urban population (% of total population) – Papua New Guinea, Solomon Islands, Burundi.* data.worldbank.org/indicator/SP.URB.TOTL.IN.ZS?locations=PG-SB-1Wandmost_recent_value_desc%3Dfalse-BI&most_recent_value_desc=false.

World Bank. (2022). *Total natural resources rents (% of GDP) – Papua New Guinea, World, Pacific island small states.* data.worldbank.org/indicator/NY.GDP.TOTL.RT.ZS?locations=PG-1W-S2&most_recent_value_desc=true.

8

Communication, information and the media

Amanda H. A. Watson

Abstract

This chapter discusses the flows of communication and information in Papua New Guinea (PNG). It argues that communication and information are essential to all aspects of life. As such, the concepts are cross-cutting. The chapter considers whether citizens have the means to communicate their views. It also asks whether citizens have access to timely information. The chapter is a literature survey that posits the importance of communication and information for governance and effective democracy. A key component of a functioning democracy is a citizenry that is well informed and actively engaged in debates about government policies. The chapter suggests that the mainstream media in PNG has a fragile freedom but does not carry out sufficient in-depth investigations. The argument is made that urban residents are much more easily able to access the media than those living in rural villages. The chapter also looks into uses of mobile telephones, the internet and social media.

Introduction

For thousands of years, people throughout what is now Papua New Guinea (PNG) have used traditional communication techniques. In some locations, these continue to be practised. In contemporary PNG, communication remains a vital part of daily life. This chapter explores diverse contemporary communication types such as receiving a telephone call from a loved one in another part of the country, participating in a discussion on Facebook and ringing a radio station with a question for a studio guest. Intertwined with the notion of communication is the concept of information. The chapter considers how information is created and disseminated, and who has access to information.

The chapter is a literature survey that reviews relevant books, articles, research reports, news stories and other written materials. It begins by outlining the key roles of communication, information and the mass media in a contemporary democracy. It then focuses on the media in PNG, including the PNG media landscape, media access, media freedom, media investigations and gender in the media. The chapter then examines mobile telephony, which has become available in rural areas since 2007. Finally, it considers the internet and social media.

Communication, information and the media in contemporary PNG

This chapter examines contemporary trends in communication practices in PNG, while acknowledging that, in some locations, traditional communication techniques continue, such as the use of slit-drums (*garamut*) to convey messages to surrounding villages, individual family members and specific clans (Watson, 2011, pp. 98–101; Watson and Duffield, 2016, pp. 276–77). Communication is defined as imparting or conveying 'one's thoughts, feelings etc. successfully' (Turner, 1984, p. 140). A key concept that relates to communication is the notion of information, which is defined as 'what is told' (Turner, 1984, p. 356) and is generally thought of as being factual or concrete (Bennett et al., 2005, pp. 186–87), for example, news (Turner, 1984).

A key term used in this chapter is 'the media' (also referred to as 'mainstream media', 'news media' or 'mass media'), which is a 'channel for communication of information, propaganda etc.' (Turner, 1984, p. 427) and typically refers to means for transmitting packaged information to large audiences, such as newspapers (sometimes called 'the press'), radio stations and television (Turner, 1984). People gathering information and writing news media stories are known as journalists, reporters or correspondents. Journalism involves 'adherence to professional codes of ethics relating to truth' (Nash, 2013, quoted in Robie, 2014, p. 322), 'objectivity and impartiality' (McLaughlin, 2016, p. 33).

In a democracy such as PNG, communication and information have key roles for the achievement of effective governance. A key component of a functioning democracy is a citizenry that is well informed and actively engaged in debates about governance, social and economic issues, and relevant government policies. Thus, it is important that citizens have the means to communicate their views and concerns. To formulate such opinions, citizens should ideally have access to timely information. As will be explained in this chapter, the media has a crucial role to play in this regard. Good governance 'depends on people knowing what their governments are doing and therefore on an active free press' (Firth, 2006, p. 6). Relaying the truth is the 'cornerstone of the relationship between democracy and journalism' (Greensmith, 2017).

As Ketan has explained regarding traditional leadership practices in the PNG Highlands, 'transparency, accountability and equity were the principles that governed wealth distribution in ceremonial exchanges, food sharing and pig ceremonials' (2013, p. 5). In other words, pigs and other foods were cut up and distributed in public spaces so that people could witness such actions and be aware of what each family received. Thus, people were informed because the transparent process meant that they had access to information about what was taking place. Similarly, Duncan emphasised 'the public aspect of gift giving' (2011, p. 154) in leadership practices across the Pacific region. In traditional contexts, information was available publicly and there was no secrecy about leaders' actions.

Ketan argued that similar practices are desirable in the modern context, 'ensuring greater levels of accountability and transparency in the disbursement of state resources, and providing vital information for planning and budgeting purposes' (2013, p. 19). Likewise, international bodies emphasise the importance of transparency when it comes to effective governance: 'the concept of governance emphasizes the participation and interest of the public as well as strong responsiveness, equity, transparency and accountability of public officials at the centre of public management' (United Nations Department of Economic and Social Affairs, 2015, p. 7). Thus, it can be seen that communication, information and transparency have key roles in the effective functioning of a democracy, and that they resonate with traditional practices and values in PNG and other Pacific settings.

A crucial component of a democratic system is the media, which can be thought of as the fourth estate, keeping watch on the three arms of government (see Matane and Ahuja, 2005, p. 31 on the separation of the parliament, the executive and the judiciary, as outlined in the PNG constitution). The media acts 'as a civil watchdog to keep an eye on those in power' (Hirst, 2013). Importantly, the media as the fourth estate is ideally independent. In a healthy democracy with robust and inclusive debates, the 'media plays its fundamental role, which is to educate and inform the masses' (Kanekane, 2006, p. 387). The fourth estate role of the media exists 'to provide an independent forum for open dialogue by all members of a society' (Pamba, 2014, p. 2). It is not the role of the media 'to tell people who to vote for, [but] merely to give them the ability to make an informed choice' (Greensmith, 2017). The media 'can both disseminate crucial information relating to governance, and also engage people in debate that can lead to tangible action' (ABC International Development, 2014, p. 7). A survey of journalists in PNG found that they generally agreed with the notion of the media as a watchdog (Robie, 2011, p. 213).

The 'fourth estate' term refers to 'journalists' role in representing the interests of "the people" in relation to the business and political elites who claim to be doing things in our names' (Hirst, 2013). In other words, in addition to monitoring government activities and policies, the media should also be a watchdog when it comes to the business sector. Interestingly, Pamba (2014) reported that the PNG Chamber of Mines and Petroleum held a series of workshops for journalists. While this may have had some benefits in terms of informing journalists about technical aspects of the industry, Pamba (2014, p. 2) argued that the industry's 'direct involvement in aspects of training of journalists may be viewed by some as undermining the independence of the media, raising issues of transparency and accountability'. Similarly, questions have been asked about whether donor aid programs subtly steer journalists to report favourably about the activities and agendas of aid agencies (Backhaus, 2020). While the role of the media as the fourth estate is commonly considered to be important in the PNG context, it is acknowledged that some commentators question whether this notion of the media's role clashes with traditional cultures and values (M'Balla-Ndi and Obijiofor, 2020, p. 78).

The variety of media in PNG

Given the importance of the media to any country, this chapter devotes several sections to the media in PNG, beginning with this introductory one. Journalism training is offered at both Divine Word University and the University of Papua New Guinea (Robie, 2011). The Media Council of PNG was formed in 1994 'to maintain professional standards in the media industry, deal with and respond to complaints on conduct, [and] make representations on behalf of the industry' (Media Council of PNG, n.d.-b). Singh (2017, p. 7) explained that it was revitalised in 2015 after a period of limited activity. It represents newspapers, television stations, radio stations and online news portals (Media Council of PNG, n.d.-b), each of which is discussed in turn.

Print media in PNG includes newspapers and various magazines. It is common in PNG for a newspaper to be passed from person to person and thus reader numbers are likely to be higher than the print run totals (M&C Saatchi World Services et al., 2014, p. 40; Word Publishing Company Ltd, 2020). There are two daily English language newspapers, which together present an important record of events and public debates: the information they print 'is comprehensive and verifiable, being usually attributed to named sources' (Watson, 2011, p. 68; see also Cox, 2018, p. 15). The *Post-Courier* was established in 1969. It is printed in Port Moresby and distributed to most provinces. Print runs vary from 20,000 copies to 35,000 copies per day. News Corp owns 60 per cent of the *Post-Courier* and 40 per cent is owned by PNG companies (Nambawan Super, Nasfund and others). *The National* was established in 1993. It is printed in Port Moresby and Lae and distributed to most provinces. It has a circulation of about 50,000 copies per day and is owned by Rimbunan Hijau, a Malaysian logging company (Pacific Media Watch, 2011; Perottet and Robie, 2011).

There are two weekly English language newspapers. The *Sunday Chronicle* was established in 2006. It has print runs of 25,000 copies and is owned by a PNG company. In 2018, then Opposition member Bryan Kramer accused the daily newspapers of favouring the government and failing to report the Opposition's views, and he encouraged citizens to refrain from buying the two daily newspapers in protest (Gware, 2018). This inspired a PNG businessman to start a new publication, *The Sunday Bulletin*, with the aim of publishing investigative journalism. It sells 5,000 printed copies in Port Moresby and several other provinces and its owner also publishes three magazines.

The weekly *Wantok* newspaper is in the Tok Pisin language and was established in 1970 (Cass, 2020; Word Publishing Company Ltd, 2020). More than 15,000 copies of each edition are printed in Port Moresby, of which 10,000 are distributed and sold around the country. Approximately 5,000 are provided free of charge to schools, churches and other groups, and a small number are posted to subscribers. It is owned by four churches.

Until fairly recently, PNG only had one homegrown television station, a commercial operation named EMTV. In addition, in urban centres such as Port Moresby and Madang, pay television services offer a range of international stations to subscribers. In 2008, the National Broadcasting Corporation launched a television station and it gradually rolled out its transmission around the country (*The National*, 2010). In 2014, the Digicel mobile telecommunication company began offering a pay television service (Business Advantage PNG, 2014a) and another company also commenced a similar television service at around the same time called Click TV (Business Advantage PNG, 2014b). The Australian television service broadcasting to the Pacific region was cut in 2014 (Betteridge, 2014).

Neglect of the government-funded, networked local radio stations has been documented (Boden, 1995; Matbob et al., 2011, p. 5), although the National Broadcasting Corporation, as it is now known, recently launched a new transmitter in the Highlands in order to boost coverage in several surrounding provinces (NBC News PNG, 2020). The network has also launched a youth-oriented radio station (Singh, 2017, p. 7). Within the last few years, the radio signal for the network's local station in the Autonomous Region of Bougainville has been restored (Thomas et al., 2019, p. 5).

As well as government-funded radio stations, there are also commercial, privately owned radio stations and church-run radio stations. Yumi FM, Nau FM and FM100 are the most popular commercial stations and Wantok Radio Light is the most popular religious station (ABC International Development, 2019, p. 32). Talkback radio programs are particularly popular as trusted forums for community discussion (ABC International Development, 2019).

In 2017, Radio Australia shortwave broadcasts to the Pacific ended (Betteridge, 2017; Dobell et al., 2018; Duffield, 2020, p. 185) and a Chinese broadcaster now uses those shortwave frequencies (Dickey et al., 2019, p. iii). While these cuts were noticed in the region, Radio Australia nonetheless continues to provide coverage of Pacific news and current affairs through 13 local FM radio stations across the Pacific, five of which are in PNG, as well as through online platforms (Duffield, 2020, p. 185). Radio New Zealand (2020a) also broadcasts into the Pacific.

There has been a marked increase in PNG-related material that is available online in recent years. Both the daily newspapers have established websites that are updated with news stories daily (the *Post-Courier* in 2014 and *The National* in 2009). The Digicel company established an online news service called Loop PNG in about 2014 (Dorney, 2016, p. 69). The television station EMTV now posts stories online through Facebook and these are commonly shared by users in PNG. The *Sunday Bulletin*'s stories are available on its Facebook page. Some of the *Wantok*'s stories appear on its website. In mid-2020, a weekly English language newspaper for the Autonomous Region of Bougainville had its first print run, building on its Facebook presence (Radio New Zealand, 2020b).

News content about the Pacific, including PNG, is available online from the Australian Broadcasting Corporation, Radio New Zealand and the three outlets produced by the Pacific Media Centre: Pacific Media Centre Online, Pacific Media Watch and Asia Pacific Report (Robie, 2020a, pp. 27–28). A notable, recent addition to online reporting on the Pacific, including PNG, is the launch of *The Guardian*'s Australia edition, with the awarding of grant funding in 2019 for journalism focused on the Pacific (Duffield, 2020, pp. 186–87; Taylor, 2020, p. 16). Analysis on the Pacific is available through online outlets of The Australian National University, including the *Devpolicy Blog*, which has substantially increased the amount of material on PNG and by experts from PNG in recent years, and Policy Forum, which launched a Pacific section in 2020. Other Australian online outlets that include analysis of Pacific issues include the Lowy Institute's *The Interpreter*, Griffith Asia Institute's *Pacific Hub*, and the Australian Strategic Policy Institute's *The Strategist*. Economic analysis is available from Business Advantage PNG and Islands Business. Various other websites provide PNG news, such as PNG Facts, while PNGi Central produces in-depth reports by 'an informal network of academics, activists and journalists' (PNGi, n.d.).

In recent years, there have been some examples of a decrease of availability of media, such as the end of Radio Australia shortwave broadcasts, while there have also been concurrent increases in the number of television stations and in the amount of PNG-related material that is available online. In terms of types of offering, there has been a net increase overall.

Access to the media in PNG

Most people in PNG live a rural life (see Table 6.1 in Chapter 6, this volume). In some rural villages, people continue to regularly use traditional forms of communication such as *garamut* or slit-drums (Watson, 2011). Radio stations are essential sources of information in many rural villages but overall 'limited media access continues to be a major obstacle for the people of PNG' (Matbob et al., 2011, p. 6).

A recent survey in urban, peri-urban and rural areas of six provinces reported that 53 per cent of people read a newspaper at least once per week, 50 per cent of people listen to the radio weekly and 60 per cent of people watch television on at least some occasions (ABC International Development, 2019, pp. 5–6). In rural areas where the majority of households do not have televisions, some people charge entry fees to allow others to view their screens – such enterprises are known as 'village cinemas' ('*haus piksa*' or 'CD *haus*' in Tok Pisin) (Matbob et al., 2011, p. 8; Thomas and Eby, 2016). Low levels of literacy continue to present a challenge to text-based mediums, particularly newspapers (ABC International Development, 2019, p. 6; Elapa, 2011, p. 119; Logan and Suwamaru, 2017, p. 284; Matbob et al., 2011, p. 6; Perottet and Robie, 2011, p. 166; Rooney, 2017a; Williams, 2019, p. 3).

In urban areas, there are two distinct groups of people: the largest group access traditional media (newspapers, television and radio), and a growing minority access information through the internet and social media (ABC International Development, 2019, p. 5). For those who use the internet, the social network Facebook is the most popular platform (ABC International Development, 2019, p. 6; Logan and Suwamaru, 2017, p. 289; Williams, 2019, p. 6).

Research conducted in rural areas of all six districts of Madang Province involved in-depth interviews with 120 people and determined that residents value the provincial radio station that is part of the National

Broadcasting Corporation, despite reception problems in some locations (Issimel, 2011). At a similar time, a survey in Western Highlands Province looked into young people's media access in two villages: a peri-urban village and a rural village (Cangah, 2011). Sixty surveys were completed by people aged 16 to 26. In both villages, radio stations were popular. There was good access to the *Wantok* newspaper, but most respondents reported that they did not have access to the daily newspapers. Television was accessed more in the peri-urban village than the rural village (Cangah, 2011). Recent research in the Autonomous Region of Bougainville established that mobile telephone access is high, but newspapers are not available, with the exception of the *Bougainville Bulletin*, a periodic publication of the Autonomous Bougainville Government (Thomas et al., 2019, p. 5). Access to radio stations is limited across the region and those who have access to television tend to use Digicel's service (Thomas et al., 2019, p. 5).

Overall, access to the media in PNG is trending towards an increasingly wide divide between urban residents with access to the internet and rural residents. The level of access to a variety of news sources is increasing for urban internet users, with the establishment of various online news outlets as well as additional weekly newspapers and television services. Meanwhile, some people in urban areas have limited or no access to the internet. In rural areas, communication options continue to stagnate or even decline, in particular due to the end of Radio Australia's shortwave broadcasts, which had been a daily source of news for rural communities. (See also Table 6.8 in Chapter 6, this volume, for evidence of declining access to traditional media.)

Media freedom

Media freedom is 'one of the most important pillars of any functioning democracy' (Greste, 2017, p. xii). There are two components of media freedom: 'freedom to be informed and freedom of expression' (Robie, 2013, p. 101). Compared to other countries in the Pacific region, 'the PNG media industry continues to have a relative degree of independence, diversity and robustness' (Matbob et al., 2011, p. 6). Freedom of the media is protected in the constitution (Dorney, 2016, pp. 67–68; Duffield, 2006; Robie, 2013, p. 102). PNG is ranked 46th out of 180 countries on the World Press Freedom Index (Reporters without Borders, 2020a), meaning that the country's media is considered to have relative freedom to conduct enquiries and report on issues without fear (see also Dorney, 2016, pp. 67–71; Kanekane, 2006, p. 386). A concern is that 'journalists continue to be prevented from covering the fate of detainees in Australia's refugee detention centres on Papua New Guinea's Manus Island and in the capital, Port Moresby' (Reporters without Borders, 2020b). Freedom House rated PNG as 'partly free', indicating that it is a democracy with regular elections, albeit with problems of violence and corruption, where 'the judiciary retains significant independence, and the media are mostly free to criticize the government' (Freedom House, 2019). Nonetheless, 'media freedom in Papua New Guinea remains endangered' (Ubayasiri et al., 2020, p. 9).

The rights and responsibilities of the media are frequently debated in PNG. For example, respected journalist Scott Waide was suspended late in 2018 over a story critical of the government but was soon afterwards reinstated following public outcry (Wesley, 2020). In 2020, Police Minister Bryan Kramer, who has a strong 'reputation for transparency and use of online media communication' (Robie, 2020b), criticised two journalists from mainstream media outlets for inaccurate reporting of financial information and, in response, one of the outlets, Loop PNG, published an editorial defending its reporting (Robie, 2020b). There were also concerns about the media's ability to access timely information when regular media briefings were temporarily suspended during the COVID-19 global pandemic due to a positive test result at the operations centre in Port Moresby (Pacific Media Watch, 2020; Robie, 2020c). Such concerns are not new, with one informed commentator having suggested in 2006 that relations between the media and the government were at that time tense, although day-to-day interactions were cordial and the government had refrained from official censorship (Duffield, 2006; see also Freedom House, 2019; Perottet and Robie, 2011, pp. 166–67; Robie, 2019; Singh, 2017, pp. 6–7).

The Committee to Protect Journalists (n.d.-a, n.d.-b) reports on murders of journalists around the world; it indicated that there had been one murder in PNG: a foreign journalist, Per-Ove Carlsson, was murdered in Kiunga, not far from the Indonesian border, in 1992. Carlsson went 'to the region to make a film about the guerrilla organization Free Papua Movement' (Committee to Protect Journalists, n.d.-b) in West Papua. To date, there have been no arrests related to his murder (Committee to Protect Journalists, n.d.-b).

The ownership of media outlets is relevant to discussions of media freedom because owners may influence editorial policy. For example, when an enquiry was looking into land leases, many of which were held by Rimbunan Hijau, *The National* was warned by one of the enquiry's commissioners not to be biased in its reporting (Pacific Media Watch, 2011; see also Cass, 2004, p. 88). In fact, a recent report suggested that *The National* 'rarely publishes any news story or op-ed [opinion piece or editorial] critical of the logging industry' (Dickey et al., 2019, p. 22).

As Singh (2004, pp. 51–52) has explained, 'public perceptions of a medium's credibility are crucial for survival [and] any public perception of bias would hurt the credibility, and thus the marketability, of the medium'. PNG's newspapers are highly reliant on a large volume of government advertising. Thus, it could be argued that they may not wish to antagonise the government in their reportage. Even if there is no direct influence on editorial decisions, there are concerns that, for business owners, a 'profit motive overrides any consideration for improvement' (Pamba, 2004, p. 59).

The *Post-Courier* is majority owned by News Corp and its executive chairman, Rupert Murdoch, is frequently accused of 'political intervention through the use (or threatened use) of his media power in the United Kingdom, the United States, and Australia' (Hobbs and McKnight, 2014, p. 1). It is alleged that 'the company misuses its vast media power for corporate gain and to pursue political ends' (Ricketson, 2012, p. 139). For instance, it has been argued that the company's Australian newspapers 'campaigned vigorously against the re-election of the Labor government in 2013' (Hobbs and McKnight, 2014, p. 1) and again in 2019 (Dwyer and Koskie, 2019). Interestingly, one study comparing newspaper coverage found that News Corp's coverage of Australia's refugee detention centre on PNG's Manus Island was more favourable in its representation of the PNG residents than the other newspaper studied (Allen and Hoenig, 2018, p. 118). This may be because the News Corp article ran in both the *Post-Courier* and its fellow publication *The Australian* at the same time (Allen and Hoenig, 2018). According to News Corp, PNG citizens should not be worried about the *Post-Courier* being foreign owned because editorial decisions are made by PNG staff (Dickey et al., 2019, p. 22).

Although the uptake of social media will be discussed in detail later in the chapter, it is worth noting here that PNG's first cybercrime law was passed by parliament in 2016 (Dawidi, 2016; Kenneth, 2016). It 'allows the prosecution of people who publish defamatory material or incite violence on social media, raising concerns that it could be misused to punish legitimate speech' (Freedom House, 2019). Such concerns about the law imposing limits on free speech have been expressed in various forums (Kant et al., 2018, pp. 69–70; Oxford Business Group, n.d.; Singh, 2017, p. 6; Tahana, 2014; Tlozek, 2015). Addressing such concerns, it has been argued that the law is 'not the result of some sinister ploy by the Government to shut out our right to freedom of speech (which in any case, is a qualified Constitutional right) or opinions on corruption' (Dawidi, 2016). Singh (2020, p. 55) has argued that 'while governments could be accused of censorship, they have some real concerns about social media abuse, and the damage to individuals, communities and society'. Even so, it has been pointed out that the PNG law 'does not have a clear section or subsection which protects freedom of expression, specifically critical political discourse' (Kant et al., 2018, p. 70).

Media investigations

It is essential in an effective democracy 'that the media has the capacity to investigate and distil information from various stakeholders and to make sense of it for the average consumer of news' (Pamba, 2014, p. 2). This section asks about the extent to which the media is able to carry out in-depth investigations. Matbob (2011) documented a strong history of investigative journalism in PNG. For example, the former PNG weekly newspaper *The Independent* uncovered major corruption scandals through its investigative journalism while it was in operation (Kanekane, 2006, p. 385). Examples of such investigations can still be found today, especially on the PNGi website. However, there have been repeated assertions that, overall, the media in PNG fails to undertake a sufficient amount of investigative journalism (Duffield, 2006; Lasslett, 2015; Popot, 2011; Reporters without Borders, 2020b). This section considers why this is the case. The contributing factors, which will be discussed here, are monetary considerations, workplace issues, a culture of deference and the lack of a substantial presence of foreign correspondents. As will be outlined here, these factors tend to lead to a habit of reprinting or broadcasting material directly from media releases produced by government departments, businesses and others.

Monetary considerations directly contribute to a lack of investigative journalism. There is a 'lack of funding and material resources for proper investigative journalism and reporting in the field' (Reporters without Borders, 2020b). Robie (2011, p. 214) stated that lack of resources is a major challenge inhibiting the practice of investigative journalism, specifically 'lack of staff, money and time'. Firth (2006, p. 6) argued that, in PNG, 'the media is constrained, above all, by the need to make money', but this can be difficult for media businesses, due to factors such as 'low disposable incomes, limited product sales and small profit margins' (Singh, 2020, p. 58). Across the Melanesian region, there are 'dwindling resources in many newsrooms, especially for investigative journalism' (Robie, 2020a, p. 30; see also Melanesia Media Freedom Forum, 2019; Singh, 2020).

Workplace issues within media organisations in the region, including PNG, comprise 'longstanding, unaddressed issues such as underqualified and inexperienced journalists, uncompetitive salaries, [and] high journalist turnover' (Singh, 2020, p. 56). High turnover of staff is also mentioned as a problem by several other commentators (Krishnamurthi, 2020; Matbob et al., 2011, p. 11; Pamba, 2014, p. 1). Journalists' salaries in PNG are generally low, compared to other professions in PNG (Robie, 2011, pp. 212–13) and there are insufficient training opportunities (Singh, 2017, p. 1). Staff at media outlets are busy covering daily news events and therefore do not have time to undertake in-depth investigations (Duffield, 2006).

A culture of deference has also been blamed for an apparent unwillingness to undertake in-depth investigations. Recently, Transparency International PNG carried out a review of PNG newspapers. It examined stories about then Prime Minister Peter O'Neill and found that only 4 per cent portrayed him in a negative light (79 per cent were positive while 17 per cent were neutral or indifferent), 'demonstrating an overwhelming deference to the incumbent Prime Minister' (Transparency International PNG, 2020; see also Krishnamurthi, 2020). According to Lasslett (2015), there is a lack of willingness on the part of media in PNG to undertake thorough investigations: 'there is a systematic failure to inquire into, and report on, the daily scandals profoundly affecting the region'. This may, in part, be because of a culture of deference in which 'many Pacific journalists are reluctant to ask the hard questions of political leaders and those in high office' (Robie, 2020a, p. 18; see also Shaligram, 2019; Singh, 2020, p. 52). A practical reason for deferential behaviour could be to ensure access. As journalist Scott Waide has argued, limited access to information presents a challenge for the media in PNG: 'you are excluded from events or deliberately not informed' (quoted in Krishnamurthi, 2020). One way that deferential reporting has been sidestepped on occasion has been for PNG media to provide information that they are unwilling to handle to overseas outlets and, after they release the news, then report it as second-hand information (Hill, 2018).

At present, and for some years, there has only been one foreign correspondent based in PNG. While the Australian Broadcasting Corporation's correspondent has been able to generate a substantial amount of coverage of PNG for Australian audiences and others (Duffield, 2020; Ginau et al., 2011), one person cannot cover daily news and also undertake regular in-depth investigations in such a large and complex country. A greater number of foreign journalists based in PNG might increase the amount of investigative journalism completed because these people would likely be more willing to ask difficult questions and their operations would generally be better resourced. There certainly would be many possible investigations that could be embarked upon (Lasslett, 2015). The various chapters of this book have presented areas that are ripe for investigation and in-depth media coverage, including governance, economic performance and social issues.

Due to the factors outlined above, '"copy-and-paste" journalism' (Reporters without Borders, 2020b) is frequently employed by the PNG media, meaning that media releases written by government departments and corporations tend to be reprinted or broadcast in full without any analysis (Shaligram, 2019; Singh, 2020, p. 57). While not unique to PNG, this is certainly not good journalistic practice. In doing their work, 'news organisations inevitably have to quote politicians and analysts' (Greste, 2017, p. 307). However, 'a disciplined news organisation would shy away from repeating' (Greste, 2017, p. 306) the language of leaders time after time and would instead try to find other ways to describe occurrences (Greste, 2017, pp. 300–12). When the newspapers in PNG reprint press releases in full (Matbob et al., 2011, p. 8; Singh, 2020, p. 57), they fall into the trap of presenting the world in the way that others want them to, rather than examining stories from multiple perspectives.

The Media Council of PNG (n.d.-a) has a code of conduct that aims to encourage professional standards and suggests that media workers should strive 'to provide balanced coverage by providing a fair opportunity for any individual or organizations mentioned in a news story to respond to allegations or criticism before publication'. Indeed, it is important to allow 'different viewpoints [to be] expressed to enable a healthy societal debate on governance' (Transparency International PNG, 2020). In their defence, PNG newspapers do at least reproduce media releases from opposing sides of various controversies, sometimes on consecutive days.

This section has argued that there are insufficient in-depth investigations conducted by the media in PNG. Several reasons have been outlined. The result is that the practice of reprinting media releases is commonplace. To increase the number of investigations undertaken, further effort could be made to attract content funds. For instance, a PNG journalist was granted funding in 2020 to report on environmental issues (Internews, 2020). Current affairs programs on television or radio, or collaborations across media outlets, could potentially provide avenues for thorough investigations through which bureaucrats, politicians and companies could be held to account.

Gender and media

Popot (2011) examined articles referring to gender-based violence in the two daily newspapers. In nearly all of the 113 stories analysed, the only source for the articles was a police report: 'most of the stories were very brief and reported just the assaults, without doing further interviews' (Popot, 2011, p. 77). Several years later, media coverage of gender-based violence continued to be a contested issue, with one commentator suggesting that there should be allocation of funding 'to the media industry to support timely, accurate and independent reporting on these issues' (Rooney, 2017b).

More female journalists might increase the presence of female voices in media reportage and could enable more effective reporting of issues such as gender-based violence (e.g. because female victims may feel more comfortable talking to female journalists rather than males) (Valencia-Forrester et al., 2020, p. 72). According to Dorney (2016, p. 64), the composition of the media workforce has changed: when he began work in the PNG media in 1974, management positions and coveted political reporting assignments were all occupied by males, but there are now many female journalists and media managers. A survey conducted in 2001 found that about half of journalists in PNG were female (Robie, 2011, p. 207).

A recent study identified that within the PNG media sector women hold a third of content-maker positions and a third of decision-making roles but only a small percentage of board positions (Media for Development Initiative, 2018, p. 2; see also Melanesia Media Freedom Forum, 2019; Valencia-Forrester et al., 2020). A 2010 study also found 'evidence of the general under-representation of women in power and decision making structures' (Global Media Monitoring Project, 2015, p. 7) in the PNG media sector.

It has been claimed that female journalists have been silenced in various ways – for instance, because editors have rejected their stories or because sources have refused to be interviewed by females (Valencia-Forrester et al., 2020, pp. 69–70). In addition, 'facing threats of violence and suppression is a daily occurrence for many female journalists' (Valencia-Forrester et al., 2020, p. 70). There are significant concerns about workplace culture and insufficient handling of reported sexual harassment: 'safety concerns, lack of managerial and organisational support for effective safety practices and extensive accounts of harassment and sexual harassment dominate the experiences of women working in the media sector' (Media for Development Initiative, 2018, p. 2). It has been suggested that journalists' typically low salaries tend to be even lower for women than their male colleagues (Valencia-Forrester et al., 2020, p. 68), although further research is required on this issue (Global Media Monitoring Project, 2015, p. 5).

Several media products have made deliberate efforts to present positive images of women. *Stella* magazine produced four editions per annum from 2012 to 2016. *Lily* magazine launched in 2013 and continues to print two to three editions each year. Since 2012, a television program presented by Jennifer Baing-Waiko has aimed at encouraging healthy eating habits. The *Lewa Show* is an online television show that commenced in 2019 in which women's issues are discussed. Nonetheless, there is room for improvement with regard to the portrayal of women by the media. Writing about a sexist cartoon that appeared in one of the newspapers, Rooney (2017a) suggested that the cartoon 'only serves to reinforce social, cultural and political challenges women face … and the PNG mainstream media should lead efforts to strengthen equitable and fair coverage of women'. Indeed, the media could play a role 'in sustaining a national conversation about important issues such as gender equality' (Rooney, 2017a).

Mobile telephones

The chapter transitions now from the media to more interactive forms of communication, starting with the mobile telephone. Until 2007, most people in PNG had to travel to the nearest town to queue at a public telephone if they wanted to make a telephone call. The government telecommunication provider, Telikom PNG, held a monopoly (Barker, 2008; Foster and Horst, 2018, p. 1; Jorgensen, 2018, p. 54; Marshall, 2007) and had established mobile network coverage only in urban areas (Barker, 2008; Watson, 2011, p. 47; Watson and Duffield, 2016, p. 271). The monopoly ceased when the Independent Consumer and Competition Commission opened up the market, granting licences to two companies. Digicel, which advertised extensively, expanded its network across the country quickly and offered cheap handsets. GreenCom, the other licensee, never actually offered any mobile telephone service (Watson, 2011, p. 47).

Digicel commenced operations in PNG on 1 July 2007 and rapidly expanded mobile network coverage to all provinces, starting with provincial capitals and extending to rural areas. Initially, uptake increased at an astonishing rate – Digicel signed up 600,000 customers by March 2008 (Marshall, 2008). In the first few years of its operations in PNG, mobile telephone uptake reportedly led to increases in the gross domestic product (Watson, 2011, p. 48). Figure 8.1 shows the number of mobile telephones in use in PNG over the past two decades.

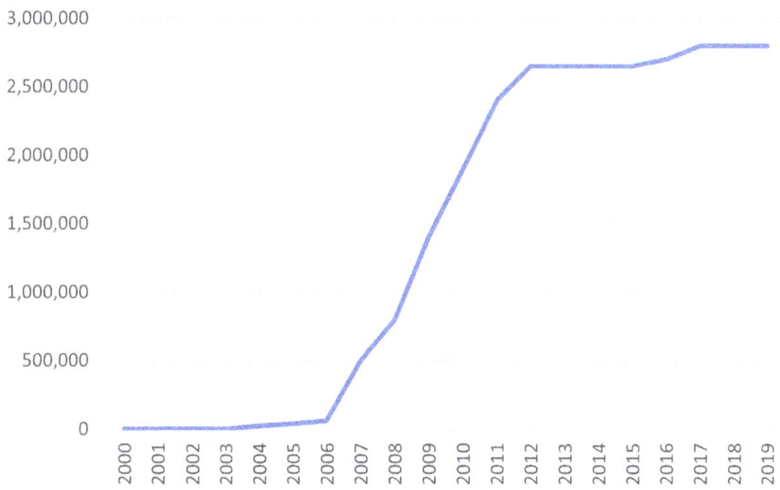

Figure 8.1: Mobile telephones in use in PNG over time.

Source: Author's calculations.

In research conducted in rural villages during 2009, when the Digicel network coverage was a novel phenomenon generating new experiences, it was 'found that the introduction of mobile telecommunications has generally been viewed positively, although several negative concerns have been strongly felt' (Watson, 2011, p. iii). People were delighted to be able to hear the voices of loved ones residing in other parts of the country and appreciated the usefulness of mobile telephony during time-critical emergencies (Watson, 2011). Worries related to affordability and concerns about the impact of the introduction of a means for private communication (Watson, 2011). For example, random telephone calls to unknown numbers can lead to 'phone friendships' (Lipset, 2018, p. 24; Wardlow, 2018), which may fall outside of the rules governing communities.

There are three mobile network licences available in PNG. In 2008, there was a partial sale of bmobile, which was initially a subsidiary of Telikom PNG, with the PNG Government retaining an interest. Telikom PNG launched its Citifon service in 2011. Citifon was replaced by Telikom PNG's 4G LTE service in 2016. This meant that, for a number of years, the PNG Government had, in effect, an interest in two competing mobile networks: bmobile and Telikom PNG's offering (first Citifon and later 4G LTE). At the time of writing, a process of merging these two entities is ongoing. The idea is to create one competitive market player out of the two entities with PNG Government involvement (Watson and Patel, 2017), although additional funds are required to complete the technical aspects of merging the two networks (Moi, 2020). The merger has made the third licence available and there are indications that a Fijian company is likely to enter the PNG market in the near future because the Asian Development Bank recently announced funding for it to set up a mobile network in PNG (Asian Development Bank, 2020).

Currently, Digicel has a 92 per cent market share, with approximately 2.5 million mobile telephone users (Highet et al., 2019, pp. 18–19). It has 'an effective monopoly [because it] is the only network that covers rural and remote locations' (Watson and Fox, 2019). Despite its parent company carrying a substantial amount of debt, Digicel's PNG operations are 'remarkably profitable' (McLeod, 2020b). Its competitor (the merged bmobile/Telikom entity) has a large amount of debt and is loss making (Wall, 2020).

Two-thirds of people now live within mobile network coverage (Highet et al., 2019, p. 19). The coverage can be intermittent though, with recent research in the Autonomous Region of Bougainville having identified frequent mobile network outages, particularly in Central and South Bougainville (Watson, Miller et al., 2020). There are 2.8 million active mobile telephones in PNG (Highet et al., 2019, p. 24). This suggests that, although access to telephones has increased since 2007, many people do not own or use a mobile telephone. The majority (55 per cent) of the mobile telephones in use in PNG are second generation (2G) handsets, which means that they are suitable for telephone calls and text messaging (Highet et al., 2019, p. 18). Twenty-three per cent are third generation (3G), which is suitable for browsing the internet, and 22 per cent are fourth generation (4G), which enables faster internet speeds (Highet et al., 2019, p. 18).

In many countries, 'digital connectivity, internet access and smartphone services are weak or even non-existent in deep, rural regions, such as small, remote islands' (Watson and Park, 2019). It is important to note that less than 15 per cent of the PNG population has reliable access to electricity (Highet et al., 2019, p. 11). This means that mobile telephone owners regularly struggle to keep their handset batteries charged (Highet et al., 2019, p. 23; Wardlow, 2018, p. 41; Watson and Duffield, 2016, p. 275; Watson, Miller et al., 2020, p. 8; Yamo, 2013, pp. 96–97). A survey conducted with more than 1,000 households in rural and remote locations around PNG found that 65 per cent of households had reliable mobile network coverage but more than half of the households had no mobile telephone (Benson, 2019, pp. 2–5). As might be expected, 'households that own a solar panel or generator are more likely to own a phone' (Benson, 2019, p. 6). Households with high educational attainment levels are more likely to have mobile telephones than those with lower education levels and 'richer households are more likely to own mobile phones' (Benson, 2019, p. 6).

Most of the mobile telephones in use are prepaid (Highet et al., 2019, p. 19), which means that 'users assume fiscal responsibility for managing their phone credits' (Foster, 2018, p. 109). For example, one user expressed frustration at the slow pace of her relatives' speech because of her awareness that every second of a telephone call costs her money (Foster, 2018, pp. 111–12). At the time of writing, a government policy of compulsory registration of mobile telephone owner details is ongoing and could potentially result in some users being excluded from mobile telephone access, at least temporarily (Watson, 2020b).

There are three key opportunities for use of mobile telephones to promote development that will be discussed here in turn, using relevant examples from across PNG: (1) effective two-way communication for government workers and others; (2) information dissemination; and (3) citizen reporting.

First, two-way communication will be considered using two examples from the health sector. Yamo (2013) explored the establishment by the Western Highlands Provincial Health Authority of a list of mobile telephone numbers and a system through which health workers and managers could communicate with one another as needed. The system was found to be beneficial, particularly during time-sensitive medical emergencies, but it was evident that improvements could be made in its management to maximise its effective use, reduce costs and enhance internal organisational communication (Yamo and Watson, 2014). In Milne Bay Province, a maternal health hotline was established so that rural-based health workers could telephone the labour ward at Alotau Provincial Hospital during time-critical childbirth emergencies. The hotline was found to save women's lives (Watson et al., 2015) and continues to operate (Highet et al., 2019, p. 39).

Second, regarding information dissemination, a project undertaken by the non-government organisation Population Services International, which consisted of weekly health tips in the form of text messages, was the first attempt to use mobile telephony to disseminate information to community members in PNG (Highet et al., 2019, p. 40). This was a free service available to Digicel users. At least 30,000 people subscribed to the service but it 'eventually ceased due to funding and questions about impact' (Highet et al., 2019, p. 40; see also Cullen, 2017, p. 327). In other words, it cost money to send tens of thousands of text messages every week and there was no way to know whether those receiving the text messages read them, liked them or considered adopting healthy behaviours as a result of receiving them.

Another example of information dissemination was a project of the Department of Education called SMS Story. Elementary teachers at selected rural and remote schools in two provinces received daily text messages containing short stories and lesson plans to aid them in teaching English to students. Research revealed that the reading ability of students whose teachers received the materials improved more than the ability of students whose teachers did not receive them (Kaleebu et al., 2017). Since then, the SMS Story model has been used in India and Bangladesh (Kaleebu et al., 2017, p. 643) as well as Uganda.

Third, in terms of citizens reporting information, a useful example is the Department of Finance's Phones against Corruption project, which allows reporting of alleged corruption free of charge through text messaging (Watson and Wiltshire, 2016). The project has led to at least two arrests, but district treasury officers reported no prior knowledge of the service and recommended enhanced and targeted promotional activities about it (Watson and Wiltshire, 2016).

Through informal communication networks, there are also likely many instances in which telephone calls and text messaging are used by community members to engage in two-way communication, disseminate relevant information and perhaps report local issues or provide feedback on policies. An example of effective informal communication involves coastal villagers communicating with relatives in town during tsunami alerts. Prior to the introduction of mobile telephone networks in rural areas, tsunami alerts led to panic among villagers, but since mobile telephones have been available, villagers have been able to liaise with educated, urban relatives to access timely information (Watson, 2012). A critical component of this example, which links with the next section of this chapter, is use of the internet by urban residents to find accurate information to pass on to rural-based relatives through telephone calls (Watson, 2012). The villagers had 2G network coverage and basic handsets that they could use to make telephone calls to relatives with internet access through desktop computers at their workplaces in urban centres.

The spread of mobile telephone networks throughout rural and remote parts of PNG since 2007 heralded a notable change in people's communication options and information access. While there have been some keenly felt concerns regarding the introduction of a private communication tool (Watson, 2011), there have also been noticeable benefits. For many people though, usage challenges remain, such as limited electricity and weak, patchy or inconsistent mobile network coverage (Watson, Miller et al., 2020). Despite early praise and appreciation for Digicel's network coverage in rural areas, concerns have emerged about Digicel's effective monopoly (Logan and Forsyth, 2018; Watson and Fox, 2019; World Bank, 2020, pp. 61–62) and some of the services it provides (Foster, 2017; Logan and Forsyth, 2018; Rooney et al., 2020). There are also concerns that competition is being limited due to 'the government's ownership of a number of telecommunications companies, combined with the presence of government-owned companies across the entire value chain' (World Bank, 2020, p. 61).

Internet and social media

Since about 2012, an increasing number of people in PNG have had internet access, most commonly through a mobile device. This change has been driven by the introduction of 3G network coverage in some places, and 4G in urban areas, and by the availability of cheap smartphone handsets. The latest figures indicate that there are about 600,000 smartphones in use in PNG (Highet et al., 2019, pp. 18–19). With regard to internet access, some groups are less likely to be connected, 'namely residents outside of urban areas, women and older citizens' (ABC International Development, 2019, p. 5; see also Sagrista and Matbob, 2016; Watson and Park, 2019). There are 750,000 people in PNG using Facebook, of which 39 per cent are women (Highet et al., 2019, p. 33).

To date, the internet in PNG has been costly, slow and unreliable (Deloitte Touche Tohmatsu, 2016; Logan and Suwamaru, 2017; Watson, 2020a; Williams, 2019, p. 5). PNG continues to rank very poorly compared to other countries in terms of internet affordability (World Bank, 2020, p. 50). An undersea cable connecting PNG to Australia was completed late in 2019 and a domestic undersea cable connecting numerous provinces of PNG was completed in 2020 (Coral Sea Cable System, n.d.; *The National*, 2020; Watson, 2020a; Watson, Airi et al., 2020; Williams, 2019). It is anticipated that the new cables may make the internet cheaper, faster and more reliable for consumers (Watson, Airi et al., 2020; Williams, 2019). In the first half of 2020, there was no improvement in price and several factors may influence whether there is a discernible price reduction in the future, including the need to recover the costs of the new domestic cable, market competition and existing supplier contracts (Watson, Airi et al., 2020). It has also been alleged that the wholesaler has been 'restricting access' (World Bank, 2020, p. 61) to the new international cable. At the time of writing, the regulator is working to determine appropriate prices (Watson, Airi et al., 2020).

The internet and social media can be utilised for communication and for information dissemination. Regarding communication, discussion groups on the Facebook platform allow people in PNG to communicate for a range of purposes. For instance, regional and local groups are popular for discussing issues with a geographical focus (Logan and Suwamaru, 2017, pp. 289–90; Rooney, 2012). The discussion group function is commonly used for discussing current affairs: 'the PNG-based Facebook discussion groups which have the most members and are most prominent are those devoted to discussions of governance and related social issues' (Logan and Suwamaru, 2017, p. 289).

In terms of information dissemination, it has been argued that 'social media plays a crucial role in keeping the public informed on matters that the mainstream media may have missed' (Kant et al., 2018, p. 71). For instance, numerous PNG politicians share local news, opinions, media releases, government information and so on through Facebook (McLeod, 2020a). The internet can also be used for the distribution of misinformation. As Robie has noted regarding trends in several countries in Asia, and with a caution for the Pacific, 'disinformation and media manipulation are now critical issues' (2020a, p. 19). Facebook users in PNG view inaccurate or misleading information to be common and generally can recognise it, although they feel that they have on some occasions been deceived (ABC International Development, 2019, p. 12). A study of a Facebook group for the Fly River region of Western Province found that posts about COVID-19 during March to May 2020 generally shared factual information (Dwyer and Minnegal, 2020). In the main, the Facebook group seemed to play a positive role in communication and information dissemination and users 'did not take either religious tropes or conspiracy theories as primary sources of comfort or explanation' (Dwyer and Minnegal, 2020, p. 243).

In addition to misinformation, there are negative concerns about access to and use of the internet and social media for the spread of 'child abuse content [and] explicit material' (Aualiitia and Wilson, 2020). Critics argue that popular platform Facebook 'is not doing enough to stop abusive and harmful content in local languages' (Aualiitia and Wilson, 2020). There are:

> Several active PNG-based Facebook groups with thousands of members where users share hundreds of explicit images, almost always of women, sometimes depicting sexual behaviour [and] it is unclear how these images were obtained and whether the subjects have consented to their distribution. (Aualiitia and Wilson, 2020)

A research project that sought the views of children from a settlement on the fringes of Port Moresby found that they are worried about online safety and in particular 'encountering sexual or violent content (including news coverage of violent events or photos of the deceased), harmful influences, cyberbullying and hacking' (Third et al., 2020, p. 5). PNG's cybercrime law does aim to address 'a whole range of illegal online activities such as – but not limited to – hacking, data and system interference, electronic fraud and forgery, pornography, animal pornography, child pornography and defamatory publication' (Kant et al., 2018, p. 69).

Citizen journalism is the practice of citizens reporting news or events from their local area and it is a relatively new trend in Melanesia (Singh, 2020, p. 50) that warrants further investigation. As a vehicle for distributing local-level news – for example, news about instances of abuse or violence – social media can play a 'role in giving voice to the marginalised and to bringing such cases to the attention of the police, authorities and general public' (Rooney, 2017b). Distributed primarily through social media, citizen journalism can 'support and strengthen traditional journalism, but also weaken it by diverting away revenue' (Singh, 2020, p. 55). On the one hand, journalists working for the mainstream media can use social media to source story ideas, images, videos and the like. On the other hand, social media can be used by those who wish to establish a presence as independent producers of material (Newman et al., 2012). Thus, it can be seen that social media 'both helps and hobbles the practice of journalism' (Singh, 2020, p. 60).

As Logan (2012) posited, increasing access to mobile telephones, the internet and social media may have impacts upon the political sphere, although further research is required. Online and offline activism combined in the organisation of protest rallies in PNG during the Easter weekend in 2012 when there was a constitutional crisis, with two members of parliament claiming to be prime minister (Logan, 2012; Logan and Suwamaru, 2017; Rooney, 2012). It is important to note that there has been 'collaboration between Facebook discussion groups and offline community groups, such as trade unions and churches in organizing protests and other political activity' (Logan and Suwamaru, 2017, p. 291). Although further research is required on this topic in PNG, examples from the Pacific region of political engagement online include climate change activism (Titifanue et al., 2017), feminist activism (Brimacombe et al., 2018), the Free West Papua campaign (Logan and Suwamaru, 2017, p. 291; Titifanue et al., 2016), and election-related campaigning in Fiji (Tarai, 2019). An increase in the use of social media was also noticed in relation to the 2017 election in PNG, compared to previous elections (Haley and Zubrinich, 2018).

Conclusion

This chapter has presented a literature survey that has assessed the extent to which people throughout PNG have access to communication channels and to accurate, timely information – both of which are critical for democracy and development. The chapter argues that media freedom is reasonably healthy in PNG but that it has vulnerabilities and is worth safeguarding. There are a number of media outlets, yet, as a whole, the media conducts insufficient in-depth investigations. The chapter has highlighted an increase in the availability of television stations, weekly newspapers and online information in PNG in recent years. However, as the chapter has pointed out, there is a gulf between urban and rural access to communication options and information mediums. While mobile telephone access has increased since 2007, and internet access has risen since about 2012, many people remain offline, with limited access to electricity.

Acknowledgements

Various staff members at media organisations provided details for the media section of the chapter. Detailed and useful feedback was received from Jemima Garrett on a draft. Other contributors to this volume are thanked for their encouragement and ideas.

References

ABC International Development. (2014). *Governance and the role of media in Papua New Guinea* (Audience research brief 2014). www.abc.net.au/cm/lb/9200956/data/governance-and-the-role-of-the-media-in-png---audience-research-data.pdf.

ABC International Development. (2019). *PNG citizen perceptions of governance and media engagement report.* www.abc.net.au/cm/lb/12549690/data/png-citizen-perceptions-of-governance-and-media-engagement-stud-data.pdf.

Allen, A. M. and Hoenig, R. (2018). The shadow other: Representations of the Manus Island riots in two Australian newspapers. *Australian Journalism Review*, *40*(1), 109–24.

Asian Development Bank. (2020). *ADB approves $25 million cornerstone investment to improve telecom services in PNG*. www.adb.org/news/adb-approves-25-million-cornerstone-investment-improve-telecom-services-png.

Aualiitia, T. and Wilson, C. (2020). Facebook criticised for allowing illegal and harmful content in PNG languages. ABC News. www.abc.net.au/news/science/2020-08-11/png-facebook-child-abuse-misinformation-language-moderation/12511222.

Backhaus, B. (2020). Talking the talk: Navigating frameworks of development communication. *Pacific Journalism Review*, *26*(1), 164–77. doi.org/10.24135/pjr.v26i1.1070.

Barker, P. (2008, 8 April). *ICT legislation and policy: Commentary*. Paper presented to PNG Update, Goroka.

Bennett, T., Grossberg, L. and Morris, M. (2005). *New keywords: A revised vocabulary of culture and society*. Blackwell Publishing.

Benson, T. (2019). *Can mobile phone-based household surveys in rural Papua New Guinea generate information representative of the population surveyed?* International Food Policy Research Institute.

Betteridge, A. (2014, 9 May). Australia network axing: What will happen to coverage of the region? *Devpolicy Blog*. devpolicy.org/australia-network-axing-what-will-happen-to-coverage-of-the-region-20140509/.

Betteridge, A. (2017, 14 July). Public interest journalism and regional interests: Implications for the Pacific and Australian aid. *Devpolicy Blog*. devpolicy.org/public-interest-journalism-regional-interests-implications-pacific-australian-aid-20170714/.

Boden, I. (1995). Time to light up the NBC airwaves. *Pacific Journalism Review*, *2*(1), 47–49. doi.org/10.24135/pjr.v2i1.536.

Brimacombe, T., Kant, R., Finau, G., Tarai, J. and Titifanue, J. (2018). A new frontier in digital activism: An exploration of digital feminism in Fiji. *Asia & the Pacific Policy Studies*, *5*(3), 508–21. doi.org/10.1002/app5.253.

Business Advantage PNG. (2014a). Digicel PNG plans television network as it expands its mobile network. www.businessadvantagepng.com/digicel-plans-expansion-mobile-network-creating-television-network/.

Business Advantage PNG. (2014b). Two new Papua New Guinea TV players launch pay and free-to-air channels. www.businessadvantagepng.com/two-new-papua-new-guinea-tv-players-launch-pay-free-air-channels/.

Cangah, B. P. (2011). Factors influencing HIV/AIDS media awareness campaigns. In E. Papoutsaki, M. McManus and P. Matbob (Eds), *Communication, culture and society in Papua New Guinea: Yu Tok Wanem?* (pp. 92–102). DWU Press.

Cass, P. (2004). Media ownership in the Pacific: Inherited colonial commercial model but remarkably diverse. *Pacific Journalism Review*, *10*(2), 82–110. doi.org/10.24135/pjr.v10i2.808.

Cass, P. (2020). Some aspects of climate change communication and effectiveness in PNG. *Pacific Journalism Review*, *26*(1), 148–63. doi.org/10.24135/pjr.v26i1.1106.

Committee to Protect Journalists. (n.d.-a). *Papua New Guinea*. cpj.org/asia/papua-new-guinea/.

Committee to Protect Journalists. (n.d.-b). *Per-Ove Carlsson*. cpj.org/data/people/per-ove-carlsson/.

Coral Sea Cable System. (n.d.). *About the project*. www.coralseacablesystem.com.au/about/.

Cox, J. (2018). *Fast money schemes: Hope and deception in Papua New Guinea*. Indiana University Press. doi.org/10.2307/j.ctv6mtfjm.

Cullen, R. (2017). The use of ICT in the health sector in Pacific Island countries. In R. Cullen and G. Hassall (Eds), *Achieving sustainable e-government in Pacific Island states* (pp. 305–35). Springer. doi.org/10.1007/978-3-319-50972-3_11.

Dawidi, Z. (2016, 23 August). Opinion: What you need to know about Papua New Guinea's new Cybercrime Act. Business Advantage PNG. www.businessadvantagepng.com/cybercrime/.

Deloitte Touche Tohmatsu. (2016). *Why are internet prices high in Papua New Guinea?* National Research Institute.

Dickey, L., Downs, E., Taffer, A. and Holz, H. (2019). *Mapping the information environment in the Pacific Island countries: Disruptors, deficits, and decisions*. CNA. www.cna.org/CNA_files/centers/cna/cip/disinformation/IRM-2019-U-019755-Final.pdf.

Dobell, G., Heriot, G. and Garrett, J. (2018). *Hard news and free media as the sharp edge of Australian soft power*. Australian Strategic Policy Institute. www.aspi.org.au/report/hard-news-and-free-media.

Dorney, S. (2016). *The embarrassed colonialist*. Penguin Group Australia.

Duffield, L. R. (2006). Media and government relations in Papua New Guinea. In E. Papoutsaki and D. Rooney (Eds), *Media, information and development in Papua New Guinea* (pp. 95–117). DWU Press.

Duffield, L. R. (2020). Forgetting PNG? Australian media coverage of Papua New Guinea. *Pacific Journalism Review, 26*(1), 178–93. doi.org/10.24135/pjr.v26i1.1069.

Duncan, R. (2011). Governance reform in the public sector in Pacific Island countries: Understanding how culture matters. In R. Duncan (Ed.), *The political economy of economic reform in the Pacific* (pp. 139–62). Asian Development Bank. www.adb.org/publications/political-economy-economic-reform-pacific.

Dwyer, P. D. and Minnegal, M. (2020). COVID-19 and Facebook in Papua New Guinea: Fly River forum. *Asia & the Pacific Policy Studies, 7*(3), 233–46. doi.org/10.1002/app5.312.

Dwyer, T. and Koskie, T. (2019, 5 June). Press, platforms and power: Mapping out a stronger Australian media landscape. *The Conversation*. theconversation.com/press-platforms-and-power-mapping-out-a-stronger-australian-media-landscape-117987.

Elapa, J. (2011). Pasim tok: Dialogue and conflict resolution in the Southern Highlands. In E. Papoutsaki, M. McManus and P. Matbob (Eds), *Communication, culture and society in Papua New Guinea: Yu Tok Wanem?* (pp. 113–23). DWU Press.

Firth, S. (2006). Introduction. In S. Firth (Ed.), *Globalisation and governance in the Pacific Islands* (pp. 1–6). ANU Press. doi.org/10.22459/GGPI.12.2006.

Foster, R. J. (2017). *Customer care*. limn.it/articles/customer-care/.

Foster, R. J. (2018). Top-up: The moral economy of prepaid mobile phone subscriptions. In R. J. Foster and H. A. Horst (Eds), *The moral economy of mobile phones: Pacific Islands perspectives* (pp. 107–25). ANU Press. doi.org/10.22459/MEMP.05.2018.06.

Foster, R. J. and Horst, H. A. (2018). Introduction. In R. J. Foster and H. A. Horst (Eds), *The moral economy of mobile phones: Pacific Islands perspectives* (pp. 1–17). ANU Press. doi.org/10.22459/MEMP.05.2018.

Freedom House. (2019). *Freedom in the world 2019: Papua New Guinea*. freedomhouse.org/country/papua-new-guinea/freedom-world/2019.

Ginau, M., Papoutsaki, E., Duffield, L. and Watson, A. H. A. (2011). Our neighbour's view: Australian media coverage of Papua New Guinea. In E. Papoutsaki, M. McManus and P. Matbob (Eds), *Communication, culture and society in Papua New Guinea: Yu Tok Wanem?* (pp. 62–72). DWU Press.

Global Media Monitoring Project. (2015). *Who makes the news? Pacific: Global Media Monitoring Project 2015 regional report*. World Association for Christian Communication. whomakesthenews.org/wp-content/uploads/who-makes-the-news/Imported/reports_2015/regional/Pacific_Islands.pdf.

Greensmith, G. (2017, 8 March). There is a war on media, and it's time for journalism teachers to suit up. *Crikey*. www.crikey.com.au/2017/03/08/there-is-a-war-on-media-and-its-time-for-journalism-teachers-to-suit-up/.

Greste, P. (2017). *The first casualty: From the front lines of the global war on journalism*. Viking.

Gware, C. (2018). Kramer on newspaper boycott. Loop PNG. www.looppng.com/png-news/kramer-newspaper-boycott-78221.

Haley, N. and Zubrinich, K. (2018). *2017 Papua New Guinea general elections: Election observation report*. Department of Pacific Affairs, The Australian National University.

Highet, C., Nique, M., Watson, A. H. A. and Wilson, A. (2019). *Digital transformation: The role of mobile technology in Papua New Guinea*. GSMA.

Hill, B. (2018, 23 August). Information laundering in the Pacific. *Devpolicy Blog*. devpolicy.org/pacific-launder-information-20180823/.

Hirst, M. (2013, 11 December). Right to know: The 'nation', the 'people' and the Fourth Estate. *The Conversation*. theconversation.com/right-to-know-the-nation-the-people-and-the-fourth-estate-21253.

Hobbs, M. and McKnight, D. (2014). 'Kick this mob out': The Murdoch media and the Australian Labor Government (2007 to 2013). *Global Media Journal: Australian Edition*, *8*(2), 1–13. hca.westernsydney.edu.au/gmjau/?p=1075.

Internews. (2020, 26 May). *EJN awards grants for investigative environmental reporting in Asia and the Pacific*. internews.org/updates/ejn-awards-grants-investigative-environmental-reporting-asia-and-pacific.

Issimel, A. (2011). Radio Madang: Tuned in for development? In E. Papoutsaki, M. McManus and P. Matbob (Eds), *Communication, culture and society in Papua New Guinea: Yu Tok Wanem?* (pp. 147–56). DWU Press.

Jorgensen, D. (2018). Toby and 'the mobile system': Apocalypse and salvation in Papua New Guinea's wireless network. In R. J. Foster and H. A. Horst (Eds), *The moral economy of mobile phones: Pacific Islands perspectives* (pp. 53–71). ANU Press. doi.org/10.22459/MEMP.05.2018.03.

Kaleebu, N., Gee, A., Watson, A. H. A., Jones, R. and Jauk, M. (2017). SMS Story: A case study of a controlled trial in Papua New Guinea. In A. Murphy, H. Farley, L. E. Dyson and H. Jones (Eds), *Mobile learning in higher education in the Asia-Pacific region* (pp. 623–45). Springer. doi.org/10.1007/978-981-10-4944-6_30.

Kanekane, J. R. (2006). Governance, globalisation and the PNG media: A survival dilemma. In S. Firth (Ed.), *Globalisation and governance in the Pacific Islands* (pp. 385–98). ANU Press. doi.org/10.22459/GGPI.12.2006.21.

Kant, R., Titifanue, J., Tarai, J. and Finau, G. (2018). Internet under threat? The politics of online censorship in the Pacific Islands. *Pacific Journalism Review, 24*(2), 64–83. doi.org/10.24135/pjr.v24i2.444.

Kenneth, G. (2016, 12 August). Cyber law passed! *Post-Courier*. postcourier.com.pg/cyber-law-passed/.

Ketan, J. (2013). *Political governance and service delivery in Western Highlands Province, Papua New Guinea*. SSGM Discussion Paper, 2013/9. dpa.bellschool.anu.edu.au/experts-publications/publications/1390/political-governance-and-service-delivery-western-highlands.

Krishnamurthi, S. (2020, 5 May). PNG media suffers 'overwhelming deference', says freedom report. *Asia Pacific Report*. asiapacificreport.nz/2020/05/05/png-media-suffers-overwhelming-deference-says-freedom-report/.

Lasslett, K. (2015, 30 September). *The spin cycle: How Papua New Guinea's media washes dirty stories*. International State Crime Initiative. statecrime.org/state-crime-research/spin-cycle-papua-new-guineas-media-washes-dirty-stories/.

Lipset, D. (2018). A handset dangling in a doorway: Mobile phone sharing in a rural Sepik village (Papua New Guinea). In R. J. Foster and H. A. Horst (Eds), *The moral economy of mobile phones: Pacific Islands perspectives* (pp. 19–37). ANU Press. doi.org/10.22459/MEMP.05.2018.01.

Logan, S. (2012). *Rausim! Digital politics in Papua New Guinea*. SSGM Discussion Paper, 2012/9. dpa.bellschool.anu.edu.au/sites/default/files/publications/attachments/2015-12/2012_9_0.pdf.

Logan, S. and Forsyth, M. (2018). Access all areas? Telecommunications and human rights in Papua New Guinea. *Human Rights Defender, 27*(3), 18–20.

Logan, S. and Suwamaru, J. K. (2017). Land of the disconnected: A history of the internet in Papua New Guinea. In G. Goggin and M. McLelland (Eds), *The Routledge companion to global internet histories* (pp. 284–95). Routledge. doi.org/10.4324/9781315748962-20.

M'Balla-Ndi, M. and Obijiofor, L. (2020). Media freedom in Melanesia: The challenges of researching the impact of national security legislation. *Pacific Journalism Review*, *26*(1), 75–85. doi.org/10.24135/pjr.v26i1.1087.

M&C Saatchi World Services, NBC, ABC International Development and Australian Department of Foreign Affairs and Trade. (2014). *Citizen access to information in Papua New Guinea 2014*. www.abc.net.au/cm/lb/9080250/data/report---citizen-access-to-information-in-png-2014-data.pdf.

Marshall, S. (2007, 25 July). PNG mobile company to continue operation. ABC News. www.abc.net.au/news/stories/2007/07/25/1988482.htm.

Marshall, S. (2008, 27 March). PNG Govt set to create telecommunication monopoly. ABC News. www.abc.net.au/news/stories/2008/03/27/2201123.htm.

Matane, P. and Ahuja, M. L. (2005). *Papua New Guinea: Land of natural beauty and cultural diversity*. CBS Publishers.

Matbob, P. (2011). The state of investigative journalism and the growing impact of new media. In E. Papoutsaki, M. McManus and P. Matbob (Eds), *Communication, culture and society in Papua New Guinea: Yu Tok Wanem?* (pp. 20–40). DWU Press.

Matbob, P., McManus, M. and Papoutsaki, E. (2011). Introduction. In E. Papoutsaki, M. McManus and P. Matbob (Eds), *Communication, culture and society in Papua New Guinea: Yu Tok Wanem?* (pp. 1–18). DWU Press.

McLaughlin, G. (2016). *The war correspondent* (2nd ed.). Pluto Press. doi.org/10.26530/OAPEN_605051.

McLeod, S. (2020a, 7 May). Digital declarations: Political ads on PNG social media must be clear. *The Interpreter*. www.lowyinstitute.org/the-interpreter/digital-declarations-political-ads-PNG-social-media-must-be-clear.

McLeod, S. (2020b, 22 June). Debt threatens Digicel's Pacific dominance. *The Interpreter*. www.lowyinstitute.org/the-interpreter/debt-threatens-digicel-s-pacific-dominance.

Media Council of PNG. (n.d.-a). *General code of ethics for the news media*. media-council-of-papua-new-guinea.webnode.com/code/.

Media Council of PNG. (n.d.-b). *Welcome to the media council of Papua New Guinea.* media-council-of-papua-new-guinea.webnode.com/.

Media for Development Initiative. (2018). *Papua New Guinea women in the media: Research report.* www.abc.net.au/cm/lb/10469098/data/png-women-in-media-report-data.pdf.

Melanesia Media Freedom Forum. (2019). *Outcome statement.* www.griffith.edu.au/__data/assets/pdf_file/0016/910123/MMFF-Outcome-Statement.pdf.

Moi, C. (2020, 15 September). Merging almost done: Official. *The National.* www.thenational.com.pg/merging-almost-done-official/.

NBC News PNG Facebook. (2020). NBC gets K1 million to boost Highlands coverage. www.facebook.com/213810848972510/posts/1201018783585040.

Newman, N., Dutton, W. H. and Blank, G. (2012). Social media in the changing ecology of news: The fourth and fifth estates in Britain. *International Journal of Internet Science*, *7*(1), 6–22.

Oxford Business Group. (n.d.). *Cybercrime laws being updated in Papua New Guinea.* oxfordbusinessgroup.com/analysis/facing-new-realities-cybercrime-laws-are-being-updated-better-reflect-evolution-modern-technology.

Pacific Media Watch. (2011). *PNG: Commissioner warns* National *newspaper over 'bias'.* pmc.aut.ac.nz/pacific-media-watch/png-commissioner-warns-national-newspaper-over-bias-7706.

Pacific Media Watch. (2020, 23 April). Media Council calls for 'transparency' over coronavirus – PNG media tested. *Asia Pacific Report.* asiapacificreport.nz/2020/04/23/media-council-calls-for-transparency-over-coronavirus-png-media-tested/.

Pamba, K. (2004). Media ownership in Oceania: Three case studies in Fiji, Papua New Guinea and Tonga: Papua New Guinea. *Pacific Journalism Review*, *10*(2), 56–61. doi.org/10.24135/pjr.v10i2.804.

Pamba, K. (2014). *Miners 'train' journalists.* SSGM In Brief, 2014/58. dpa.bellschool.anu.edu.au/sites/default/files/publications/attachments/2015-12/SSGM_IB_2014_58.pdf.

Perottet, A. and Robie, D. (2011). Pacific media freedom 2011: A status report. *Pacific Journalism Review*, *17*(2), 148–86. doi.org/10.24135/pjr.v17i2.356.

PNGi. (n.d.). *About.* pngicentral.org/about.

Popot, G. (2011). Reporting family violence. In E. Papoutsaki, M. McManus and P. Matbob (Eds), *Communication, culture and society in Papua New Guinea: Yu Tok Wanem?* (pp. 74–82). DWU Press.

Radio New Zealand. (2020a). How to listen. www.rnz.co.nz/international/listen.

Radio New Zealand. (2020b, 19 August). New Bougainvillean paper launched. www.rnz.co.nz/international/pacific-news/423912/new-bougainvillean-paper-launched.

Reporters without Borders. (2020a). *2020 world press freedom index*. rsf.org/en/ranking.

Reporters without Borders. (2020b). *Papua New Guinea*. rsf.org/en/papua-new-guinea.

Ricketson, M. (2012). Insights into Murdoch empire. *Australian Journalism Review*, *34*(2), 137–39.

Robie, D. (2011). The campus and the newsroom: Papua New Guinean media in education profile. In E. Papoutsaki, M. McManus and P. Matbob (Eds), *Communication, culture and society in Papua New Guinea: Yu Tok Wanem?* (pp. 205–17). DWU Press.

Robie, D. (2013). 'Four worlds' news values revisited: A deliberative journalism paradigm for Pacific media. *Pacific Journalism Review*, *19*(1), 84–110. doi.org/10.24135/pjr.v19i1.240.

Robie, D. (2014). *Don't spoil my beautiful face: Media, mayhem and human rights in the Pacific*. Little Island Press.

Robie, D. (2019, 3 May). Pacific countries score well in media freedom index, but reality is far worse. *The Conversation*. theconversation.com/pacific-countries-score-well-in-media-freedom-index-but-reality-is-far-worse-116373.

Robie, D. (2020a). Key Melanesian media freedom challenges: Climate crisis, internet freedoms, fake news and West Papua. *Pacific Journalism Review*, *26*(1), 15–36. doi.org/10.24135/pjr.v26i1.1072.

Robie, D. (2020b, 12 April). Police Minister Bryan Kramer blasts two journalists in virus reporting row. *Café Pacific*. cafepacific.blogspot.com/2020/04/police-minister-bryan-kramer-blasts-two.html.

Robie, D. (2020c, 23 April). Tough coronavirus controls threaten Pacific, global media freedom. *Asia Pacific Report*. asiapacificreport.nz/2020/04/23/tough-coronavirus-controls-threaten-pacific-global-media-freedom/.

Rooney, M. N. (2012, 31 July). Can social media transform Papua New Guinea? Reflections and questions. *Devpolicy Blog*. devpolicy.org/can-social-media-transform-papua-new-guinea-reflections-and-questions20120731/.

Rooney, M. N. (2017a, 14 June). Media fail! Papua New Guinean women deserve better from the media. *Devpolicy Blog*. devpolicy.org/media-fail-papua-new-guinean-women-deserve-better-media-20170614/.

Rooney, M. N. (2017b, 1 November). Media challenges as Papua New Guinea fights gendered and sorcery related violence. *Devpolicy Blog*. devpolicy.org/media-challenges-as-papua-new-guinea-fights-gendered-and-sorcery-related-violence-20171101/.

Rooney, M. N., Davies, M. and Howes, S. (2020, 25 May). Mi gat Y: Is Digicel PNG's loan scheme predatory? *Devpolicy Blog*. devpolicy.org/mi-gat-y-is-digicel-pngs-loan-scheme-predatory-20200521/.

Sagrista, M. and Matbob, P. (2016). The digital divide in Papua New Guinea: Implications for journalism education. *Pacific Journalism Review*, *22*(2), 20–34. doi.org/10.24135/pjr.v22i2.44.

Shaligram, H. (2019, 18 October). Papua New Guinea's untold media freedom challenge. *The Interpreter*. www.lowyinstitute.org/the-interpreter/papua-new-guinea-s-untold-media-freedom-challenge.

Singh, S. (2004). Media ownership in Oceania: Three case studies in Fiji, Papua New Guinea and Tonga. *Pacific Journalism Review*, *10*(2), 47–55. doi.org/10.24135/pjr.v10i2.804.

Singh, S. (2017). *State of the media review in four Melanesian countries – Fiji, Papua New Guinea, Solomon Islands and Vanuatu – in 2015*. SSGM Discussion Paper, 2017/1. ssgm.bellschool.anu.edu.au/sites/default/files/publications/attachments/2017-04/dp_2017_1_singh.pdf.

Singh, S. (2020). The media and journalism challenges in Melanesia: Addressing the impacts of external and internal threats in Fiji, Papua New Guinea, the Solomon Islands and Vanuatu. *Pacific Journalism Review*, *26*(1), 48–62. doi.org/10.24135/pjr.v26i1.1095.

Tahana, J. (2014, 14 April). PNG's proposed cyber crime policy sparks concerns. Radio New Zealand. www.rnz.co.nz/international/programmes/datelinepacific/audio/2592554/png's-proposed-cyber-crime-policy-sparks-concerns.

Tarai, J. (2019). Social media and Fiji's 2018 national election. *Pacific Journalism Review*, *25*(1 and 2), 52–64. doi.org/10.24135/pjr.v25i1and2.476.

Taylor, L. (2020). *The Guardian*'s role in the Australian mediascape. *Australian Journalism Review*, *42*(1), 13–22. doi.org/10.1386/ajr_00016_1.

The National. (2010, 20 July). Kundu 2 launched in Aitape. www.thenational.com.pg/kundu-2-launched-in-aitape/.

The National. (2020, 13 May). DataCo lands Kumul submarine cable in East New Britain. www.thenational.com.pg/dataco-lands-kumul-submarine-cable-in-east-new-britain/.

Third, A., Lala, G., Moody, L. and Ogun, N. (2020). *Online safety in the Pacific: A report on a living lab in Kiribati, Papua New Guinea and Solomon Islands.* ChildFund Australia, Plan International Australia and Western Sydney University. www.plan.org.au/publications/online-safety-in-the-pacific/.

Thomas, V. and Eby, M. (2016). Media and public health communication at the grassroots: Village cinemas and HIV education in Papua New Guinea. In R. K. Vemula and S. M. Gavaravarapu (Eds), *Health communication in the changing media landscape: Perspectives from developing countries* (pp. 115–33). Palgrave Macmillan. doi.org/10.1007/978-3-319-33539-1_7.

Thomas, V., Kauli, J., Levy, C. and Rawstorne, P. (2019). *Bougainville audience study – Niupela Wokabaut Bilong Bogenvil: Phase 2.* Directorate of Media and Communication, Autonomous Bougainville Government and QUT Design Lab.

Titifanue, J., Kant, R., Finau, G. and Tarai, J. (2017). Climate change advocacy in the Pacific: The role of information and communication technologies. *Pacific Journalism Review*, *23*(1), 133–49. doi.org/10.24135/pjr.v23i1.105.

Titifanue, J., Tarai, J., Kant, R. and Finau, G. (2016). From social networking to activism: The role of social media in the Free West Papua Campaign. *Pacific Studies*, *39*(3), 255–80.

Tlozek, E. (2015, 22 October). PNG government accused of censorship as it moves to crack down on social media dissent. ABC News. www.abc.net.au/news/2015-10-22/png-government-cracks-down-on-social-media/6877024.

Transparency International PNG. (2020). *Media trends report preliminary statement.* web.archive.org/web/20200516174759/http://www.transparencypng.org.pg/tipng-media-trends-report-preliminary-statement/.

Turner, G. W. (1984). *The Australian pocket Oxford dictionary* (2nd ed.). Oxford University Press.

Ubayasiri, K., Valencia-Forrester, F. and Cain, T. N. (2020). Editorial: Melanesian media freedom. *Pacific Journalism Review*, *26*(1), 7–12. doi.org/10.24135/pjr.v26i1.1117.

United Nations Department of Economic and Social Affairs. (2015). *Responsive and accountable public governance: 2015 world public sector report.* United Nations.

Valencia-Forrester, F., Backhaus, B. and Stewart, H. (2020). In her own words: Melanesian women in media. *Pacific Journalism Review*, *26*(1), 63–74. doi.org/10.24135/pjr.v26i1.1104.

Wall, J. (2020, 8 September). China's 'debt-trap diplomacy' is about to challenge Papua New Guinea – and Australia. *The Strategist.* www.aspistrategist.org.au/chinas-debt-trap-diplomacy-is-about-to-challenge-papua-new-guinea-and-australia/.

Wardlow, H. (2018). HIV, phone friends and affective technology in Papua New Guinea. In R. J. Foster and H. A. Horst (Eds), *The moral economy of mobile phones: Pacific Islands perspectives* (pp. 39–52). ANU Press. doi.org/10.22459/MEMP.05.2018.02.

Watson, A. H. A. (2011). The mobile phone: The new communication drum of Papua New Guinea [Unpublished thesis]. Queensland University of Technology.

Watson, A. H. A. (2012). Tsunami alert: The mobile phone difference. *The Australian Journal of Emergency Management*, *27*(4), 46–50.

Watson, A. H. A. (2020a, 30 January). Internet prices in Papua New Guinea. *Devpolicy Blog*. devpolicy.org/internet-prices-in-papua-new-guinea-20200130/.

Watson, A. H. A. (2020b). Mobile phone registration in Papua New Guinea: Will the benefits outweigh the drawbacks? *Pacific Journalism Review*, *26*(1), 114–22. doi.org/10.24135/pjr.v26i1.1094.

Watson, A. H. A., Airi, P. and Sakai, M. (2020, 30 July). No change in mobile internet prices in PNG. *Devpolicy Blog*. devpolicy.org/no-change-in-mobile-in-internet-prices-in-png-20200730/.

Watson, A. H. A. and Duffield, L. R. (2016). From garamut to mobile phone: Communication change in rural Papua New Guinea. *Mobile Media and Communication*, *4*(2), 270–87. doi.org/10.1177/2050157915622658.

Watson, A. H. A. and Fox, R. (2019, 16 May). A tax on mobile phones in PNG? *Devpolicy Blog*. devpolicy.org/a-tax-on-mobile-phones-in-png-20190516/.

Watson, A. H. A., Miller, J. and Schmidt, A. (2020). *Preparing for the referendum: Research into the Bougainville Peace Agreement telephone information hotline.* Department of Pacific Affairs, Discussion Paper, 2020/2. dpa.bellschool.anu.edu.au/experts-publications/publications/7716/dp-202002-preparing-referendum-research-bougainville-peace.

Watson, A. H. A. and Park, K. R. (2019, 13 August). The digital divide between and within countries. *Devpolicy Blog*. devpolicy.org/the-digital-divide-between-and-within-countries-20190813/.

Watson, A. H. A. and Patel, M. (2017, 5 September). Telecommunications in Papua New Guinea – in conversation with Telikom. *Devpolicy Blog*. devpolicy.org/telecommunications-papua-new-guinea-conversation-telikom-20170905/.

Watson, A. H. A., Sabumei, G., Mola, G. and Iedema, R. (2015). Maternal health phone line: Saving women in Papua New Guinea. *Journal of Personalized Medicine*, *5*(2), 120–39. doi.org/10.3390/jpm5020120.

Watson, A. H. A. and Wiltshire, C. (2016). *Reporting corruption from within Papua New Guinea's public financial management system.* SSGM Discussion Paper, 2016/5. dpa.bellschool.anu.edu.au/experts-publications/publications/4461/reporting-corruption-within-papua-new-guineas-public.

Wesley, F. (2020). Scott Waide, Maseratis and EMTV … how a public outcry restored media freedom. *Pacific Journalism Review*, *26*(1), 43–47. doi.org/10.24135/pjr.v26i1.1083.

Williams, P. (2019). *Connecting Papua New Guinea: The dawn of the digital era.* Deloitte.

Word Publishing Company Ltd. (2020). *Wantok*. wantokniuspepa.com/index.php/about-us.

World Bank. (2020). *In the time of COVID-19: From relief to recovery*. World Bank.

Yamo, H. (2013). Mobile phones in rural Papua New Guinea: A transformation in health communication and delivery services in Western Highlands Province [Unpublished thesis]. Auckland University of Technology.

Yamo, H. and Watson, A. H. A. (2014). How to maximise value when utilising a closed user group mobile phone service in the Papua New Guinea context. *IBS Journal of Business and Research*, *10*, 9–24.

Contributors

Dr John Cox is an honorary lecturer with the School of Culture, History and Language at The Australian National University.

Dr Sinclair Dinnen is Associate Professor, Department of Pacific Affairs, Coral Bell School of Asia Pacific Affairs, The Australian National University.

Rohan Fox was formerly a research officer at the Development Policy Centre, Crawford School of Public Policy, The Australian National University.

Joshua Goa is a tutor in the Division of Social Work, School of Humanities and Social Sciences, University of Papua New Guinea.

Dr Albert Prabhakar Gudapati is Head of the Division of Economics, School of Business and Public Policy, University of Papua New Guinea.

Dr Stephen Howes is Professor of Economics and Director of the Development Policy Centre, Crawford School of Public Policy, The Australian National University.

Michael Kabuni is a lecturer in the Division of Political Science, School of Humanities and Social Sciences, University of Papua New Guinea.

Maholopa Laveil is a lecturer in the Division of Economics, School of Business and Public Policy, University of Papua New Guinea.

Dunstan Lawihin is a lecturer in the Division of Social Work, School of Humanities and Social Sciences, University of Papua New Guinea.

Luke McKenzie was formerly an associate lecturer at the Development Policy Centre, Crawford School of Public Policy, The Australian National University, and a visiting lecturer in the Division of Economics, School of Business and Public Policy, University of Papua New Guinea.

Geejay Milli is a lecturer in the Division of Political Science, School of Humanities and Social Sciences, University of Papua New Guinea.

Dr Manoj K. Pandey is a research fellow at the Development Policy Centre, Crawford School of Public Policy, The Australian National University, and a visiting lecturer in the Division of Economics, School of Business and Public Policy, University of Papua New Guinea.

Dr Lekshmi N. Pillai is Professor of Accounting and Executive Dean, School of Business and Public Policy, University of Papua New Guinea.

Dr Lawrence Sause is Deputy Executive Dean and Senior Lecturer in the Division of Public Policy Management, School of Business and Public Policy, University of Papua New Guinea.

Dek Sum is an associate lecturer at the Development Policy Centre, Crawford School of Public Policy, The Australian National University, and a visiting lecturer in the Division of Economics, School of Business and Public Policy, University of Papua New Guinea.

Dr Lhawang Ugyel is a lecturer at the School of Business, University of New South Wales, Canberra, and was formerly a visiting lecturer in the Division of Public Policy Management, School of Business and Public Policy, University of Papua New Guinea.

Dr Grant W. Walton is a fellow at the Development Policy Centre and senior lecturer with the Policy and Governance Program, Crawford School of Public Policy, The Australian National University.

Dr Amanda H. A. Watson is a research fellow at the Department of Pacific Affairs, Coral Bell School of Asia Pacific Affairs, The Australian National University, and was formerly a visiting lecturer in the Division of Public Policy Management, School of Business and Public Policy, University of Papua New Guinea.

Dr Terence Wood is a research fellow at the Development Policy Centre, Crawford School of Public Policy, The Australian National University.

www.ingramcontent.com/pod-product-compliance
Lightning Source LLC
Chambersburg PA
CBHW040149270326
41929CB00033B/3418
9781760465025